Gertrude Hoyt Memorial

PUBLIC SECTOR ECONOMICS

Public Sector Economics presents studies of public sector pricing and investment problems as well as theoretical and empirical analyses of public decision-making.

The book begins with "A Public Enterprise Pricing Primer" setting the stage for the following positive and empirical investigation of electricity and telecommunication pricing problems. These contributions develop new methodological approaches which should also be of interest in other applied work. Then the role of public interest firms in oligopolistic markets is discussed. Thereafter, public sector pricing is related to investment problems.

The final chapters of the volume should increase our understanding of public decision-making. The issues are introduced by a survey on the contribution of the public choice literature to public utility economics. One of the issues – distributional versus efficiency objectives – is then analyzed in depth. The volume closes with an empirical study of public policy towards pollution control.

Dr Jörg Finsinger, the editor, is Research Fellow at the International Institute of Management, Berlin. He has contributed articles on theoretical and applied microeconomics as well as on competition policy to professional publications.

PUBLIC SECTOR ECONOMICS

Edited by
Jörg Finsinger
Research Fellow
International Institute of Management, Berlin

Foreword by
Bernhard Gahlen
Director
International Institute of Management, Berlin

St. Martin's Press   New York

ISBN 0–312–65567–3

Library of Congress Cataloging in Publication Data

Main entry under title:

Public sector economics.

"Contributions . . . presented at the Regulation
Conference and during the subsequent Regulation Workshop,
held at the International Institute of Management
of the Science Center, Berlin, 1–15 July 1981"—Foreword.
Includes index.
Contents: Public sector policy analysis / Jörg
Finsinger—A public enterprise pricing primer /
Gerald R. Faulhaber—Electricity consumption by
time of use in a hybrid demand system / Bridger M.
Mitchell and Jan Paul Acton—[etc.]
   1. Public utilities—Congresses.   2. Government
business enterprises—Congresses.   I. Finsinger,
Jörg.   II. International Institute of Management.
HD2763.P78   1983   338.4′73636   82–42576
ISBN 0–312–65567–3

For Gini

Contents

Foreword

The contributions to this book were presented at the Regulation Conference and during the subsequent Regulation Workshop, held at the International Institute of Management of the Science Centre, Berlin, 1–15 July 1981. The conference was supported by a generous grant from the Thyssen Foundation, for which we are extremely grateful.

The objective of the conference was twofold: first, it provided an opportunity for the exchange of the latest developments in economic research on an international level. Secondly, by emphasizing policy-relevant research it was intended to be of help to decision-makers. For the most part, this conference volume contains papers focusing on current issues in economic policy. Often, government policies are criticized and policy changes are suggested. Of course, in some cases the papers in this volume give only indirect guidance for decision-makers. Occasionally, it is demonstrated only that current public sector policies lead to outcomes quite different from policy objectives. But such insights are none the less extremely useful.

I would like to thank Dr Jörg Finsinger, Research Fellow at the International Institute of Management, for organizing the conference and the workshop. He also edited this book. Furthermore, I want to thank our staff, especially our secretary, Gisela Spivey, for her patient assistance during the conference preparation and accomplishment.

Berlin   BERNHARD GAHLEN

Notes on the Contributors

Jan Paul Acton is a Senior Staff Economist at the Rand Corporation. He has been principal investigator on research projects in the economics of health and on several studies of energy policy, including the Los Angeles Electricity Rate Study. He has published papers in the economics of health, benefit–cost analysis, energy and pricing in regulated industries, and is co-author of *Peak-Load Pricing: European Lessons for U.S. Energy Policy*. He has testified in rate cases in the United States and Canada and before the US Congress.

Charles B. Blankart is Professor of Public Finance at the University of the Federal Armed Forces in Munich. Previously he was professor of economics at the Free University of Berlin. His research interests are focused on the political economy aspects of public and regulated enterprises. He is author of the book *Ökonomie der öffentlichen Unternehmen* ('Economics of Public Enterprises') and various articles in the field of regulation and public enterprises.

Dieter Bös graduated from the University of Vienna, Austria, where he was assistant from 1965 to 1971. He was then Professor of Economics at the Universities of Graz (1971–5) and Vienna (1975–9). In 1979 he became Professor of Economics at the University of Bonn. He has lectured on public enterprise economics at the London School of Economics since 1976. He has been managing editor of the *Zeitschrift für Nationalökonomie* since 1973. He has published books and papers on most fields of public economics. His recent books include *The Economic Theory of Public Enterprise* and *Public Production* (edited with R. Musgrave and J. Wiseman).

Ronald R. Braeutigam is Associate Professor of Economics at Northwestern University. He holds an undergraduate degree in petroleum engineering and a master's degree in engineering–economic systems. He received his PhD in economics from Stanford University in 1976.

Professor Braeutigam has worked in private industry as a petroleum engineer, and has served as a staff economist in the White House Office of Telecommunications Policy. He has also taught previously at Stanford University and the California Institute of Technology, and is currently a research fellow at the International Institute of Management, Berlin. He has published numerous works dealing with regulation.

Robert E. Dansby is a Member of the Economics Research Center at Bell Laboratories and has taught at Rutgers University. His published papers have dealt with peak-load pricing theory, theory of market concentration indexes, pricing under uncertainty and theory of regulation. His current research is focused on the economics of intellectual property.

Gerald R. Faulhaber is Director of Microeconomic Studies at the American Telephone and Telegraph Co. and Adjunct Associate Professor at New York University; previously he was Head of Economics and Financial Research at Bell Laboratories. His research interests are in the economics of regulation, public enterprise pricing and market structure. He is the author of several articles on cross-subsidy in public enterprise pricing.

Bridger M. Mitchell is a Senior Staff Economist at the Rand Corporation and an Associate Fellow of the International Institute of Management, Berlin. He has been a member of the economics faculties at Stanford University and the University of California at Los Angeles. His research articles in the fields of telecommunications, energy and regulatory policy have appeared widely, and he is principal author of *Peak-Load Pricing: European Lessons for U.S. Energy Policy* (with W. G. Manning Jr and Jan Paul Acton) and co-editor of *Regulated Industries and Public Enterprise: European and United States Perspectives* (with Paul R. Kleindorfer).

Karl-Heinz Neumann is Research Assistant at the University of Bonn. His research is in the fields of telecommunications economics.

Roger G. Noll is Institute Professor of Social Science at the California Institute of Technology. He has also served as a Senior Staff Economist at the President's Council of Economic Advisers and as Senior Economist and Co-Director of Studies in the Regulation of Economic Activity at the Brookings Institution. Professor Noll's published research includes studies of communications regulation, energy and environmental policies, safety regulation, formal political theory and the theory of the regulatory process. In 1980 he served on the Executive Committee of the President's Commission for a National Agenda for the Eighties.

Urs Schweizer is Professor of Economics at the University of Bielefeld, Federal Republic of Germany. His research is in the fields of economic theory, welfare economics and regional policy. He is the editor of *Regional Science and Urban Economics*.

Ingo Vogelsang is Associate Professor of Economics at Boston University. Before that he was Wissenschaftlicher Assistant at the University of Bonn. Until 1975 he had served as a manager in the international coal trade. He has published several articles on incentives mechanisms with Jörg Finsinger and is co-author of *Staatliche Regulierung*. He is currently completing *Anreizmechanismen zur Regulierung der Elektrizitätswirtschaft*.

C. Christian von Weizsäcker is Professor of Economics at the University of Bern, Switzerland. He is leading a research project on telecommunications economics. He also does research on the economics of competition and competition policy. Before he moved to Bern he taught in Basel, Heidelberg, MIT, Bielefeld, Amsterdam and Bonn.

Part I
Introduction

1 Public Sector Policy Analysis

JÖRG FINSINGER

Increasingly, government policies are criticized for failing to achieve their objectives. It is not always appropriate simply to call for deregulation. Often deregulation is not politically feasible. Also, the 'invisible hand' does not always work better than regulation as, for example, where environmental quality is concerned. In those cases regulation will be with us for some time to come. Of course, the performance of regulatory institutions should continually be evaluated. If performance is not satisfactory more efficient policies have to be designed. Positive as well as normative analysis of regulatory institutions was presented at a conference held at Berlin in July 1981. A selection of papers addressing three major topics is contained in this volume:

pricing issues in the public sector;
investment and pricing under regulation;
public decision-making.

At least as long as there are public enterprises, the pricing issues discussed in Part II are of interest to policy-makers and economists. Gerald R. Faulhaber summarizes the essentials of the public enterprise pricing problem taking into account the recent literature. He points out that rate regulation has often led to substantial efficiency losses. In some cases welfare losses result from distribution policies. Faulhaber argues that, although society may be willing to pay this efficiency cost for more distributional equity, usually there are far less costly ways to achieve these objectives. In addition, redistribution via public enterprise prices often has unintended effects. The subsidized group of consumers may turn out to be quite different from the deserving poor. More importantly, rate structures designed to achieve distributional objectives may induce firms to enter this market, or the market for close substitutes, unless such entry is foreclosed by additional regulations. Therefore, such rate structures may not be consistent with deregulation or with the objective of minimal regulatory restrictions.

The chapter by Bridger M. Mitchell and Jan Paul Acton reports results from the Los Angeles Electricity Rate Study, which was designed to yield information about the effects of alternative pricing structures. Mitchell and Acton focus on the demand response of residential consumers to time-of-use rates. They separate the effects of prices, demographic factors, appliances and weather on electricity consumption and, thus, provide an analytic framework for forecasting purposes which should be of interest to electric utilities and to policy-makers alike.

Part II contains another empirical analysis of rate structures. Karl-Heinz Neumann, Urs Schweizer and C. Christian von Weizsäcker analyze the telecommunication tariffs in the Federal Republic of Germany. Current tariffs, it seems, are not designed to promote economic efficiency. Consumers could be made much better off with a higher rate for local calls and lower rates for long distance calls. These findings reflect the technological progress in long distance transmission where transmission costs have steadily declined. But Neumann, Schweizer and von Weizsäcker do not just propose a tariff change, they estimate the welfare gain associated with various rate changes. For this purpose they develop an estimation technique which allows the evaluation of tariff structures in the face of scarce cost and demand data. The estimates suggest that the German postal monopoly would be well advised to collect and make available more precise cost and demand data, so that Neumann, Schweizer and von Weizsäcker can relax some of their admittedly strong assumptions. More precise data would most likely reveal additional distortions of the telecommunication tariffs. Corrections of these distortions would result in even higher welfare gains from tariff reforms than the Neumann, Schweizer, von Weizsäcker estimates suggest. The message for policy makers is obvious. They should require public enterprises to disclose more data so that public enterprise performance can be better evaluated, and so that more efficient prices can be calculated.

A similar data problem exists regarding the performance of so-called public interest firms (Gemeinwirtschaftliche Unternehmen). Ingo Vogelsang's chapter examines the pricing behaviour of firms owned by trade unions. In Germany these firms are considered to pursue public interest objectives besides benefiting their shareholders. In oligopolistic markets such union-owned firms supposedly set lower prices than other firms. However, there is little empirical evidence for such beneficial behaviour. Also, it is not clear why trade unions should have an interest in using their own firms to promote competition. Vogelsang's chapter establishes the conditions under which such behaviour is plausible. He also compares union firms with cooperatives and shows that a cooperative can gain from offering service to non-members. Two further results on trade union firms deserve mentioning. First, trade union firms may price below marginal cost if union members represent a sufficiently large share of buyers in the market. Second, the presence of trade union firms does not necessarily improve welfare. There are cases, where profit maximizing behaviour would lead to a better allocation of resources than the trade union firm behaviour.

Part III of the book deals with pricing and investment strategies in regulated markets. The chapter by Ronald R. Braeutigam, introduces the time dimension into the Ramsey model for second best pricing. He assumes that the factors of production can be varied over time though not without cost. He then derives the optimal time paths for factor inputs and prices and finds a number of differences and similarities relative to the optimal values in the classical static model.

Robert E. Dansby studies a related problem in his chapter. Recent deliberations by state and federal regulatory agencies have raised several public policy issues concerning the methods used in the telecommunications industry to finance research and development. His paper provides insight concerning the question: What are the welfare economic consequences of alternative methods of allocating R&D cost among technology producers and users? The focus is on the apparent concern of regulatory agencies that R&D costs be shared by utility firms and their customers in a manner that 'promotes the public interest'. Similar policy questions are relevant to the German Postal Service's specification of contractual terms for the development and purchase of new equipment.

Consider the alternative flows of technology and costs from R&D activity to final consumers depicted in Figure 1.1. One alternative is to have the technology producers (for example, German electronics suppliers) bear the R&D cost through their pricing of technology. Alternatively, the producer of final services (for example, the German Postal Service) could bear the R&D cost and recover this cost through pricing of its final product. (In this case the Postal Service contracts to pay electronics firms to do the R&D and to purchase equipment at its

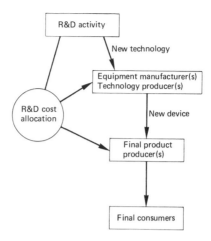

FIGURE 1.1

marginal production cost while raising telephone prices to cover the R&D cost.) Thus, a fundamental trade-off exists. Allocating R&D cost to technology producers may distort technology prices and lead to higher final product prices. Reducing the R&D cost allocated to technology users may increase their incentive to adopt new technology and lead to welfare gains from the savings in final production costs. Dansby shows that the R&D cost allocations that balance these tradeoffs depends crucially on the market structure and internal organization of the technology producers and users; he derives the optimal allocation for three alternative market structure–internal organization scenarios. If technology producers and users are vertically integrated, centrally managed monopolists, then a case is made for allocating all R&D cost to downstream technology users. However, if the vertically integrated monopolists operate at 'arms length', that is, decision making is decentralized, then it is shown that the integrated firm and its customers may be better off if some of the R&D cost is allocated to technology producers. Similar results hold if the upstream, technology producing industry is competitive, and there are several differentiated downstream competitive industries which can use the new technology in their production process.

Part IV of the book addresses the problem of public decision making. Charles B. Blankart summarizes the contributions of the public choice literature to public utility economics. He begins by investigating the collective decision processes leading to regulation. Why are certain markets regulated whereas other markets remain free? The next question to be answered is how collective decisions are taken under regulation, for example, how prices and profits are regulated. Finally, the role of the economist as adviser of collective decision making bodies is discussed. Blankart also focuses on the question of why some public utilities are publicly owned while others are private.

In contrast to normative theories of public utility pricing the public choice approach tries to model the actual collective decision process. This is why issues of fairness and equity cannot be neglected. Dieter Bös's chapter examines the outcome of a vote between a tariff which is uniform across all customers and a social tariff which discriminates between customers of different income. Such a social tariff, however, is not the only way to attempt a correction of the income distribution via public utility pricing. Price discrimination between customers of different incomes is not always possible. However, the multi-product public utility can discriminate between different goods. As long as the rich and the poor have different usage patterns a limited correction of the income distribution may be possible. Bös distinguishes necessities and non-necessities and compares their prices under different policy regimes such as welfare maximization, distributionally weighted consumers' surplus maximization and pricing under majority rule.

Quite a different aspect of public decision making is presented in Roger G. Noll's chapter, which deals with the design of policies toward pollution control, clearly a most important issue in all developed and many under-developed countries. Some governments and most representatives of industry argue that current environmental policies impose too heavy a burden on the economy. Considering the cost of environmental regulation in the US, estimated to be in the range of thirty to fifty billion dollars annually, it is worth while looking for the least cost policies to achieve desirable environmental quality levels. Noll restricts his analysis to air pollution control, but the results are relevant for other kinds of pollution. He first summarizes the standard air pollution regulation in effect until 1977. This regulation translated federal ambient air quality standards into appropriate standards for each source of pollution. These standards specified the abatement technology as well as maximum permissible emissions from a source of pollution. Noll describes the shortcomings of this regulatory policy and then analyzes the advantages and problems associated with the new, more decentralized, market-oriented policy. Under the new policy many public decisions are replaced by individual firm decisions; firms can rearrange the pattern of emissions by exchanging their permits and choosing any abatement technology. Polluting firms, as a group, still have the same incentive to reduce emissions, but each firm can buy and sell permits until its environmental protection outlays are minimal. Provided the market for permits works well, the total cost of achieving a given air quality standard is minimized. This is demonstrated by a case study of the regulation of sulfur oxide emissions in the Los Angeles air shed. Finally, the problems of transition and implementation are discussed.

Part II
Pricing Issues in
the Public Sector

2 A Public Enterprise Pricing Primer

GERALD R. FAULHABER

INTRODUCTION

The past decade has seen a substantial amount of scholarly activity in the US devoted to the economics of pricing in regulated (or public) enterprises subject to increasing returns to scale. More recently, this interest in public enterprise pricing has been actively shared by economists and policymakers in Europe, especially West Germany and Great Britain. While much of this work has been somewhat technical, it is aimed directly at the pricing issues of greatest concern to managers and regulators of public enterprises. In this paper, some of these pricing policy concerns are explored in a non-technical format, drawing upon the 'new literature' where appropriate. Our purpose here is not to report new research, but rather to consider those broad pricing issues that recur across different countries, different industries and different times, and what light economics can shed on such issues.

The focus of this paper is on industries in which both price and entry are tightly regulated by the state, particularly the traditional public utility industries in which goods are provided to consumers through a franchised monopoly, either public or private. The recent trend toward deregulation in the United States has seriously questioned the need for such regulation, even in the core public utility industries such as telecommunications and rail transport. While the scope of pervasive regulation may be substantially reduced in the months and years ahead, it is most unlikely that it will be eliminated altogether. Thus, public enterprise pricing issues will be with us for some time to come.

It would be naive to suggest that once the regulator has been armed by the economist with the 'correct' pricing principles, his problems are over. In fact, price regulation of public enterprises is more closely akin to trench warfare, with various interest groups, industry spokespersons, consumerists and others all clamouring that the regulator meets their 'needs' for low prices/high profit. Application of *any* pricing principle almost invariably results in winners and losers; good principles tend to result in more and bigger winners than losers, but the fact remains that it is nearly impossible in practice to have nothing but winners. Further, articulate losers can and will denounce the offending action of the regulator, and care little about 'principle'. The economist can offer little balm to the regulator constantly exposed to such slings and arrows. Nevertheless, economists would be remiss should we not offer what we can to those whose decisions have such a profound impact on our economies.

THE HEART OF THE CONTRACT

Economists, lawyers, public utility regulators and managers have traditionally viewed price as the essential piece of any transaction. While many other matters press for the attention of regulators, such as the quality of service, speed of delivery, obligation to serve all, and so on, price has rightly been considered the key variable. The price of a good or service informs each consumer of the market value of the good, and permits him to adjust his consumption of this good relative to other goods and his total income, so that each consumer maximizes his own net benefit. The price also signals firms how much of each good to produce, what markets to enter or leave, when and where to introduce or discontinue products and when and where to build new facilities, in order to produce maximum returns. Indirectly, signals are provided to investors as well, who direct capital expenditures to those activities with the greatest return. Thus, the 'right' price insures that the right goods will be produced in the right amounts and be directed to the right consumers. In short, prices are a tool to ensure that society's scarce resources are used in the most economically efficient fashion.

WHAT IS AT STAKE?

In a competitive market, inter-firm rivalry over price for the business of consumers can be expected to keep the price 'right', that is, assure that scarce resources are allocated efficiently. If prices and entry are publicly controlled, however, there is no such assurance. Public regulators are correct in their concern over pricing matters; if they do not set prices 'correctly', serious direct consequences may be observed:

(1) chronic shortages in underpriced commodities (such as natural gas in the US prior to deregulation);
(2) too many resources (capital investment, labour, and so on) devoted to underpriced goods and too few resources devoted to overpriced goods;
(3) imbalances in research and development efforts, towards highly profitable markets and away from subsidized markets;
(4) inefficient firms may enter certain markets and efficient firms may leave other markets;
(5) the structure of supply may be significantly distorted from the cost-minimizing structure (such as US surface freight).

In short, inappropriate pricing can be expected to result in *efficiency losses*. Briefly, an efficiency loss results when economic resources are directed away from consumers or producing units where those resources have the largest benefit (as measured by willingness-to-pay less actual payment), and toward consumers or producing units which value those resources less. While it is dangerous to generalize across the broad range of regulatory experience, the empirical work of many economists suggests that US regulation has not succeeded in avoiding pricing distortions, and that the efficiency cost of these distortions can be very large indeed. Policy-makers with pricing responsibility are well advised to gain some familiarity with the results of the extensive literature on the efficiency costs of regulation. A recent such study is Levin[1] on railroad regulation in the US, but economists have studied these problems for at least two decades.

If there are no close substitutes available for the goods in question, and if the regulators have foreclosed easy entry and exit in the industry, then the price-setting behaviour of regulators is not constrained by market forces, but may be shaped by forces of political expediency: interest groups which have access to political decision makers can obtain favourable price treatment for goods they use intensively. For example, agricultural interests in the US were successful for many years in maintaining particularly low rates for the rail transport of farm goods through the Interstate Commerce Commission. There are, however, many forms of political intervention for lower rates that might be seen as serving broader social goals: lower prices for goods consumed primarily by low income households, handicapped persons, retired persons, students, veterans and so on. ('Lifeline' rates in the US, for example). This may also take the form of special discounts for targeted groups (such as reduced public transport fares for students and retired persons). In short, public enterprise pricing must consider *distributional* concerns. Recent work in this area includes the excellent Chapter 9 in this volume by Professor Dieter Bös as well as the paper by Robert Willig and Elizabeth Bailey, 'Income Distributional Concerns in Regulatory Policy-Making'.[2] The key principle that must always be borne in mind is that pricing distortions for distributional or any other purpose virtually *always* benefit the favoured group *less* than it costs the consumers who must provide the subsidy. Indeed, this is the meaning of efficiency loss.

Economists (and political scientists) have traditionally been wary of using public utility prices to attain distributional objectives. As noted above, price distortions can generally be expected to cause efficiency losses, even when such price distortions are made to fulfil certain distributional objectives, such as transferring income from the well-off to the poor. In fact, society may be quite willing to pay this efficiency cost in order to have a more just and equitable society. Usually, however, we would expect that there are far less costly ways to achieve the desired redistribution of income than through the manipulation of public enterprise prices. We would expect that to achieve a given level of income transfers to the poor, increasing the progressiveness of the income tax (or inheritance taxes) would involve less efficiency losses than distorting, say, electricity or telephone prices. Further, price reductions for certain goods used intensively by the poor can have unintended subsidy effects. The introduction of Lifeline telephone rates in certain states in the US (very low monthly rates with a charge for every call made, designed to subsidize low-use customers who needed a phone in the house) subsidized low-use customers, *not* the poor. Indeed, many poor use the telephone as a substitute for more expensive intra-city travel, and have very high calling rates. Conversely, many well-off persons maintain second homes or apartments, in which the telephone is used very little, so that Lifeline rates, at least in part, subsidize vacation homes for the rich, hardly its intended purpose.

Whenever some goods are subsidized for distributional reasons, the price of other goods must be raised (or 'taxed') in order to pay for the transfer. Should prices be increased sufficiently for these other services, firms may be induced to enter the market for these services, even if they are inefficient, simply by the presence of the subsidy. If entry is foreclosed, either *de jure* or *de facto*, by regulations, firms may spend considerable resources to either subvert or break down these regulatory restrictions and divert the attention of regulators from other activities. Thus the assiduous pursuit of distributional objectives in pricing will tend to create distorted entry signals to other firms, which can result in inefficient use of resources.

More broadly, policymakers concerned with income distribution have many instruments at their command, including taxes on income, real property, wealth, inheritance, wages and commodities, including public utility services. As a general rule legislators and tax experts have not singled out public utility prices as a particularly effective way of redistributing income. Thus, policymakers concerned with the regulation of public enterprises should perhaps leave income redistribution to their legislatures unless specific and unusual circumstances (or a direct legislative mandate) dictate to the contrary. Indeed the argument can be made that explicit attempts by regulators to use prices for distributional purposes directly subverts national taxation policy and objectives, no matter how good-hearted the regulators.

In the enabling statutes of most regulatory bodies, it is often stated that prices should be 'just and reasonable', or 'fair and equitable', without explaining precisely what is meant by these terms. Typically, regulators have interpreted *fairness* in several ways.

(1) Fairness between owners of the enterprise and consumers of the enterprise. Thus, the revenues collected from the consumers should be at least equal to the cost of resources consumed in providing services to these consumers, including an adequate return to risk investment capital, but no more.
(2) Fairness among various consumers of the firm. This is perhaps the most controversial, least understood notion of fairness, and can represent the regulators' and managers' most difficult decisions. We devote the next section to a discussion of this crucial issue.

FAIRNESS AMONG CONSUMERS

The issue of fairness in public enterprise pricing can take several forms, not all of which are mutually consistent:

(1) does the price of each good or service cover the cost of providing that good or service?
(2) does the amount that consumers pay (both individually and collectively) cover the cost of serving those consumers?

(3) are prices non-discriminatory?
(4) are prices uniform across consumers?
(5) can everyone (or almost everyone) afford access to the services of the enterprise?

Costs

The first two concepts of fairness are most strongly related to the idea of cross-subsidy. Assuming the enterprise is producing revenues just sufficient to cover its economic costs of production, are some consumers paying too much, while others pay too little? Are the prices of the goods and services sufficient to cover the added costs (marginal or incremental costs) of producing them? If not, consumers who purchase goods priced below cost are being subsidized by other consumers purchasing goods priced above cost. If the production technology exhibits constant returns to scale in each good, then prices set equal to marginal costs will insure that the enterprise's revenues will just cover its economic costs, and involve no cross-subsidy. In this case, both economic efficiency and fairness (in the sense of no cross-subsidy) are achieved.

Should the production technology be characterized by increasing returns to scale (more precisely, cost sub-additivity), then marginal cost pricing will most likely be insufficient to cover total costs, and the regulators must decide whether to maintain marginal cost pricing and subsidize the enterprise from other sources (for example, tax revenues) or to increase prices sufficiently above marginal costs to cover total cost.

Experience in the USA with external subsidies for increasing-returns industries (for example, the postal service) is perceived as less than successful (although the author is not aware of specific empirical studies supporting such a result). Operationally, marginal costs are estimated only imperfectly, and it can be quite a difficult job determining whether or not prices have actually been set at marginal costs. Further, if any deficits of the enterprise are made good out of the public treasury, there is little incentive for the managers to minimize costs, possibly leading to a very inefficient operation. Requiring that total revenues cover total cost has been the rule in the USA for non-governmental public enterprise (telecommunication, electric power, water, and so on), and appears to be at least an objective even for such government agencies as the US Postal Service. Under these circumstances, subsidy-free prices are those prices which insure revenues for each service (and for each group of services) at least as much as the incremental cost of providing these services (we assume here that the enterprise is regulated to earn just its cost of capital).[3] As a rule, there will be many price vectors which are subsidy-free, any of which cover total costs and generate revenues sufficient to cover incremental costs. Thus, the regulator is often confronted with a choice of prices, all of which are subsidy-free, if the enterprise is characterized by increasing returns to scale.[4]

In such circumstances, can economics provide guidance as to which of the many subsidy-free prices to choose? If economic efficiency is important to the regulator, then the use of Ramsey prices should be considered. Briefly, Ramsey prices are those prices for a multi-commodity enterprise which are the most efficient prices (that is, maximize consumers plus producers surplus) which also cover total costs. Briefly, if marginal cost prices do not cover total costs, prices must be sufficiently above marginal costs (some more, some less) in order to cover total costs. Ramsey prices deviate from marginal costs in such a way as to minimize changes in quantities consumed from those which obtain at marginal costs. Since aggregate social benefit depends upon quantities consumed, Ramsey prices insure that revenues cover total cost with the very least loss in social benefit. As a result, we would expect that Ramsey prices for goods and services which are least price-sensitive (inelastic) would depart furthest from marginal cost, while Ramsey prices for goods and services which are most price-sensitive (elastic) would depart least from marginal cost.[5] It should be noted, however, that in certain circumstances, Ramsey prices may not be subsidy-free. Should this be the case, the regulator may face a trade-off between efficiency in the form of Ramsey pricing, and equity in the form of subsidy-free pricing. He may choose to resolve this dilemma by using the most efficient prices which are subsidy-free (that is, accepting the constraint of subsidy-free, and maximizing surplus subject to this constraint), or simply using Ramsey prices even though a cross-subsidy is thereby involved.

If distributional issues are important, the regulator may wish to choose prices from the set of subsidy-free prices which favour certain classes of consumers (say, retired persons or students). In doing so, the regulator should bear in mind a number of things: (a) achieving distributional goals through public enterprise pricing will almost always have an efficiency cost – whether that loss of efficiency is small or large will depend on the circumstances of the case at hand; of course, but should be of interest to the regulator, and (b) for a given distributional objective, there are almost certainly other means to achieve this objective which involve less efficiency loss than tampering with prices (for example, income or wealth taxes); the regulator should be satisfied that the case at hand admits of no other solution than that of pricing.

As long as redistribution is accomplished within the context of subsidy-free prices, the question is simply that of who gets the marginal cost price. On the other hand, the political pressures for redistribution can force a specific, targeted subsidy of one service by the others. In this case, redistributional notions of fairness may be perceived to outweigh the notion of fairness that each should pay the cost they impose on the system. For example, it may be 'fair' that each good or service pay the cost of providing that service, while at the same time, it may also be considered 'fair' that retired persons or students are served free or at below-cost rates. While such views are not mutually consistent in a logical sense, they are often simultaneously held by large numbers of people.

Should the regulator decide on prices which involve cross-subsidy (either to achieve efficiency, to achieve redistribution, or as a result of a dumb mistake), he may expect more than charges of unfairness. If the subsidies are substantial, there will be groups of consumers whose demands can be satisfied at a lower cost to them than they are being charged; not only will such consumers complain, but we would expect other firms to see the opportunities for profitable entry into these markets. The regulator is then placed in the situation of either permitting free entry and eroding the revenue base for his designed subsidy, or excluding free entry and justifying his action to the potential beneficiaries of such entry. To avoid this embarrassment, the regulator needs to choose prices which are *sustainable*, that is, can sustain the natural monopoly against inefficient, non-innovating entry.[6] While sustainable prices and subsidy-free prices are not always identical, we may normally expect that substantial cross-subsidy will encourage entry, and entry attempts are a signal that cross-subsidy is present.

The concept of subsidy-free prices is related to the goods and services of the public enterprise. In order that it be a proper notion of fairness, it should be related as well to the consumers of the enterprise, and not just the products of that enterprise. It is easy to extend the definition to consumer subsidy-free prices as those prices for which all consumer groups produce revenues sufficient to cover the incremental costs of serving them. In theory, prices which are subsidy-free (by product) need not be consumer subsidy-free, and vice versa. A somewhat stronger notion is that of anonymous equity: prices are anonymously equitable if *all possible* consumer groups generate revenues in excess of their incremental costs. Empirically, it is almost impossible to determine directly whether prices are consumer subsidy-free, but under certain circumstances (determined by the production technology), if prices are subsidy-free (by product), then they are anonymously equitable, and hence consumer subsidy-free. Under these circumstances, a showing that each *service* covers its incremental cost is sufficient to prove that each *consumer group* covers its incremental cost.[7]

Non-Discrimination

In the case of natural monopoly (more generally, any case in which total revenues raised by marginal cost prices do not cover total costs), the weak condition of subsidy-free prices may not be wholly satisfactory as a means of insuring that prices are fair. For example, suppose we have an enterprise with fixed costs of $100, (constant) marginal costs for product 1 of $1, and (constant) marginal cost for product 2 of $2. Assume inelastic demands of 500 for each product; what are 'fair' prices (p_1, p_2)? It could be argued that each price should cover its marginal cost, so that p_1 should be at least $1 and p_2 at least $2 (subsidy-free), and that the overhead should be divided 'fairly'. Suppose each unit sold carried the same amount of allowed fixed cost ($100 divided by total units sold = $0.10). Then p_1 should be $1.10 and p_2 should be $2.10. This could be labelled non-discriminatory in that each unit of production is assigned the same share of the fixed cost. On the other hand, since product 2 is more expensive to produce than product 1, it could be argued that each unit should be assigned fixed costs proportional to its marginal cost. Such a rule would lead to a fixed percentage markup over marginal costs, with p_1 set at $1.067 and p_2 set at $2.133.

Which of these two methods is 'fair', or 'non-discriminatory'? Unfortunately, we can offer no advice here, except to say each method is equally arbitrary. Both, of course, are subsidy-free; they differ in the non-discriminatory rule used to assign the overhead costs to products. We could also have a rule which assigned *all* overhead costs to, say, product 1, so that p_1 would be $1.20, and p_2 would be $2.00. While these prices are subsidy-free, it would likely be argued that they are not fair since product 1 pays more than its 'fair share' of the overheads. Beyond such assertions, however, it is impossible to select an allocation scheme on pure non-discrimination grounds. The problem is even more complicated when the product or service in question has multiple attributes. To take an example (due to Baumol); suppose we wished to allocate the fixed right-of-way costs for a railroad amongst three different types of freight shippers: diamonds, feathers, and crushed stone. We could choose to allocate the fixed costs on the basis of weight, volume, or value; each of the three methods would result in different prices for each of the three shippers, and these shippers would have very definite preferences as to which allocator they preferred. (See Table 2.1.)

Not only is there no 'natural' method of non-discriminatory pricing of fixed overheads, each 'non-discriminatory' method will have strong advocates and strong opponents prepared to use their resources to influence public regulators for their own private gain. Regulators can not escape such pressures by appealing to notions of fairness based on non-discrimination.

Under special circumstances, some weak evidence can be found to support the constant-percentage mark-up allocator (that is, allocating fixed costs in proportion to incremental costs), either for efficiency reasons or for consistency reasons. In the special case of a multiproduct firm in which *demands* are *independent* and demand *elasticities are equal*, then the constant-percentage mark-up allocator leads to efficient (Ramsey) prices.

Should elasticities be not too different from one another this method could be defended as a reasonable approximation which did not require estimating demand elasticities. Of course, this is hardly a fairness argument, but a weak efficiency argument.[8]

Another circumstance favouring the constant percentage markup allocator comes from the work of Billera and Heath on consistent allocators.[9] The authors find that if an allocator of total costs must:

(1) allocate *all* costs;
(2) allocate no less cost to a service if demand increases for that service;
(3) if two goods are identical up to a scalar multiple, the allocated costs should be the same scalar multiple;

TABLE 2.1

Allocation method	Commodity shipped		
	Diamonds	*Feathers*	*Stone*
Weight	M	L	H
Volume	L	H	M
Value	H	M	L

H = high price
M = medium price
L = low price

(4) if the total cost function can be written as the sum of two or more cost functions, then allocating total costs to services should lead to the same answer as allocating the separate cost functions to services and then adding across functions.

Billera and Heath propose these conditions as minimal consistency conditions for any allocator, and then proceed to demonstrate that if the cost function is differentiable everywhere, there is a unique allocator that satisfies conditions (1)–(4). This unique allocator corresponds to the Aumann–Shapley value of a 'trading game' with very many infinitesimal consumers.[10]

It is easy to demonstrate that if the cost function is homothetic,[11] then this unique Aumann–Shapley allocator is the constant-percentage mark-up allocator. Again, this is not a fairness argument, but rather a weak consistency argument.

In sum, the search for fairness via 'non-discriminatory' pricing of fixed overhead costs can be frustrating for the public regulator, and economists hold out little hope for this approach.

Uniformity

It is often asserted that it is 'fair' if all consumers pay the same price for a certain service, such as access to the telephone network, medical insurance premiums, and so on, even if the costs of providing service are substantially different. While this appears to be a non-discrimination argument at first blush, a little thought shows it to be just the opposite. It is rather an argument for average pricing. In the USA, most areas served by telephone companies offer a 'flat rate' service which gives the consumer an unlimited number of local calls for a fixed monthly rate. While all consumers are charged the same, some consumers use the service much more than others, thereby imposing higher costs on the system, and thus raising the rate that must be charged to cover total costs. The rate, then, is an average cost over a distribution of usage across consumers.

Economic theory tells us that such averaging is (a) inefficient and, therefore (b) will attract competitive entry toward those consumers with lower use, and (c) may involve a cross-subsidy of high-use consumers by low-use consumers. Economic practice, however, tells us that in all industries, some price averaging must take place, simply to maintain a price structure that human beings can understand. Should the efficiency costs of such averaging be greater than the transactions and information cost savings realized by averaging, we would expect competitive entry.

In sum, price uniformity is not a good proxy for non-discriminatory pricing, and may indeed mask important cost differences. Price uniformity may be sensible when cost differences are small, simply to increase consumers' understanding of prices.

Universal Access and Affordability

A powerful and recurring theme in public enterprise regulation, especially public utilities, is that it is 'unfair' if only certain persons can afford access to the services of the enterprise. This notion of fairness has a geographical component: every town, city and village should have a railway station, an airport, a telephone exchange and a public education system. It also has a price component; all (or most all) persons should be able to afford to use it, that is, it should have a low price for access.

This concept of fairness seems to have several sources; one is that certain goods and services constitute a kind of social infrastructure, so that an individual without access to them is somehow disenfranchised. It may be thought that every citizen is 'entitled to' a phone, access to a public transport network, a decent education, and so on. The good or service in question (or at least access to it) becomes a social right; exclusion from it is 'unfair'. While such notions are usually beyond the purview of economics, the impact of 'economic justice' concepts in regulated industries has been explored by E. E. Zajac.[12]

The provision of access to unprofitable markets may be thought of as a 'merit good', as that term is traditionally employed in public finance. In many regulated industries, provision of a ubiquitous service at unprofitable prices has often been subsidized by higher, non-sustainable prices in profitable markets. In the US airline market prior to deregulation, it appears that airlines were sometimes awarded profitable routes on condition that they also served certain unprofitable routes or airports, thereby providing access to geographically isolated communities to the domestic air network at low prices. A similar, more severe subsidy appears to be present in US telecommunications in which the highly profitable long-distance (interstate) message service supports the underpriced provision of access to the telephone network through a complicated interjurisdictional mechanism called separations and division of revenues. In all such cases, relaxation of entry restrictions has caused substantial entry into the high-profit markets, thus attacking the revenue base for the subsidy. In the long run, of course, competition can and will erode such subsidies.

Alternative, and more efficient, ways of insuring universal access abound. If cost-based access prices are deemed too high for certain classes of citizens, those classes can be directly reimbursed by the government for telephone service, or receive a tax deduction or credit for such service. Alternatively, local governments could pay for the provision of access facilities (airports, railway spurs, small telephone switching centers), perhaps with Federal aid, to lower the private costs of access to the system. While such arrangements are no doubt more efficient from an economic perspective, governments have been reluctant to implement direct and highly visible subsidies (for which they can be held accountable) when the option exists to implement indirect (and largely invisible) subsidies via public utility prices.[13]

Another source of this concept of fairness has been more recently developed by J. H. Rohlfs,[14] as well as many others, and is called the network (or access) externality. If a consumer joins a communication or a transport network, he not only receives his own private benefit, but bestows benefits to those who are already on the network, who may now call him, visit him more easily, or ship goods to him. Thus, a social, or public, benefit is bestowed over and above the private benefit realized by the individual consumer. Economic theory suggests that in such circumstances, social efficiency may be served by pricing access below what it might otherwise be. Of course, such prices may not be sustainable and may attract competitive entry into the subsidized markets. The importance of this externality in terms of how much prices need to be altered is an empirical issue, and may or may not be important depending on the specific case.

PUBLIC UTILITY PRICING, PUBLIC FINANCE, AND TAXATION

It has long been recognized that the economic analysis of public utility prices bears a strong formal resemblance to that of the taxation and public finance literature. In fact, the basic efficiency principle of Ramsey pricing was originally made by Frank Ramsey in 1927 as a contribution to the taxation literature, not to that of public utility pricing. Similarly, we have alluded to pricing for distributional purposes as related to, or a substitute for, tax policy.

While this correspondence between utility pricing and taxation has been particularly clear on the demand side (for example, the use of the inverse elasticity rule for Ramsey prices/taxes), recent work by Panzar and Willig strongly establish this correspondence on the supply side as well.[15] Specifically, they establish that if economies of scope exist in a multiproduct firm (that is, if it is cheaper to produce a group of products together rather than individually), then there must exist inputs to the production process that are sharable among the group of products. Such inputs are called *quasi-public*, in that they may be used by two or more products without complete congestion. An extreme example is the generating capacity of an electric utility, which may be shared among different hours of the day (or days of the week). The use of the capacity during off-peak hours does not diminish the availability of that capacity during peak hours. Thus, the quasi-public input is analogous to the traditional 'public good' of public finance: a good or service, such as national defense, public parklands and so on, whose benefit to one citizen is not reduced by its consumption by others. Such goods are typically financed by the public sector via taxes. In the case of quasi-public, or sharable, inputs, we would expect its cost to be financed via 'taxes' levied on the goods and services which share the input. Thus, Ramsey pricing can be viewed as an internal taxation scheme to cover the cost of the quasi-public inputs.

With this insight, it is possible to consider any public enterprise pricing scheme as equivalent to a taxation scheme; whatever has been said or written concerning 'fair' and 'equitable' tax burdens applies with equal force in the pricing context. The principles which are compelling in the realm of tax policy are equally compelling in the realm of public enterprise price policy.

SUMMARY

There are many pressures brought to bear on regulators and managers of public enterprises in establishing prices. The economist can offer a principle for determining objective baseline prices with at least some claim to social desirability: Ramsey prices are those prices which lead to the most efficient use of society's resources. Should price-setters be tempted to deviate from such baseline prices for reasons of distributive justice, fairness, demands from special interest groups for favourable treatment and so on, they would be well-advised to examine some key issues.

(1) What is the efficiency cost to the economy of the proposed deviation?

(2) Who pays the cost? Who receives the benefit?

(3) Are there less costly means of accomplishing the same objective?

(4) Are price-setters willing to accede to the demands of others who offer similar justifications of social 'need', 'fairness', 'justice' and the like?

(5) Will the proposed prices encourage potential inefficient entrants? If they are excluded *de jure*, how can that be justified? If not, how can the inefficiency be justified?

(6) Are the notions of fairness being used consistent and acceptable to all parties? Are there alternative notions? If so, what are their effects?

Clearly, economists do not have the final answers to these questions, which must often be answered in the glare of social controversy. At best, our discipline can offer principles and general guidance to the policy-maker. It is the purpose of this paper to summarize those principles in a fashion which is both comprehensible and cogent to the intended audience; it is the hope of the author that this ambitious purpose is at least in part fulfilled.

NOTES AND REFERENCES

1. R. C. Levin, 'Railroad Rates, Profitability, and Welfare Under Deregulation', *Bell J. Econ.*, Spring 1981.
2. Robert Willig and Elizabeth Bailey, 'Income Distributional Concerns in Regulatory Policy-Making', in G. Fromm (ed.), *Studies in Regulation* (Cambridge, Mass.: MIT Press, 1981).
3. It is easy to show that these conditions for prices to be subsidy-free are the same as insuring that the revenue from each service (and group of services) is no greater than the cost to provide that service (or services) on a stand-alone basis. Whichever form of the test is to be used is a matter of practical convenience (assuming, of course, no excess profit).
4. For a precise definition and characterization of subsidy-free prices, see G. R. Faulhaber, 'Cross-Subsidization in Public Enterprise Pricing', *American Economic Review*, Dec. 1975.
5. See W. Baumol and D. Bradford, 'Quasi-Optimal Departures from Marginal Cost Pricing', *American Economic Review*, Sept. 1970.
6. See J. C. Panzar and R. D. Willig, 'Free Entry and the Sustainability of Natural Monopoly', *Bell Journal of Economics*, Spring, 1977.
7. The subsidy relationship between products and consumer groups is discussed in G. R. Faulhaber and S. B. Levinson, 'Subsidy-Free Prices and Anonymous Equity', *American Economic Review*, December, 1981.
8. It has been used as such by G. Knieps, J. Müller and C. C. von Weizsäcker, 'Telecommunications Policy in West Germany, and Challenges from

Technical and Market Development', forthcoming in *Zeitschrift für National Ökonomie.*

9. L. Billera and D. Heath, 'A Unique Procedure for Efficient Allocation of Shared Costs', Technical Report # 430, School of Operations Research and Industrial Engineering, Cornell University, July, 1979.
10. It is related to similar Shapley value results of earlier work by S. C. Littlechild, 'A Game Theoretic Approach to Public Utility Pricing', *Western Economic Journal*, 1980, and E. T. Loehman and A. B. Whinston, 'A Generalized Cost Allocation Scheme', in S. A. Lin (ed.), *Theory and Measurement of Economic Externalities*, (New York: Academic Press, 1976), both of which recommend the use of the Shapley value for cost allocation, but of a 'game' in which the services, or goods are the 'players'.
11. A cost function is homothetic only if at any scale of operation, the cost-minimizing output proportions are the same.
12. E. E. Zajac, 'Is Telephone Service an Economic Right?', in H. Trebing (ed.), *Energy and Communications in Transition*, (East Lansing: Michigan State Univ., 1981).
13. The tendency of regulators to opt for indirect subsidies has been explored by R. A. Posner, 'Taxation by Regulation', *Bell Journal of Economics*, Spring 1971.
14. J. H. Rohlfs, 'A Theory of Interdependent Demand', *Bell Journal of Economics*, 1974.
15. J. C. Panzar and R. D. Willig, 'Economics of Scope', *American Economic Review*, May 1981.

3 Electricity Consumption by Time of Use in a Hybrid Demand System

BRIDGER M. MITCHELL
and JAN PAUL ACTON[1]

INTRODUCTION

Peak-load pricing has long been advocated for the sale of electricity and other services in which periodic variations in demand are jointly supplied by a common plant of fixed capacity. Time-of-use (TOU) electricity rates have been widely used in Europe for several decades to reflect peak-load cost variations. By contrast, in the USA TOU rates began to receive serious consideration only following the 1973–74 Arab oil embargo.[2]

To better understand the likely consequences of TOU pricing for residential users, several US electric utilities undertook a series of rate trials beginning in 1975.[3] Most of these 'demonstration projects' had very limited variation in experimental prices and did not permit own- and cross-price effects of a TOU rate to be determined. However the more ambitious studies were designed to yield detailed data on electricity consumption under a variety of experimental rates and different levels of major variables affecting electricity use – household appliances, economic and demographic characteristics and weather conditions.

Several analytic approaches are available to estimate the own- and cross-price effects of TOU rates in order to forecast changes in electricity use and measure net welfare effects.[4] The principal effects can be determined from an analysis of variance or covariance of independently estimated equations for each rate period. Such estimation techniques impose a minimum of structure, but they fail to exploit the implications of utility maximizing behaviour from neoclassical demand theory and cannot calculate changes in consumer surplus, which require estimated demand curves. At the other extreme, highly structured systems of demand equations can be estimated in order to extract more information from the experimental data. Such systems impose restrictions on the demands for electricity across different rate periods and frequently between electricity and other goods as well.[5] However, these systems require highly restrictive or untestable assumptions that increase the risk of obtaining spurious empirical findings.[6]

Another limitation of neoclassical consumer theory is its lack of guidance regarding the effects of weather, appliance ownership and a number of household characteristics on electricity demand. Indeed, in many specifications the dependent variable becomes 'weather-adjusted consumption' or 'relative demand per electrical appliance'; under these conditions, there is no compelling reason to expect Slutsky symmetry, homothetic separability or other features of demand system theory to hold.

To reliably estimate TOU rate effects we proceed cautiously and employ a hybrid approach to modelling and estimating TOU electricity demand. First, we estimate the basic pattern of demand with minimal restrictions to see if consumer behaviour is broadly consistent with economic theory. Then, we incorporate greater structure and restrictions after the basic pattern of response has been determined. This staged approach offers the advantage of being able to test some simple implications of rational behaviour – for example, greater consumption under more extreme weather conditions and reduced consumption in the face of higher overall prices – before the consumer's response is represented by a large number of parameters which require simultaneous interpretation. Furthermore, this approach allows us to assess whether the estimated components of the demand estimates – for example, the predicted use by different types of appliances – are reasonable when compared to information from other sources such as end-use measurements. The hybrid approach also allows us to separate the effects of weather, appliance holdings and other explanatory factors from the effects of prices. This permits greater flexibility in applying the estimates to another forecasting situation where exogenous estimates of non-price demand can be easily incorporated.

In the remainder of this chapter we develop the model for estimating electricity demand under TOU pricing and apply it to data from the Los Angeles Electricity Rate Study. The next section presents a brief description of that study and its data base. The third section outlines the hybrid modelling approach and some of its advantages. The fourth section presents the empirical results. The final section summarizes the results in terms of demand elasticities and compares them with estimates obtained from other studies.

THE LOS ANGELES EXPERIMENT AND DATA BASE

The Los Angeles Electricity Rate Study, jointly undertaken by the Los Angeles Department of Water and Power and The Rand Corporation over the 1975–80 period, included extensive variation in rate forms and rate levels so that statistically identified own- and cross-price effects could be determined over a wide variety of costing and demand conditions. The study had two major components – a seasonal experiment, in which the price was constant throughout the day but varied between winter and summer, and a time-of-use experiment, in which rates varied over three hour rating periods.[7] The present analysis treats only TOU demand.[8]

Design of the TOU Experiment

In all, 1268 households were available for TOU analysis. Nine hundred and thirty-one households were observed on one of 17 TOU rates that apply either 5 or 7 days per week (for a total of 34 different rate structures). An additional 337 households faced either seasonal, flat or declining-block rates but had their use recorded continuously; they served as 'control' households for TOU customers and their consumption could be included in much of the analysis. Magnetic tape cassette meters recorded the electricity use every 15 minutes for these 1268 households.

Table 3.1 shows the distribution of experimental households by rate plans. Five congruent rate periods (09–12, 12–15, 15–18, 18–21, 21–09) permit data from the 17 TOU rate plans to be analyzed simultaneously in a single demand system.

Participation in the study was voluntary. Households were first interviewed to determine basic household demographics and appliance ownership. If they were eligible for the study (that is, paid their own electricity bill, no family member worked for Rand or the Los Angeles Department of Water and Power and so on), they received an offer to join the study and pay for electricity under an experimental rate. Our desire to estimate demand curves that might apply in future circumstances led to plans under which some households could have been worse

TABLE 3.1   *Rate plans and number of households*

No.	Peak period			Prices per kWh (cents)			Number of households on peak rates	
	i	Hours	Peak	Peak	Off-peak	Average*	Mon. – Fri.	Mon. – Sun.
00	—	00–24	Conventional Declining Block Rate			—	—	175‡
0S	—	00–24	Seasonal†			—	—	68‡
0A	—	00–24	2		2	2	—	56‡
0B	—	00–24	5		5	5	—	38‡
1	1	09–12	5		2	2.35	37	34
2	1	09–12	9		2	2.81	24	27
3	1	09–12	13		2	3.27	9	9
4	2	12–15	9		2	2.87	18	16
5	2	12–15	13		2	3.36	10	10
6	3	15–18	5		2	2.43	9	9
7	3	15–18	9		2	3.01	34	35
8	3	15–18	13		2	3.59	29	39

9	4	18–21	5	2	2.55	9	10
10	4	18–21	9	2	3.29	27	26
11	4	18–21	13	2	4.03	26	25
12	5	21–09	5	2	3.30	72	71
13	3–4	15–21	7	2	3.34	16	15
14	2–4	12–21	5	2	3.36	49	56
15	2–4	12–21	9	2	5.17	27	27
16	1–4	09–21	5	1	3.27	27	30
17	1–4	09–21	9	1	5.54	35	34
Totals						458	810

* Average price per kWh computed for the reference load curve at a flat rate.
† Households with seasonal plans and cassette meters are used in the share analysis but not in the total consumption analysis.
‡ Households with recording meters.

off if their electricity use remained unchanged. Those households were offered quarterly compensation in the form of 'participation payments' based on their pre-experimental level and time-of-day pattern of use; the payments were unaffected by experimental use. Although self-selection bias is an appropriate concern in such voluntary experiments, over 92 per cent of the eligible households offered an experimental rate plan accepted it and we make no adjustment in the results reported below.[9]

Household Information

Extensive household-specific information was collected in three surveys made at the beginning, the midpoint and the end of the study. Data on household composition, appliance ownership, income and attitudes were collected during each 30-minute interview. In the present analysis, we use the responses provided in the first two surveys, which apply most directly to the 24-month period of data used for the empirical analysis. Household values for income, family size and housing rental value are updated from the end-project survey.

Weather Data

Hourly weather data are collected in each of three climate zones in the city of Los Angeles: (1) a mild coastal zone with moderate summer and winter temperatures, (2) an inland valley zone with more extreme temperatures in both summer and winter, and (3) a civic centre area with intermediate temperatures. We reflect weather through heating and cooling degree hours, taken as deviations from 65°F.[10] This use of hourly measures of temperature captures the detailed variation in weather over a day. In contrast, the more familiar heating or cooling degree-day – which is based on mean daily temperature – takes on a single value in a 24-hour period, which masks the differences between two days with identical mean temperature but very different high and low temperatures.

OVERVIEW OF THE ANALYTIC APPROACH

Our basic model of electricity consumption by time of use may be schematically represented by three types of systematic components plus unmeasured factors (random error)

$$(\text{electricity}_{hjt}) = f(\text{weather}_{hjt}, \text{household}_{hj}, \text{price}_{hj}, \text{error}_{hjt}) \quad (3.1)$$

Consumption in kilowatt hours at hour h, by household j, in month t depends on the weather; on that household's characteristics in terms of electrical appliances, behavioural patterns, and economic resources; and on the prices by time of use charged for electricity.

The primary objective of a TOU electricity pricing experiment is to accurately measure the price component of electricity consumption so that the changes in load resulting from proposed TOU rates can be estimated and the economic benefits of such pricing evaluated. To do so, however, the weather and the household-specific components of consumption must be accurately accounted for.

The Hybrid Model of Demand

In this chapter we adopt a three-stage approach. First, we estimate the variation in hourly consumption that results from the month-to-month variation in weather and adjust each household's consumption to a level corresponding to average weather conditions. Second, we determine how the adjusted consumption, including the mean weather effects, is distributed over the hours of the day. Because hourly consumption data were not measured prior to the introduction of TOU rates in the Los Angeles experiment, it is necessary to separate the 'permanent' or normal use in each time period from the response to TOU rates. To accomplish this we estimate a reference load curve (for a household of given characteristics at average weather) that indicates the proportions of daily electricity consumption used in each period of the day when a uniform price for electricity is charged at all hours. The experimental TOU rates are then used to explain deviations from this load curve. Finally, in the third stage of analysis, we explain the level of total electricity consumption by the household's characteristics and the average price of electricity in peak and off-peak hours.

Two Analytic Approaches

We report estimates of the price-component effects based on two types of analysis. A straightforward approach to assessing TOU rates is to first standardize all households to a common reference load curve and then to measure separately, for each of the 17 weekday TOU rates in the Los Angeles experiment, the effect of each rate on (1) consumption in each period of the day, and (2) total consumption. This *analysis of covariance* method imposes a minimum number of assumptions when processing the original data and reveals the basic patterns of response produced by the experiment. It amounts to assuming that the responses to the TOU rates of the 17 groups of households have nothing in common.

In fact, the empirical results suggest common regularities among the different groups that are consistent with the theory of consumer demand. We therefore introduce a two-level *demand system* and estimate its complete set of parameters. The demand system equations simultaneously explain both the distribution of consumption by rate period and the overall level of consumption as a function of all TOU prices. These estimates yield own-price and cross-price effects on demand for five weekday rate periods and permit prediction of load shifts due to proposed TOU rate plans, including rates not directly tested in the experiment. The estimated coefficients measure the change in relative loads. Full price elasticities calculated from these coefficients permit comparison with estimates from other models and data sources, and the estimated load curve shows the overall effect of a representative TOU tariff.

Advantages of Hybrid Model

The hybrid model allows estimation with minimal structure imposed on the data before proceeding with more restrictive analysis. The decomposition of demand into a weather component, a demographic and appliance component and a behavioural response to TOU prices permits greater flexibility and forecasting accuracy when analyzing TOU effects under different circumstances.

Using a weather-adjusted reference load curve removes one important source of variation for which economic theory offers little guidance. The price-related and household-specific estimates are more useful for forecasting loads that have had weather effects removed. In applying these experimental results to another utility service area, the analyst can either use a predicted reference load curve (based on the weather component estimated with Los Angeles data) or a local reference load curve (perhaps based on a load study) which may more accurately represent local weather-related effects.

Second, by separating relative consumption by time-of-use from total electricity consumption, exogenous estimates or assumptions of long-run effects that may be unmeasurable in an experimental context can be introduced. For example, if the analyst thinks secular trends or price-induced changes in appliance ownership will produce a shift in total consumption, he can combine that information with the estimates that capture the behavioural shifts by the time of use conditional on a given stock of appliances. In addition, if it is anticipated that future appliances may contain features that assist adaptation to TOU rates (for example, built-in timers), the coefficients on those appliances can be adjusted within the model's equations to account for those effects.

Unit of Analysis

The household is the unit for present analysis. Consumption data for each household are available for each 15-minute interval over the 30 months of its participation in the experiment (which covered the period July 1976–June 1979 – approximately 100 million observations). The data available to explain electricity use are of two basic types: *time-dependent variables*, chiefly measures of weather conditions, but also the occurrence of vacations and changes in household appliances and demographic factors; and *household-dependent variables*, which are effectively constant over the life of the experiment. Household-dependent variables are the price of electricity by time of day and the household's appliances and demographic and economic character-istics.[11]

As a practical matter, such voluminous data require aggregation prior to analysis. For this report we have used 24 months of data from January 1977 to December 1978, a period during which nearly all households faced only their experimental rates. We aggregated the raw 15-minute observations in each period, K_{hjt}, into the average daily consumption in each rate period for each month. Using the 10 rate periods in Table 3.2

TABLE 3.2   *Time of use rate periods*

Hours	Weekday	Weekend
09–12	1	6
12–15	2	7
15–18	3	8
18–21	4	9
21–09	5	10

our initial data unit is the kilowatt-hour measure

$$\tilde{X}_{ijt} = (1/n_{hjt}) \sum_{h \varepsilon H(i)} K_{hjt} \qquad (3.2)$$

where h is the index of 15-minute intervals,

$H(i)$ is the set of 15-minute intervals in rate period i,

j indexes the household,

t indexes the month,

n_{ijt} is the number of effective 24-hour days of observations per
             month[12]

Note that the daytime periods 1–4 and 6–9 are each 3 hours long; however, the overnight periods, 5 and 10, are each 12 hours long because there is no price variation within these overnight periods. Unless stated otherwise, all analysis in this chapter refers to average daily consumption in each period.

This level of data aggregation strikes a balance between the detail needed to detect the effects of specific rate plans and the costs of processing daily or hourly observations.[13] For particular questions of special interest, subsequent analysis might use less aggregated data – for example, hourly loads for selected days of the year.

EMPIRICAL RESULTS

In the hybrid model of demand, we first estimate the weather component of electricity use and adjust each household's consumption to a level corresponding to that at average weather. The weather-adjusted data determine a reference load curve for each household. The effects of household characteristics and TOU rate plans on electricity use by time of day and on total consumption are estimated as deviations from this load curve. In this section we present model-free estimates of demand based on an analysis of covariance and then present estimates of total demand for electricity and its distribution by time period using a complete system of demand equations. Finally, we report some miscellaneous empirical results of electricity use under experimental circumstances.

Weather-sensitive Consumption

The primary cause of month-to-month variation in electricity consumption that is measurable with available explanatory variables is weather. Temperature differences cause electricity use to vary by time of day, and this variation is largely independent of the price of electricity.[14] For households whose price of electricity does not vary over the hours of the day, we assume that consumption $\tilde{X}_{ijt}$ in period i can be decomposed into a weather component, $W_i(\cdot)$, plus a component for household j that is invariant to weather conditions, a_{ij}.

To estimate each weather component, we follow work reported earlier and assume that the effective stock of weather-sensitive appliances varies with their capacity, the area to be cooled or heated and outside temperature.[15] The air-conditioning variable (AC) is an index that combines central, wall and evaporative units weighted by their relative consumption rates and house size. The variable ($HEAT$) measures the availability of space heating and house size.[16] The heating and cooling appliances are affected quadratically by the monthly mean temperature ($TEMP$) in each rate period, measured in cooling degree-hours for air-conditioning and in heating degree-hours for space heating. Hourly temperature readings are available for three distinct climatic zones in Los Angeles, but not at each residence; the degree-hour variable for a household is that measured for its zone in the city. The other time-dependent variables that influence monthly consumption are whether an adult member of the household is normally at home during the period ($HOME$) or is on vacation in that month (VAC).[17]

Ten weather equations, one for each rate period, take the following general form

$$\tilde{X}_{ijt} = a_{ij} + W_i(AC_{jt}, HEAT_{jt}, TEMP_{ijt}, VAC_{jt}, HOME_{jt}) + e_{ijt}$$
(3.3)

$$i = 1, \ldots, 10 \text{ (rate period)}$$

$$j = 1, \ldots, n \text{ (household)}$$

$$t = 1, \ldots, T \text{ (month)}$$

The detailed specification is shown in Table 3.3.

The weather equations are estimated using 24 months of data from the 337 households on flat, seasonal and declining-block rates. For computational convenience, the parameters are estimated using deviation from household means as observations. Ordinary least-squares (OLS) estimates, assuming the unobserved error e_{ijt} to be independently distributed with constant variance, explain 18–53 per cent of the variation in mean monthly weekday and weekend consumption by rate period.

The weather component W_i is the mean consumption of electricity used for cooling or heating at a given outside temperature. Table 3.4 shows that when the temperature in the morning is 80°F, households with central air-conditioning use an average of 0.75 kWh per hour for space cooling. This value falls at midday and then rises substantially in

TABLE 3.3   *Specification of weather-sensitive consumption equations**

$$\tilde{X}_{ijt} = a_{ij} + \beta_{1i}AC_{jt}\cdot CDH_{ijt} + \beta_{2i}AC_{jt}\cdot CDH_{ijt}^2 + \gamma_{1i}HEAT_{ji}\cdot HDH_{ijt}$$
$$+ \gamma_{2i}HEAT_{jt}\cdot HDH_{ijt}^2 + \delta_i VAC_{jt} + \rho_i HOME_{jt} + e_{ijt}$$

$$i = 1, \ldots, 10 \qquad \text{(rate periods)}$$
$$j = 1, \ldots, n \qquad \text{(households)}$$
$$t = 1, \ldots, T \qquad \text{(months)}$$

Definition of variables

$$AC_j = [1 + \log(ROOMS_j/\overline{ROOMS})]\cdot ACSTOCK_{jt}$$

$ACSTOCK\dagger =$ $1\cdot$central electricity or combination gas/electric AC
     $+ 0.60\cdot$central gas AC
     $+ 0.37\cdot$central evaporative AC
     $+ 0.18\cdot$number of wall refrigerative AC
     $+ 0.12\cdot$number of wall evaporative AC

$$HEAT_{jt} = [1 + \log(ROOMS_j/\overline{ROOMS})]\cdot HEATSTOCK_j$$

$HEATSTOCK =$ $1\cdot$heat pump
     $+ 1\cdot$central electric space heat
     $+ 1\cdot$central combination gas/electric space heat

$VAC_{jt} =$ number of days household j was empty in month t.

$HOME_{jt} = 1$ if an adult is usually at home daytime on weekdays in the week-day equations. A similar variable $= 1$ for weekends.

$ROOMS_{jt}, \overline{ROOMS} =$ number of (and mean) rooms (including kitchen, excluding bath).

---

* Equation estimated by OLS with all variables as deviations from household-specific means; for example $(\tilde{X}_{ijt} - (1/T)\sum \tilde{X}_{ijt})$ where T_j is the number of months of data available for household j. Total observations = 7024.
† Coefficients represent the mean relative consumption of various types of air-conditioning units.

the afternoon and evening periods. The variation in mean rates of consumption undoubtedly reflects the increased probability that the home is occupied in the later hours of the day and also, perhaps, the increased energy required to cool unoccupied rooms that have heated up by late afternoon.

For space heating, the weather component of mean consumption at 55°F on weekdays is relatively constant. (The projected negative consumption during the warmest period of the day is beyond the range

TABLE 3.4 *Weather-sensitive consumption: households with central air conditioning and electric space heating*

Period		Mean weekday consumption (kWh/hr)	
i	hours	Cooling (at 80° F)	Heating (at 55° F)
1	09–12	0.75	1.48
2	12–15	0.23	−0.32*
3	15–18	1.01	1.33
4	18–21	2.33	1.08
5	21–09	0.30	0.46

* Temperature is outside range of average monthly data at midday.

of average temperatures at those hours.) This regularity, and the lower mean rate of consumption in the overnight period, is consistent with a constant daytime thermostat setting that is set back to a cooler level overnight. Because electric space heating is not widely used in Los Angeles these estimates are somewhat less reliable than those for air-conditioning.

Time-of-use and Total Consumption in an Analysis of Covariance Framework

To put all households on a comparable basis we use the estimated weather components to adjust each household's electricity use to the estimated level that would prevail if temperatures were at the city-wide average levels $\overline{TEMP_i}$ in the ith rate period

$$X_{ijt}^{adj} = \hat{X}_{ijt} - W_i(AC_{jt}, HEAT_{jt}, TEMP_{ijt} - \overline{TEMP_i}, VAC_{jt}, HOME_{jt}) \tag{3.4}$$

These adjusted consumption values, which fluctuate monthly due to unmeasured random effects, are averaged over 24 months for each household

$$\alpha_{ij} = (1/T) \sum_t X_{ijt}^{adj} \tag{3.5}$$

to obtain the household-specific component of electricity consumption at each rate period. The components α_{ij} incorporate the jth household's pattern of consumption that is due to its appliance and demographic characteristics, its estimated consumption at average weather conditions, and its responses to its rate plan. Because all of the major time-dependent explanatory variables have been incorporated into the estimated weather component, the remaining analysis is conducted using average 24-month consumption values and explanatory variables that are essentially constant for each household j.

Kilowatt hour Share Equations

We are now in a position to analyze the distribution of household j's consumption by time of day in terms of its relative load curve. For the five weekday rate periods in the experiment, this load curve is given by the household's weekday consumption component α_{ij} in each period divided by its total daily consumption, or

$$s_{ij} = (\alpha_{ij}/\alpha_j); \quad i = 1, \ldots, 5 \quad \text{and} \quad \alpha_j = \sum_1^5 \alpha_{ij} \tag{3.6}$$

These consumption shares s_{ij} vary systematically with household characteristics; they are also changed by TOU rates.[18]

We estimate share equations for each of the five rate periods of the form

$$s_{ij} = f(PLAN_j, APPL_j, DEMO_j) + e_{ij}$$

$$= a_i + \sum_m b_{im} PLAN_{mj} + \sum_k f_{ik} APPL_{kj} + \sum_k g_{ik} DEMO_{kj} \tag{3.7}$$

$$i = 1, \ldots, 5$$

The vector of dummy variables ($PLAN_m$) indicates which rate plan is assigned to the household, and vectors of appliance ($APPL_k$) and demographic ($DEMO_k$) variables allow us to standardize relative loads across households with different characteristics. These equations are estimated by ordinary least squares with the same set of explanatory variables in each equation, ensuring that the sum of the estimated shares is 100 per cent for each household. They explain 24–36 per cent of the variations in mean weekday relative loads.[19]

The plan, appliance and demographic variables are all important determinants of the household load curve. For economy of exposition, we report only the plan effects from the analysis of covariance and discuss the demographic and appliance variables later in the context of the demand system model.

TOU Price Effects on Relative Loads

In the share equations (3.7) the effect of prices is represented by separate dummy variables $PLAN_m$ for each type of plan.[20] For households on the '2¢-flat' plan who paid 2¢/kWh at all hours, all of the $PLAN$ dummy variables take zero values. Thus, the average consumption of those households on the 2¢-flat plan constitutes the mean *reference load curve* against which the effects of other plans are compared.[21] At the mean values of the weather, demographic and appliance variables for the experimental households, the weekday reference load curve is

Period	i :	1	2	3	4	5
Share (per cent)	s_i :	10.7	11.5	15.3	19.7	42.3

The covariance analysis specification is effectively 'model-free' in prices and allows each TOU rate plan to have an independent effect on the relative load in each of the five rate periods.[22] In Table 3.5 we summarize these effects in terms of the change in consumption relative to the 2¢-flat reference load, using estimated coefficients b_{im} in the peak periods.[23] The first two rows of the table are for the 2¢ and 5¢ flat-rate plans in which there is no incentive to shift loads. In subsequent rows the TOU plans are grouped by peak period, in ascending order of peak price within each group. The upper portion of Table 3.5 reports the 12 TOU plans with a single three-hour peak period. The reported values are the mean (percentage-point) changes in the peak period shares. For example, plans 1, 2 and 3 have peak prices of 5¢, 9¢ and 13¢ per kWh respectively at 9 am to noon. These rates reduce the consumption share at this period by 1.5, 2.4 and 3.4 percentage points. The estimated pattern is highly consistent: relative to the reference load at a 2¢ flat rate, TOU rates reduce the share in every peak period, and in most cases higher TOU prices result in greater reductions. Most of the estimated effects differ significantly from the load at a 2¢ flat rate. Moreover, as shown in the lower part of the table, plans with 6-, 9- and 12-hour peak periods (plans 13–17) cause reductions during every three-hour period that the peak rates are in effect.

At most of the peak price periods, there are two or three separate TOU plans with different price levels. The experimental design thus permits us to interpret the effects of each TOU rate plan in terms of the incremental

TABLE 3.5   *Time-of-use price effects relative to consumption at 2¢-flat plan*

Plan No.	No. of House-holds	Peak periods i	Peak periods Hours	Prices per kWh Peak	Prices per kWh Off-peak	Change in peak period weekday share	t-ratio	Change in total monthly consumption kWh(%)	t-ratio
0A	56	—	00–24	2¢	2¢	—	—	—	—
0B	38	—	00–24	5¢	5¢	—	—	−3.7	(−0.4)
					Single period peak plans				
1	71	1	09–12	5¢	2¢	−1.53	(−3.0)	−5.3	(−0.8)
2	51	1	09–12	9¢	2¢	−2.40	(−4.3)	−0.0	(−0.0)
3	18	1	09–12	13¢	2¢	−3.39	(−4.4)	−10.0	(−1.0)
4	34	2	12–15	9¢	2¢	−2.41	(−3.7)	−4.2	(−0.5)
5	20	2	12–15	13¢	2¢	−1.07	(−1.4)	−7.1	(−0.7)
6	18	3	15–18	5¢	2¢	−1.36	(−1.5)	0.7	(0.1)
7	69	3	15–18	9¢	2¢	−1.30	(−2.8)	−6.8	(−1.0)
8	68	3	15–18	13¢	2¢	−2.02	(−3.3)	−5.9	(−0.8)
9	19	4	18–21	5¢	2¢	−0.40	(−0.4)	1.0	(0.1)
10	53	4	18–21	9¢	2¢	−1.99	(−3.0)	−8.2	(−1.0)
11	51	4	18–21	13¢	2¢	−0.86	(−1.3)	−6.3	(−0.8)
12	143	5	21–09	5¢	2¢	−0.85	(−0.8)	−0.1	(−0.0)

Multiple-period peak plans

						Periods					
						1	2	3	4		
13	31	3–4	15–21	7¢	2¢			−1.62	−2.53	−10.1	(−1.1)
14	105	2–4	12–21	5¢	1¢		−1.69	−1.19	−0.87	1.3	(0.2)
15	54	2–4	12–21	9¢	1¢		−1.30	−1.92	−1.63	−7.5	(−0.9)
16	57	1–4	09–21	5¢	1¢	−1.55	−1.07	−0.69	−0.73	−5.1	(−0.7)
17	69	1–4	09–21	9¢	1¢	−2.03	−2.18	−2.55	−0.80	−15.6	(−2.0)

change that successively higher peak prices have on relative peak loads. For example, in Table 3.5 TOU Plan 1 was estimated to reduce the 9 am to noon load 1.53 percentage points. Table 3.6 shows the plan-by-plan effects on the basis of incremental price effect.[24] Plan 1 has a 3¢ (5¢ − 2¢) differential between peak and off-peak prices so the estimated rate of change in the peak period weekday share per 1¢ increase in the peak period price is − 0.51. This value is shown as the first entry in Table 3.6. Plan 2 (9¢ peak, 2¢ off-peak) increases the price differential by an additional 4¢ = 9¢ − 5¢ and causes a further reduction in the 9 am to noon load share at the rate of − 0.22 per 1¢ difference in price. Plan 3 causes a similar − 0.25 incremental rate of load reduction. Thus, at the 9 am to noon peak period the estimated effects are consistent with a negatively sloped demand curve that becomes steeper at higher prices. In only a few cases is an incremental effect of a higher peak period price statistically different from zero. Thus, the overall pattern of estimated effects in most rate periods appears to be one in which the maximum rate of response results from the initial price difference, with notably smaller incremental effects occurring at higher price differentials.

TOU Price Effects on Total Consumption

The preceding results establish that TOU rates systematically alter the time of day distribution of the daily load. To determine whether TOU rates also affect total consumption, we first calculate monthly consumption at mean weather conditions for a month with the average 21.7 weekdays and 8.6 weekend days

$$\overline{X}_j = 21.7 \sum_{i=1}^{5} \alpha_{ij} + 8.6 \sum_{i=6}^{10} \alpha_{ij} \tag{3.8}$$

We then estimate an equation for total monthly consumption that is similar in form to the share equations

$$\overline{X}_j = f(PLAN_j, APPL_j, DEMO_j) + e_j \tag{3.9}$$

$$= a + \sum_m b_m PLAN_{mj} + \sum_k f_k APPL_{kj} + \sum_k g_k PLAN_{kj} + e_j$$

Because total consumption varies across households from one hundred to several thousand kWH per month, we use an extensive set of appliance and demographic variables to capture systematic differences

TABLE 3.6 Rate of change in peak period weekday share per 1¢ difference between peak and off-peak price

Peak period i	Hours	Single peak period plans	Multiple peak period plans		
			2 period	3 period	4 period
1	09–12	−0.51* (5/2)† −0.22 (9/2) −0.25 (13/2)			−0.39* (5/1) −0.12 (9/1)
2	12–15	−0.34* (9/2) 0.33 (13/2)		−0.42* (5/1) 0.10 (9/1)	−0.27* (5/1) −0.28* (9/1)
3	15–18	−0.45* (5/2) −0.09 (9/2) −0.08 (13/2)	−0.33* (7/2)	−0.30* (5/1) −0.18 (9/1)	−0.17 (5/1) −0.46* (9/1)
4	18–21	−0.13 (5/2) −0.40* (9/2) 0.28 (13/2)	−0.51* (7/2)	−0.22 (5/1) −0.19 (9/1)	−0.18 (5/1) −0.02 (9/1)
5	21–09	−0.28 (5/2)			

* Significant at 95 per cent confidence level, one-tailed test.
† Peak/off-peak prices in ¢ per kWh are shown in parentheses.

across households. Overall, the equation explains 72 per cent of the variance in monthly weather-adjusted consumption between households.

The estimated effects of each TOU plan on total monthly consumption relative to consumption under a 2 ¢ flat rate are shown in the last two columns of Table 3.5. The coefficients are negative in all but three cases and indicate that higher average rates per kWh do reduce overall electricity use. However, one coefficient is significantly different from zero and the joint hypothesis of no TOU plan effect on total consumption cannot be rejected.

Summary of Analysis of Covariance

The covariance analysis of TOU price effects provides strong evidence that TOU rates alter the time-of-day distributions of residential loads and, less clearly, suggests that the rates also affect total consumption.

In an actual application of TOU rates, households will generally move from a declining-block or flat rate to a TOU rate that, on average, raises the same total revenue (apart from changes in level of use). Thus, it is not clear, *a priori*, whether total consumption can be expected to increase, fall, or remain constant – only a complete demand system analysis can address that question. But the expected effect of decreased peak and increased off-peak use is clear, and the covariance analysis of the experimental data is broadly consistent with the anticipated effects. Considering the relatively small number of households per experimental plan, the pattern of mean responses across rate plans is highly consistent with predicted economic behaviour.

Demand System Analysis

To more fully exploit the rich experimental design of the Los Angeles experiment, we now specify the price effects in terms of a two-level system of demand equations. Congruence of the rate periods over all 17 TOU plans allows all households to be pooled into a single sample. The demand equation for each rate period includes major appliance and demographics variables that standardize the relative load curve across households with varying characteristics. The parameter estimates that we obtain enable us to reliably estimate the magnitude of the effects of each rate period's price on both total consumption and its distribution over the day.

In principle, one can postulate a utility function and derive a demand curve for each rate period. Each consumer would have a utility function containing the services of electricity consumed in each period and a composite commodity representing all non-electricity consumption. When maximized subject to a budget constraint, the utility function would imply restrictions on the specification and coefficients of the individual demand equations. This approach has been applied to several sets of data from TOU rate demonstration projects.[25] However, formally derived consumer demand systems are not easily adapted to the demand for intermediate goods and services. In practice such models have required either very strong assumptions on the structure of the underlying utility function or arbitrarily introducing other parameters – such as appliance stocks – into the utility function.

Our approach in this chapter is less formal. We model TOU effects at two levels – the effect on total consumption and on consumption by time of day relative to the reference load curve of a household at a 2 ¢ flat rate. By this artifice we usefully decompose a single reality – the change in kWh consumption at each rate period. We measure total consumption in kilowatt hours. This aggregate, rather than the total expenditure on electricity that is used in neoclassical demand systems, allows straightforward comparison of results with previous estimates of electricity demand.

Introduction of a TOU rate will generally affect consumption in every rate period. First, a TOU rate will change the average price of electricity and thereby total monthly electricity consumption. Based on the household's consumption shares in each rate period at a 2¢ flat rate, the household's price index $\bar{p}$ for total kilowatt hours will change from $\bar{p} = 2.0$ to some new $\bar{p} = f(p_1, \ldots, p_{10})$. Along with this overall reduction in total consumption is a shift in the relative load curve – the kWh shares at each period. For example, if the TOU rate has its peak price $p_1 = 5 ¢$ in period 1 and off-peak prices $p_2 = \ldots = p_{10} = 2 ¢$ in other periods, the expected effect is a reduction in both total use and the percentage of total consumption that occurs in period 1. The reduced share in period 1 will necessarily increase the percentage share in one or more other periods.

Relative Demand Estimates

In the complete demand system the kWh share equations are similar to equation (3.7) estimated in the covariance analysis, except that the dummy variable treatment of plan effects is replaced by a set of price terms, $b_{ik}p_k^*$, so that the kWh share equations become

$$s_{ij} = a_i + \sum_k b_{ik}p_k^* + \sum_k f_{ik}APPL_{kj} + \sum_k g_{ik}DEMO_{kj} + e_{ij} \quad (3.10)$$

The TOU prices are entered in relative form as

$$p_k^* = \log(p_k/p_5), \ k = 1, \ldots, 4 \text{ weekdays} \quad (3.11)$$

$$p_k^* = \log(p_k/p_{10}), \ k = 6, \ldots, 9 \text{ weekends}$$

The implicit assumption is that consumers adjust consumption shares on the basis of the ratio of prices in different periods. The logarithmic transformation of this price ratio reflects the pattern observed in the covariance analysis – a diminishing proportional load-shifting effect as the absolute differences between peak and off-peak prices increase.

The five weekday and five weekend share equations were first estimated as specified in (3.10) by OLS with price variables p_k^* and the same demographic and appliance variables used in the analysis of covariance. The estimated own-price share coefficients were all negative and highly significant on a one-tailed ($P = 0.05$) t-test; most of the cross-price effects were positive, but only 6 of 15 were statistically significant by a two-tailed test.

Next, we tested to see whether households with particular appliances are sensitive to TOU rates. We augmented specification (3.10) to include additional sets of coefficients for the TOU prices interacted with major appliance variables. Statistically significant effects were found for both swimming pools and air conditioners; with this specification the estimated share equations are

$$s_{ij} = a_i + \sum_k (b_{ik} + c_{ik}POOL_j + d_{ik}AC_j)p_k^* + \sum_k f_{ik}APPL_{kj}$$

$$+ \sum_k g_{ik}DEMO_{kj} + e_{ij} \quad (3.12)$$

The estimates of these coefficients appear in Table 3.7. TOU rates have quite modest effects on the relative loads of households having neither a pool nor an air conditioner: only two of the estimated own-price share coefficients differ significantly from zero. In contrast, nearly all of the coefficients for households with a pool are significant, indicating that such customers do respond to TOU rates in both the peak and off-peak

TABLE 3.7 *Weekday demand system price coefficients*

Rate i	period Hour	k	Coefficient of $\ln(p_k/p_s)$ 1	2	3	4	Coefficient of $\ln(p_k/p_s)\cdot$ POOL 1	2	3	4	Coefficient of $\ln(p_k/p_s)\cdot$ AC 1	2	3	4	R^2
1	09–12 s_1		−0.36 (−2.22)	−0.00 (−0.02)	−0.00 (−0.01)	0.12 (0.61)	−3.01 (−8.48)	−0.89 (−1.76)	1.43 (3.64)	0.42 (0.98)	−0.72 (−1.86)	−0.17 (−0.30)	0.40 (0.94)	0.24 (0.53)	0.40
2	12–15 s_2		0.00 (0.00)	−0.22 (−0.93)	0.10 (0.53)	0.06 (0.30)	0.34 (0.89)	−2.33 (−4.35)	−0.28 (−0.67)	0.47 (1.02)	0.87 (2.13)	−0.88 (−1.51)	0.28 (0.63)	−0.37 (−0.78)	0.35
3	15–18 s_3		−0.12 (−0.64)	−0.14 (−0.54)	−0.19 (−0.90)	0.07 (0.30)	1.73 (4.09)	−0.60 (−1.34)	−1.52 (−3.27)	−0.04 (−0.08)	0.77 (1.66)	0.99 (1.52)	−1.14 (−2.27)	−0.60 (−1.12)	0.24
4	18–21 s_4		0.09 (0.49)	−0.24 (−0.91)	0.17 (0.79)	−0.44 (−1.89)	1.48 (3.42)	0.13 (0.21)	−0.77 (−1.62)	−0.85 (−1.62)	−0.01 (−0.01)	0.96 (1.44)	−0.17 (−0.32)	−0.50 (−0.91)	0.27
5	21–09 s_5		0.38 (1.01)	0.61 (1.16)	−0.08 (−0.19)	0.19 (0.42)	−0.53 (−0.63)	3.90 (3.25)	1.15 (1.24)	−0.00 (−0.00)	−0.91 (−1.00)	−0.90 (−0.70)	0.63 (0.63)	1.24 (1.16)	0.26

NOTE *t*-ratio in parentheses

hours. Air-conditioned households are also significantly responsive but at somewhat smaller magnitudes. Rather than analyze these estimates in detail here, we will assess the TOU price effects in terms of full price elasticities after establishing the effect of TOU rates on total consumption.

Total Consumption Estimates

The Los Angeles experimental design was not limited to 'revenue-neutral' TOU rates, and the final rates included considerable variation in the average price per kWh (see Table 3.1). This key feature enables us to obtain estimates of the effect of TOU rates on total consumption as well as its relative distribution by period.

Specification of the total consumption equation in the demand system is also similar to that used in the analysis of covariance (equation (3.7)) except that the set of dummy variables for TOU plans is replaced by a single price index $\bar{p}$ of total kilowatt hours of electricity

$$\bar{X}_j = a + b\bar{p}_j + \sum_k f_k APPL_{kj} + \sum_k g_k DEMO_{kj} + e_j \qquad (3.13)$$

In these total consumption equations, price is in natural units; for example, for households on 2¢ and 5¢ flat rates, the index is $\bar{p} = 2¢$ or $\bar{p} = 5¢$. For household j on a TOU plan, facing TOU prices $p_{1j}, \ldots, p_{10j}$, the price index is constructed to measure the *ex ante* costliness of electricity under its TOU rate plan. The household's reference load curve at the 2¢ flat rate, given its demographic and appliance characteristics, has the estimated shares s_{ij}^* from equation (3.12). The price index

$$\bar{p}_j = \sum_i s_{ij}^* p_{ij} \qquad (3.14)$$

gives household j's average cost per kWh under the TOU rates prior to load shifts induced by the rates.[26] The estimated price index coefficient is -21.2 ($t = 3.4$), implying a price elasticity of total consumption of -0.13 at mean levels of consumption and prices. The air conditioner and pool variables interacted with the price index do not result in significant coefficients, indicating that changes in total consumption are similar for all households at the same price index value.

The experimental results thus establish that TOU rates do change total consumption in the direction predicted by consumer demand theory. Because the overall elasticity of -0.13 is estimated by controlling for an extensive list of major appliances and demographic factors, it approaches a 'pure utilization' measure of price response. It compares, for example, with price elasticity estimates of -0.06 to -0.08 in Lillard and Acton's analysis of the seasonal component of the Los Angeles experiment and -0.35 to -0.50 in Acton, Mitchell and Sohlberg's (1980) analysis of non-experimental data in Los Angeles county. The much larger elasticity estimates reported by other researchers using non-experimental data, such as those summarized in Taylor's (1975) survey, were obtained in more aggregative studies that contain only limited adjustment for variation in appliance stocks.

Appliance and Demographic Effects

Because the total monthly consumption equation (3.9) is specified in linear form the estimated coefficients provide direct estimates of the mean consumption rates of each type of appliance. These values, reported in Table 3.8, are reliably estimated for most of the major appliances and are consistent with the results obtained from small-sample studies of individual household appliances in nearly all cases.[27] For example, an electric water heater is estimated to consume 140 kWh/month (exclusive of its use with a clothes washer or dishwasher) and a colour television set 46 kWh/month. The coefficients for air conditioners (163 kWh/month) and space heaters 111 kWh/month) are the estimated average monthly (year-round) consumption for a household with these appliances facing average Los Angeles temperatures.

The results for the demographic variables in Table 3.8 confirm the importance of housing characteristics and family size, as well as income, in explaining household-specific variation in electricity use. Because the services of electricity are not consumed directly, these variables are proxies for unmeasured appliances, rates of utilization, and tastes that affect overall consumption. The implied income elasticity, 0.11 at the sample mean, is perhaps best interpreted as the combined effect of greater utilization of a given stock of major appliances plus ownership of minor, unmeasured appliances. The principal effect of income is probably reflected through the long-run decisions to purchase appliances and determine housing characteristics.

Major appliances and demographic characteristics also affect the timing, as well as the level, of a household's electricity consumption. The

TABLE 3.8   *Effects of appliances and demographic variables on total monthly consumption*

Item	Monthly consumption (kWh)	t-Ratio
Appliance variables		
Swimming pool (at mean area of 120 ft^2)	368	13.8
Water heater	140	2.7
Clothes washer (with electric water heater)	73	1.2
Dishwasher (with electric water heater)	50	0.8
Clothes dryer	65	3.4
Stove:		
all electric	71	4.2
combination	58	1.6
Microwave oven	51	2.4
Refrigerator	64	1.8
Frost-free refrigerator	149	3.3
Freezer	104	6.1
Black and white television	18	1.9
Colour television	46	4.0
Air conditioner	163	6.7
Electric space heater	111	3.4
Demographic variables		
	Coefficient	
Family income (ln)	60	4.7
Family size (ln)	174	7.6
Number of rooms (ln)	99	2.6
Housing rental value (ln)	108	5.1

estimated coefficients of these variables for the five weekday share equations are shown in Table 3.9. They indicate, for example, that relative to the reference load curve, a flat-rate household with a swimming pool consumes some 4 percentage points more of its electricity (which is greater in aggregate) during the morning and early afternoon (periods 1 and 2), about 1 percentage point more in the late afternoons, and a lesser share in periods 4 and 5. Similarly, households with electric dryers and washing machines have higher relative loads in the early part of the day and lower loads in the evening and overnight periods. The relative load curve is also shifted in the expected way by the weather-sensitive appliances. At mean temperatures the presence of an air conditioner increases the relative load from noon to 9 pm, with the

TABLE 3.9 *Coefficients of weekday share equations (at 2¢ flat rate)*

Item	Coefficients in period*				
	1	2	3	4	5
Appliance variables					
Pool	4.06	4.11	1.05	−2.94	−6.28
Electric water heater	1.35	0.55	−0.43	−1.57	0.10
Clothes dryer	1.24	0.52	0.25	−0.54	−1.47
Clothes washer (with water heater)	0.62	1.01	0.28	−0.75	−1.16
Stove (all electric or combination)	0.22	−0.04	1.24	−0.29	−1.12
Microwave oven	0.08	0.05	−0.61	−0.33	0.81
Frost-free refrigerator (increment over refrig.)	0.83	0.69	−0.19	−1.57	0.23
Freezer	0.36	0.03	−0.15	−0.99	0.76
Colour television	0.07	0.09	0.04	0.03	−0.22
Air conditioner	−0.28	0.95	1.74	0.25	−2.72
Heater	0.54	−0.11	−0.50	−0.06	0.13
Demographic variables					
Income (ln)	−0.15	−0.44	−0.63	0.15	1.07
Family size (ln)	−0.11	0.72	1.11	0.10	−1.82
Rooms (ln)	−0.43	−0.56	−1.13	−0.39	2.50
Monthly or housing value (ln)	0.05	−0.23	−0.15	0.55	−0.22

* Italicized coefficients are significant at the 0.05 level.

greatest effect occurring in mid-afternoon. Electric space heating causes relative loads to be higher in the morning and overnight. Multi-person households have higher afternoon loads when children are likely to be at home.

Miscellaneous Results

The richness of the Los Angeles experimental data base invites numerous tests of special hypotheses. We report very briefly a few that have been conducted to date.

Testing for Weekday to Weekend Load Shifts

For one-half of the TOU households the price during all weekend hours was the off-peak price. For the other households the peak hours and prices applied seven days a week. The first group ('five-day' households) therefore had some incentive to shift weekday electricity consumption into weekend hours. If such shifting occurs, it will reduce the total consumption on weekdays by five-day households relative to seven-day households. It could also alter the distribution of weekday shares.

We tested for such effects in the demand system by separately estimating total weekday and total weekend consumption equations, distinguishing the five-day households by a dummy variable. The dummy-variable coefficients in both the weekday and weekend equations were positive and insignificant. When the five-day dummy variable is included in the kWh share equations it is also insignificant. There is therefore no evidence that off-peak weekend rates shift load out of weekday periods.

Effect of Lump-Sum Compensation Payments

Some households, at their rates of consumption for one year prior to the beginning of the experiment, would have incurred a higher annual electricity bill under their experimental rate plan. These households received quarterly lump-sum checks for this difference throughout the experiment, regardless of their level or pattern of electricity use during the experiment. If households 'earmarked' their compensation payment for the higher bill they would otherwise pay on TOU rates, they might display no response to the TOU rate. To test this hypothesis, households receiving compensation were randomly split into two groups, with 178 receiving full quarterly payments. The second group of 75 households received one-half of their compensation payments quarterly and the balance in a lump sum at the termination of the experiment 30 months later.[28] If earmarking were taking place, households receiving half-payments quarterly should have responded differently to TOU rates than those receiving full payments after accounting for all other factors.

Dummy variables indicating those households that received full payment and those receiving half-payment are significantly positive in the total consumption equation. Although this might suggest that households receiving payments were less responsive to the marginal prices of electricity, the positive coefficients may simply reflect the positive correlation across the sample between consumption and the occurrence of a compensation payment: because of the declining-block rate in effect prior to the experiment, households receiving compensation payments were predominantly large consumers of electricity who previously had the lowest average price per kilowatt hour. The coefficients of the full and half-payments variables are statistically indistinguishable. This result refutes the earmarking hypothesis and allows us to assume that households receiving compensation payments do not differ from other experimental households in their responses to TOU rates.

Relative Price Specification

In equation (3.12) we assume that the quantity shares in each rate period are functions of TOU prices in relative terms (for example, p_i/p_5). Thus, standardizing for household characteristics, the relative loads of households on 2¢ flat rates and on 5¢ flat rates should be the same. A test of this hypothesis is provided by including a dummy variable for 5¢ flat plans in equation (3.12). It was insignificant in each rate period.

TOU DEMAND ELASTICITIES

In this concluding section we report the matrix of full own- and cross-price elasticities of demand that are obtained from the hybrid model. We compare these estimates to own-price elasticities obtained in demand system studies of other TOU experiments. Finally, we illustrate the use of the hybrid model to predict the changes in load that would attend the introduction of a particular TOU rate plan not tested in the experiment itself.

Price Elasticities of Demand

After the effects of weather (and other time-dependent variables) have been netted out, electricity demand (x_i) in period i is a function of the vector of TOU prices (p) and a vector of household-specific characteristics (Z). The demand system takes the general form

kWh share equations

$$s_i = x_i/x = s_i[(p_1/p_n), \ldots, (p_{n-1}/p_n); Z], i = 1, \ldots, n \quad (3.15)$$

Total consumption equation

$$x = x(\bar{p}; Z) \quad (3.16)$$

where

$$\bar{p} = \sum_k s_k^* p_k, s_k^* = s_k[(p_1^0/p_n^0), \ldots, (p_{n-1}^0/p_n^0); Z]$$

is the price index of the vector of TOU rates p evaluated using the kWh shares at a reference price vector p^0 (for example, 5¢ flat rate).

The price elasticity η_{ij} of consumption in rate period i with respect to a change in the price in period j can be represented in terms of the elasticities of the share equations

$$\varepsilon_{p_j}^{s_i} \equiv (\partial s_i/\partial p_j)(p_j/s_i) \tag{3.17}$$

and the elasticity of the total consumption of equation

$$\varepsilon_p^x \equiv (\partial x/\partial \bar{p})(\bar{p}/x) \tag{3.18}$$

To see the relation between share elasticities and total elasticity of demand define

$$w_j = (p_j x_j)/\bar{p}x \tag{3.19}$$

the expenditure in period j relative to the cost of total consumption at the index price. Then the full elasticity can be written

$$\eta_{ij} = \varepsilon_{p_j}^{s_i} + \varepsilon_p^x w_j \quad ^{29} \tag{3.20}$$

The resulting elasticity η_{ij} is a 'full, uncompensated' price elasticity that includes the changes in total expenditure on electricity and in real income that result from a change in the period j price.

The matrix of full price elasticities for the weekday model are reported in Table 3.10. Because the price elasticity of total consumption is sensitive to the level of the price index, we evaluate the full price elasticities in terms of a reference price of 5¢. At this level the total consumption elasticity is -0.19.[30] The parameters are first calculated at the mean consumption shares observed in the sample, assuming no swimming pool or air conditioner. These appliances are then introduced separately and together. The results show the sensitivity of TOU response to these appliances; when a household has either a pool or an air conditioner it has both a different initial relative load curve and a greater propensity to shift load.

TABLE 3.10   *Full price elasticities of demand (at $p_i = 5\text{¢}/kWh$)*

Weekday kWh in period Hour	*i*	*Price in period*				
		1	*2*	*3*	*4*	*5*
		Households without pool or air conditioner				
09–12	1	−0.06	−0.02	−0.04	−0.03	−0.08
12–15	2	−0.02	−0.05	−0.03	−0.03	−0.08
15–18	3	−0.03	−0.04	−0.05	−0.07	−0.07
18–21	4	−0.02	−0.04	−0.02	−0.07	−0.08
21–09	5	−0.01	−0.01	−0.03	−0.04	−0.13
		Households with pool and without air conditioner				
09–12	1	−0.27	−0.07	0.08	0.03	0.11
12–15	2	0.01	−0.17	−0.07	0.02	0.09
15–18	3	0.09	−0.07	−0.16	−0.01	0.03
18–21	4	0.08	−0.04	−0.05	−0.10	−0.02
21–09	5	−0.02	0.09	0.03	−0.02	−0.20
		Households without pool and with air conditioner				
09–12	1	−0.12	−0.08	0.04	−0.03	0.02
12–15	2	0.06	−0.21	0.08	−0.03	−0.05
15–18	3	0.03	0.00	−0.09	−0.05	−0.05
18–21	4	−0.02	0.04	−0.03	−0.08	−0.07
21–09	5	−0.03	0.01	−0.04	−0.00	−0.10
		Households with pool and air conditioner				
09–12	1	−0.32	−0.12	0.13	0.03	0.17
12–15	2	0.06	−0.28	0.01	0.02	0.09
15–18	3	0.13	−0.03	−0.19	−0.04	0.02
18–21	4	0.07	0.05	−0.07	−0.13	−0.03
21–09	5	−0.04	0.12	0.02	0.01	−0.20

For households with no pool or air conditioner the own-price elasticities are quite small, −0.05 to −0.13. The cross-price elasticities are smaller and negative. Such households tend to make small reductions in loads in all periods when any TOU price is increased.

Households with a pool, an air conditioner or both are considerably more responsive. Own-price elasticities range up to −0.13 to −0.32 with greater values found in the morning and afternoon and lowest values in the period 6 pm – 9 pm. Even at this early evening period, the own-price elasticity for households with both pool and air-conditioner is roughly double that for households lacking both pieces of equipment. Cross-price elasticities are also larger and of mixed signs. Households with these appliances increase net loads in some off-peak periods.

Comparison with other TOU Price Elasticity Estimates

Using data from the first 18 months of the Los Angeles experiment, Manning and Acton (1980) conducted exploratory data analysis using Box–Cox transformations and selected a log-linear specification for single equation estimation. Their demand equations make consumption in each weekday rate period a function of weather, appliance and demographic variables, and TOU prices alone and with appliance interactions. The own-price elasticities for households at the mean characteristics of the sample range from -0.05 to -0.10; cross-price elasticities are generally insignificant. When mean household characteristics are combined with a swimming pool, own-price elasticities lie between -0.07 and -0.46 during daytime hours. These values are in general agreement with the hybrid model estimates in Table 3.10.

Data from the Connecticut, Arizona and Wisconsin TOU experiments have been analyzed in neoclassical demand system models by several research groups.[31] These models typically estimate 'partial' elasticities that are conditional on a fixed amount of expenditure on electricity. As Hendricks and Koenker (1980) make clear, the value of the partial elasticity in a given rate period is a direct function of both the quantity share and the TOU price in that period. Consequently, partial elasticities cannot be compared across rate periods or across different experiments.

By accounting for the price elasticity of total consumption one can calculate full (unconditional) price elasticities from the estimated partial elasticities. However, in the case of these three experiments there was insufficient variation in the average price per kWh to obtain reliable estimates of the aggregate price elasticity. Nevertheless, Hendricks and Koenker assumed that the elasticity of total consumption is -0.10 and computed full TOU price elasticities for the various demand system studies. With this assumption they find that the range of own-price full TOU elasticities is approximately -0.1 to -0.3.

The estimate of the total consumption price elasticity in our hybrid model at a 5¢ flat rate is -0.19, somewhat greater than that assumed by Hendricks and Koenker. The full own-price elasticities estimated here range from -0.05 to -0.13 for households with no pool or air conditioner, and from -0.13 to -0.32 for households with both (Table 3.10). Overall, the own-price elasticities from the various experiments appear to be in general agreement.

No full cross-price elasticities have been published for the demand system models of the other experiments. As a result, we have no direct basis for comparing our cross-elasticity estimates, which show that most of the load shifting induced by TOU rates is due to households with pools or air conditioners.

An Illustrative TOU Rate

Suppose that initially a 5¢/kWh flat rate prevails. In the Los Angeles sample households with the mean appliance and demographic variables and both a pool and air conditioner would use an average of 954 kWh per month at average weather conditions. The weekday distribution of this load is shown in Table 3.11.

TABLE 3.11 *Weekday load changes of an illustrative TOU rate: average household with pool and air conditioner*

Item	Period 1	Period 2	Period 3	Period 4	Period 5
			Flat rate		
Price per kWh	5¢	5¢	5¢	5¢	5¢
Share (%)	13.7	15.5	17.5	17.5	35.7
kWh/day	4.4	5.0	5.6	5.6	11.4
			TOU rate		
Price per kWh	3¢	9¢	9¢	9¢	3¢
Share (%)	15.4	12.1	13.7	15.7	43.1
kWh/day	4.8	3.8	4.3	4.9	13.5

Introduction of a 9¢/kWh rate from 09–18 daily and 3¢/kWh at other hours would establish peak prices during three rate periods. Although this particular tariff was not included as one of those tested experimentally, the hybrid model can readily be used to predict the household's new load curve. Based on the average household's load under the flat rate, the TOU rate would raise the average price per kWh from 5¢ to 5.94¢ and reduce total monthly consumption to 934 kWh. The effect on loads in each rate period is calculated from the respective share equations by inserting the 9¢ and 3¢ prices in the appropriate periods. As shown in the table the net effect would be to decrease loads in each of the three peak price periods and increase usage in the off-peak hours.

NOTES

1. We thank Don Negri for contributions to the model presented here. He and Karl Schwenkmeyer provided assistance with the computations. Andrew Buck, Dan Kohler, Michael Ward and Dennis Whitney made very useful comments on an earlier draft. Becky Goodman's editorial skills improved several drafts of the chapter.

   We gratefully acknowledge the support of the Los Angeles Department of Water and Power and especially Michael T. Moore, the original project officer. A grant from the John A. Hartford Foundation is permitting us to extend this analysis into a more national focus.

2. See Mitchell, Manning and Acton (1978) for a review of European pricing and Joskow (1977) for a history of recent US pricing.

3. In all, about 15 'rate demonstrations' were undertaken with the encouragement and partial support of the Federal Energy Administration (and later the Department of Energy). Their principal features are reviewed in Hill et al. (1979) and Aigner and Poirier (1980).

4. Typically, conventional meters currently cost $20–$30 plus installation while TOU meters presently cost $100–$150 plus installation. Thus, introducing TOU rates raises an important benefit/cost question for smaller residential users.

5. See Aigner and Poirier (1980) for a general review of demand systems available for estimating TOU electricity consumption and a critique of their application in a number of TOU studies.

6. For example, using Monte Carlo techniques Kohler (1980) demonstrated that estimates using an indirect translog utility function with homothetic separability imposed can yield 'significant' price response coefficients even when none are present in the actual data.

7. Optimal experimental design followed procedures developed by Conlisk and Watts (1969), and individuals were assigned to particular procedures developed by Morris (1979). See Acton, Mitchell and Manning (1977) for an overview of the study and its policy objectives; Manning, Mitchell and Acton (1979) for a description of the statistical design; and Chow and Mitchell (1979) for a description of the sampling procedures.

8. See Lillard and Acton (1980) for an analysis of seasonal demand.

9. In exploratory data analysis using the first 18 months of experimental data, Manning and Acton (1980) found that making a correction for selection bias reduced own-price elasticities in evening and night-time consumption periods by a few percentage points.

10. Cooling degree-hours (CDH) = max $(T°F − 65°, 0)$; heating degree-hours (HDH) = max $(65° − T°F, 0)$. Both are averaged over the month in the relevant rate period.

11. Household demographic and economic variables – family size, income, housing value, and the like – can change during the study. We employ average values of these variables to explain permanent level of use. Appliance holdings can also change during the study. In the monthly weather regressions, these variables change monthly. In the remainder of the analysis, the dependent variable is a measure of average consumption and an average value of each appliance is used.

12. Missing observations occur because of blackouts, meter failures, magnetic tape defects, and the like. Calculating the mean consumption per period by dividing by the actual number of observations corrects for the missing data.

13. Two alternatives to the data aggregation employed here were illustrated in analysis of the Connecticut rate study. Hendricks, Koenker and Poirier (1978) fit a smooth periodic function (a cubic spline) to the hourly data over a week. They can explain the parameters of this function in terms of household demographics, price and so on. At the other extreme, Granger *et al.* (1977) estimate hourly regressions with no aggregation of the data.

14. In addition to temperature, humidity and the amount of natural illumination alter electricity use. These secondary factors are not incorporated into the estimates presented here except to the extent that they vary systematically by weather zone.

15. See Acton, Mitchell and Sohlberg (1980).

16. Because only 6 per cent of the experimental households reported any form of electric space heating no attempt was made to distinguish different types of heating units.

17. Our fixed-coefficient model assumes that the same weather component W_i applies to all households facing the same temperature and having similar heating and cooling equipment. Considering the coefficients as random variables allows an alternative specification that would permit the weather-sensitive consumption to vary by household. For an application of this approach in the context of seasonal electricity pricing see Lillard and Acton (1980).

18. For expository convenience we refer to weekday loads and shares. A similar analysis is carried out for weekend consumption.

19. Because the share values for each household are 24-month averages there is little to be gained from using a logit estimator. As the same explanatory variables appear in each equation, OLS and seemingly unrelated regression estimates are equivalent.

20. We do not distinguish plans that apply peak prices five days per week from plans with the same peak rates that apply seven days per week. At the end of the section we present evidence supporting this grouping for weekday consumption.

21. Two cents per kWh is merely a convenient reference value from which measure load changes. The average price per kWh for experimental households on TOD rates was 3.47¢. During the experimental period the lowest price for Los Angeles households on standard rates rose from about 2.4¢/kWh to over 5¢/kWh.

22. Subject, of course, to the constraint that the sum of the effects over all five periods is zero.

23. The effect of plans on total consumption is discussed in the next subsection.

24. These estimates are obtained by estimating equation (3.7) with the *PLAN* dummy variables redefined as price differences. Thus, $PLAN_1 = 5¢ - 2¢$, $PLAN_2 = 9¢ - 5¢$, $PLAN_3 = 13¢ - 9¢$, ..., $PLAN_{14} = 5¢ - 1¢$, $PLAN_{15} = 9¢ - 5¢$, ...

25. See, for example, the studies surveyed by Aigner and Poirier (1980) and Hendricks and Koenker (1980).

26. This definition of $\bar{p}$ avoids the simultaneity bias that would be introduced by using *ex post* share weights s_{ij}.
27. See, for example, Parti and Parti (1980).
28. Households receiving compensation payments were randomly allocated to the full or half-compensation schemes with a 50:50 probability, subject to the restriction that no household would receive less than \$1 quarterly if assigned to the half-compensation scheme.
29. Write $x_i = s_i x$. Then

$$
\begin{aligned}
n_{ij} &= (\partial x_i/\partial p_j)(p_j/x_i) = (\partial s_i/\partial p_j)(p_j/x_i)x + s_i(\partial x/\partial p_j)(p_j/x_i) \\
&= (\partial s_i/\partial p_j)(p_j/s_i) + (x_i/x)(\partial x/\partial \bar{p})(\partial \bar{p}/\partial p_j)(p_j/x_i) \\
&= \varepsilon_{p_j}^{s_i} + (x_i/x)\{(\partial x/\partial \bar{p})(\bar{p}/x)\}(x/\bar{p})(\partial \bar{p}/\partial p_j)(p_j/x_i) \\
&= \varepsilon_{p_j}^{s_i} + \varepsilon_{\bar{p}}^{x}\{(s_j p_j)/\bar{p}\} = \varepsilon_{p_j}^{s_i} + \varepsilon_{\bar{p}}^{x} w_j
\end{aligned}
$$

30. This value of price elasticities for total consumption differs from the value reported above (-0.13) because the former value corresponded to an average TOU price index value of 3.47¢/kWh.
31. See Aigner and Hausman (1978), Atkinson (1977, 1978), Caves and Christensen (1980), Lau and Lillard (1978), Lawrence and Braithwait (1977) and Miedema *et al.* (1978).

REFERENCES

Acton, Jan Paul, Bridger M. Mitchell and Willard G. Manning (1977) 'Lessons from the Los Angeles Rate Experiment in Electricity', in J. L. O'Donnell (ed), *Adapting Regulation to Shortages, Curtailment, and Inflation* (East Lansing, Mich.: Michigan State University).

Acton, Jan Paul, Bridger M. Mitchell, and Ragnhild Sohlberg (1980) 'Estimating Residential Electricity Demand Under Declining-Block Tariffs:. An Econometric Study Using Micro-data', *Applied Economics*, Vol. 12, No. 2 (June), pp. 145–62.

Aigner, Dennis J. and Dale J. Poirier (1980) *Electricity Demand and Consumption by Time-of-Day: A Survey.* (Palo Alto: EPRI) report EA-1294.

Aigner, Dennis J. and Jerry A. Hausman (1978) 'Correcting for Truncation Bias in the Analysis of Experiments in Time-of-Day Pricing of Electricity', *The Bell Journal of Economics*, Vol. 11, No. 1 (Spring), pp. 131–42.

Atkinson, Scott E. (1977) 'Responsiveness to Time-of-Day Electricity Pricing: First Empirical Results', in *Forecasting and Modelling Time-of-Day and Seasonal Electricity Demands*, Anthony Lawrence (ed.) (Palo Alto, CA: Electric Power Research Institute) EA-578-SR.

Atkinson, Scott E. (1978) 'A Comparative Analysis of Consumer Response to Time-of-Use Electricity Pricing: Arizona and Wisconsin', Paper presented at the EPRI Workshop on Modelling and Analysis of Electricity Demand by Time-of-Day, San Diego, CA, June 12–14, 1978.

Caves, Douglas W. and Laurits R. Christensen (1980) 'Residential Substitution of Off-Peak for Peak Electricity Usage Under Time-of-Use Pricing', *The Energy Journal*, Vol. 1, No. 2 (April), pp. 85–142.

Chow, Winston and Bridger M. Mitchell (1979) *Sample Selection in the Los Angeles Electricity Rate Study* (Santa Monica: The Rand Corporation) R-2430.

Conlisk, John and Harold Watts (1969) 'A Model for Optimizing Experimental Designs for Estimating Response Surfaces', *Proceedings of the Social Statistics Section*, American Statistical Association, pp. 150–156.

Granger, Clive W. J., Robert Engle, Ramu Ramanathan and Alan Anderson (1977) 'Residential Load Curves and Time-of-Day Pricing: An Econometric Analysis', Discussion Paper No. 77–16, Department of Economics, University of California, San Diego, CA.

Hausman, J. A., M. Kinnucan, and D. McFadden (1979) 'A Two-Level Electricity Demand Model: Evaluation of the Connecticut Time-of-Day Pricing Test', *Journal of Econometrics*, Vol. 10, pp. 263–89.

Hendricks, Wallace, and Roger Koenker (1980) 'Demand for Electricity by Time-of-Day: An Evaluation of Experimental Results', in *Issues in Public-Utility Pricing and Regulation*, M. A. Crew (ed.) (Lexington, Mass.: D.C. Heath).

Hendricks, W., R. Koenker and Dale J. Poirier (1978) *Residential Demand for Electricity by Time of Day: An Econometric Approach*, (Palo Alto: Electric Power Research Institute) Report No. EA-704.

Hill, Daniel H. *et al.* (1979) *Evalution of the Federal Energy Administration's Load Management and Rate Design Demonstration Projects* (Palo Alto: Electric Power Research Institute) Report EA 1152.

Joskow, Paul L (1977) 'Electric Utility Rate Structures in the United States: Some Recent Developments'. Paper presented at the Seventh Michigan Conference on Public Utility Economics.

Kohler, Daniel F. (1980) *Essays in Applied Demand Analysis*, PhD Dissertation, University of Michigan.

Lau, Lawrence J. and Lee A. Lillard (1978) 'A Random Response Model of the Demand for Electricity by Time-of-Day'. Paper presented at the EPRI workshop on Modeling and Analysis of Electricity Demand by Time-of-Day, San Diego, CA, June 12–14, 1978.

Lawrence, Anthony and Steven Braithwait (1977) 'The Residential Demand for Electricity by Time-of-Day: An Econometric Analysis', in *Forecasting and Modeling Time-of-Day and Seasonal Electricity Demands*, Anthony Lawrence (ed.) (Palo Alto, CA: Electric Power Research Institute) EA-578-SR.

Lillard, Lee A. and Jan Paul Acton (1980) 'Seasonal Electricity Demand Analysis With A Variable Response Model', *Bell Journal of Economics*, Vol. 12, No. 1 (Spring), pp. 71–82.

Manning, Willard G. and Jan Paul Acton (1980) *Residential Electricity Demand Under Time-of-Day Pricing* (Santa Monica: The Rand Corporation) R-2426-DWP.

Manning, Willard G., Bridger M. Mitchell and Jan Paul Acton (1979) 'Design of the Los Angeles Peak-Load Pricing Experiment for electricity', *Journal of Econometrics*, Vol. 11, No. 1 (Sept.), pp. 131–94.

Miedema, Allen K., *et al.* (1978) 'Time-of-Use Electricity Prices: Arizona', Report prepared for the Department of Energy, Office of Utility Systems.

Mitchell, Bridger M., Willard G. Manning, Jr. and Jan Paul Acton (1978) *Peak-Load Pricing: European Lessons for the U. S. Energy Policy*, (Cambridge, Mass.: Ballinger).

Morris, Carl (1979) 'A Finite Selection Model for Experimental Design of the Health Insurance Study', *Journal of Econometrics*, Vol. 11, No. 1 (Sept.), pp. 43–62.

Parti, Michael and Cynthia Parti (1980) 'The Total and Appliance-Specific Conditional Demand for Electricity in the Household Sector', *Bell Journal of Economics*, Vol. 11, No. 1 (Spring), pp. 309–21.

Taylor, Lester D. (1975) 'The Demand for Electricity: A Survey', *Bell Journal of Economics*, Vol. 6, No. 1 (Spring), pp. 64–110.

4 Welfare Analysis of Telecommunication Tariffs in Germany

KARL-HEINZ NEUMANN
URS SCHWEIZER
C. CHRISTIAN von WEIZSÄCKER

INTRODUCTION

In this chapter the theory of optimal pricing is adapted and used for an empirical welfare analysis of the telecommunication tariffs in the Federal Republic of Germany. Though only rough estimates of marginal costs and demand elasticities are currently (1979) available, all empirical evidence seems to suggest that the present structure of tariffs is not optimal in any sense whatever. Prices are set above marginal costs and huge profits arise which then are used to cover deficits from postal services and as subsidies to the governmental budget. But even at the 1979 level of profits it seems possible to lower social losses considerably simply by restructuring telecommunication tariffs.

Estimates of these losses in welfare will be given in the fifth section of this chapter. They are based on the best estimates of cost and demand parameters we could obtain. More accurate data could be sought out by those who have access to internal files, and, of course, better data lead to more accurate estimates of the welfare losses. But our results are, hopefully, sufficiently significant to spur further investigation by those who do have access.

Our welfare analysis follows the Ramsey–Boiteux theory of optimal pricing under the constraint of a profit target. First, the profit of the telecommunication sector will be kept fixed at its 1979 level while prices are changed such that the consumers' surplus increases. Numerical estimates of such changes in prices and welfare are given. Second, the case of zero profits will be examined. Here, additional gains are possible by moving prices closer to marginal costs. Finally, welfare implications of prices proportional to marginal costs will be discussed. Such prices have been proposed by Knieps, Müller and Weizsäcker (1981) on the ground that only they are compatible with competition within the telecommunication sector. Here again, the analysis will be carried out for 1979 and zero profit levels.

The chapter is organized as follows. In the second section it is shown how marginal price changes affect welfare and which data are needed to evaluate them. Following that a model with linear cost and demand structure is introduced. This model will be used to evaluate global changes in prices and to arrive at numerical values for Ramsey–Boiteux prices and the corresponding gains in welfare. The linear case allows for simple calculation and, if compared to convex demand functions, leads to a lower bound of the possible welfare gains. This result will be established in the fourth section. Finally, all numerical results are derived and fully discussed, and conclusions are drawn.

THE WELFARE EFFECT OF MARGINAL PRICE CHANGES

Let us consider a public enterprise such as the German Bundespost in the telecommunication sector, which produces n different services or commodities. The (1979) tariff structure is denoted by

$$\mathbf{p}^o = (p_1^o, \ldots, p_n^o)$$

It is assumed that the aggregate demand functions

$$\mathbf{x}(\mathbf{p}) = \{x_1(\mathbf{p}), \ldots, x_n(\mathbf{p})\}$$

are known at least for prices $\mathbf{p}$ sufficiently close to current prices $\mathbf{p}^o$. Let $k(x)$ denote the cost function which is also known in a neighbourhood of current demand $\mathbf{x}^o = \mathbf{x}(\mathbf{p}^o)$. Profits at prices $\mathbf{p}$ are given as

$$R(\mathbf{p}) = \mathbf{p}\mathbf{x}(\mathbf{p}) - k\{\mathbf{x}(\mathbf{p})\}$$

Suppose now that the observed demand functions $\mathbf{x}(\mathbf{p})$ can be written as the sum

$$\mathbf{x}(\mathbf{p}) = \sum_{i=1}^{H} D_i(\mathbf{p}, \mathbf{q}, y_i)$$

of individual demand functions D_i over H different households. Here $\mathbf{q}$ denotes the vector of prices of all other commodities and y_i the income of household i. The indirect utility function of household i is denoted by $V_i = V_i(\mathbf{p}, \mathbf{q}, y_i)$. It is assumed that prices $\mathbf{q}$ and incomes y_i do not depend on the prices $\mathbf{p}$ charged by the public enterprise. They are kept fixed throughout and, therefore, do not appear explicitly as arguments of the aggregate demand functions.

In this section, only marginal changes in prices are considered and for that, only data in the neighbourhood of the current situation are needed. The following discussion is related to the results of Guesnerie (1977) and of Willig and Bailey (1979).

Let $d\mathbf{p}$ denote a marginal change in prices for the commodities produced by the public enterprise. It will be shown that the price change $d\mathbf{p}$ leads to a potential Pareto improvement if

$$dR - \mathbf{x}^o d\mathbf{p} > 0 \qquad (4.1)$$

For that to be true, it must be possible to distribute the gain dR in profits (losses if negative) among the households such that all of them will be better off. But this can be simply done. All we need to know is the current demand $D_i^o = D_i(\mathbf{p}^o, \mathbf{q}, y_i)$ of the different households. Let us define.

$$dy_i = D_i^o d\mathbf{p} + (dR - \mathbf{x}^o d\mathbf{p})/H \qquad (4.2)$$

It follows immediately that

$$\sum_{i=1}^{H} dy_i = dR$$

Moreover, Roy's identity implies that

$$V_i(\mathbf{p}^o + d\mathbf{p}, \mathbf{q}, y_i + dy_i) = V_i(\mathbf{p}^o, \mathbf{q}, y_i) + (\partial V_i/\partial y_i)(dy_i - D_i^o d\mathbf{p})$$

Since marginal utility of money $\partial V_i/\partial y_i$ is positive, and since $dy_i - D_i^o d\mathbf{p}$ must be positive if (4.1) holds, it can be easily seen that utility

$$V_i(\mathbf{p}^o + d\mathbf{p}, \mathbf{q}, y_i + dy_i) > V_i(\mathbf{p}^o, \mathbf{q}, y_i)$$

increases for all households, as was to be shown.

Condition (4.1) can be expressed in a slightly different way. If dE_i denotes the equivalent variation of household i under the price change d$\mathbf{p}$, which is defined by

$$V_i(\mathbf{p}^o, \mathbf{q}, y_i + \mathrm{d}E_i) = V_i(\mathbf{p}^o + \mathrm{d}\mathbf{p}, \mathbf{q}, y_i)$$

then, again by Roy's identity, $\mathrm{d}E_i = -D_i^o \, \mathrm{d}\mathbf{p}$. It follows that

$$-x_o \mathrm{d}\mathbf{p} = \sum_{i=1}^{H} \mathrm{d}E_i$$

and, hence, that the price change d$\mathbf{p}$ leads to a potential Pareto improvement if the sum over all equivalent variations and the change in profits is positive.

In the fifth section of this chapter this result is applied to the current tariff structure of the telecommunication sector. There we assume that all cross price elasticities of demand $\mathbf{x}(\mathbf{p})$ vanish. For that case, some more specific formulas can be obtained in the following way. Let

$$\varepsilon_j^o = (p_j^o/x_j^o)(\mathrm{d}x_j/\mathrm{d}p_j)$$

denote the price elasticity of the demand for commodity j at the price structure $\mathbf{p}^o$. Marginal costs at current demand are given as

$$c_j^o = \partial k(x^o)/\partial x_j$$

It follows that

$$\mathrm{d}R = \sum_{j=1}^{n} (1 + \alpha_j^o) x_j^o \, \mathrm{d}p_j \tag{4.3}$$

and, hence, that

$$\mathrm{d}R - \mathbf{x}^o \mathrm{d}\mathbf{p} = \sum_{j=1}^{n} \alpha_j^o x_j^o \, \mathrm{d}p_j \tag{4.4}$$

where

$$\alpha_j^o = (p_j^o - c_j^o)\varepsilon_j^o / p_j^o$$

At a Ramsey–Boiteux optimum, all the numbers α_j have to be equal as follows from the well known Ramsey rule. If, however, at least two of these numbers – we call them Ramsey numbers – are different at $\mathbf{p}^o$, then the tariff structure cannot be optimal, not even with the profit level r^o as a target. In this case explicit formulas for the proper change in prices and the induced gain in welfare are available. For example, suppose

$$\alpha_1^o > \alpha_2^o \tag{4.5}$$

In the following, only price changes for commodities 1 and 2 are considered. According to (4.3), profit remains unchanged if

$$(1 + \alpha_1^o)x_1^o \, dp_1 + (1 + \alpha_2^o)x_2^o \, dp_2 = 0 \tag{4.6}$$

It then follows from (4.4) that

$$dR - \mathbf{x}^o \, d\mathbf{p} = \{(\alpha_1^o - \alpha_2^o)/(1 + \alpha_2^o)\} x_1^o \, dp_1 \tag{4.7}$$

If (4.5) holds, then an increase in the price of commodity 1 together with the proper decrease in price 2 will leave the profit of the public enterprise unchanged while the social welfare expressed as $dR - x_o \, d\mathbf{p}$ necessarily increases.

Formulas (4.6) and (4.7) play an important role in our empirical analysis (see the fifth section). If cross price elasticities of aggregate demand can be assumed to vanish, data requirements are as follows: in order to calculate the Ramsey numbers, price elasticities of demand as well as marginal costs have to be known at the current situation. It is then possible to determine the set of all marginal price changes which leave the profit unchanged. Without further information, those price changes can be picked out which increase social welfare and lead to a potential Pareto improvement. To arrive at an actual Pareto improvement, incomes have to be redistributed according to (4.2). For that, only current demand of the different households (or classes of households) has to be known.

A LINEAR MODEL TO EVALUATE GLOBAL WELFARE EFFECTS

In the last section, welfare effects of marginal price changes have been examined. Marginal changes, however, would typically not be enough to arrive at optimal tariffs, unless the current situation itself is close to the optimum. To evaluate larger price changes, some information about the global structure of demand and cost functions is needed. In this section we consider the case where demand as well as cost functions are linear. For the linear case, local data will be enough to evaluate global changes. Though demand functions for telecommunication services are more likely to be convex (see the next section), the empirical analysis will be carried out under the assumption of linear demand functions. However, it will be shown in the next section that welfare losses evaluated within the linear framework form a lower bound if compared with the case of convex demand functions. In this sense, the linear case can be understood as a reference point.

For the linear case, the demand for the n commodities supplied by a public enterprise can be written as

$$x = x^L(p) = b - Ap$$

Hereby b is a positive n vector and A is a $n \times n$ matrix with fixed coefficients. The following analysis will be restricted to the situation, where the matrix A is symmetric and positive semi-definite. This, of course, would be true if all cross price elasticities of demand vanish. But it is also true if x can be interpreted as a system of compensated demand functions as is well known from the theory of demand.

Let $S = S(p)$ denote consumers' surplus. For the vector $\partial S/\partial p$ of partial derivatives the following equation holds

$$\partial S/\partial p = -x = -b + Ap$$

Integration leads to

$$S = \text{constant} - pb + (1/2)pAp \tag{4.8}$$

We assume that $S(p)$ measures the distance in consumers' welfare between prices p and zero prices. The constant in (4.8) then disappears and $S(p)$ attains negative values only.

In the linear case, the cost function can be expressed as

$$k(x) = f + cx$$

where c denotes the n vector of constant marginal costs and f represents fixed costs.

As for f, a different interpretation is possible which plays an important role for the empirical analysis. f can be understood as representative for the economies of scale as well as for the costs which are not attributable to output. For a given output x, attributable costs z are defined as $z = cx$. If the cost function is non-linear then, of course, the vector $c = c(x)$ of marginal costs depends on the level of output. To determine the ratio of attributable to total costs, the function

$$h(\lambda, x) = k(\lambda x)$$

is introduced. Differentiating h with respect to the real variable λ at $\lambda = 1$ leads to

$$h'(1, \mathbf{x}) = c(\mathbf{x})\mathbf{x} = z$$

and hence to

$$z/k = h'(1, \mathbf{x})/h(1, \mathbf{x})$$

h'/h corresponds to the relative increase in costs if all outputs are increased by one per cent and is called the degree of cost degression. Thus the degree of cost degression allows us to determine explicitly the ratio of attributable to total costs. This result will be used in the fifth section of this chapter to estimate the numerical value of the coefficient f of the cost function.

Now we come back to our discussion of the linear model. At the first best solution, prices must be equal to marginal costs. The first best solution consists of a price vector $\mathbf{p}^* = \mathbf{c}$ and of an output bundle $\mathbf{x}^* = \mathbf{b} - \mathbf{A}\mathbf{p}^*$. Social welfare

$$W(\mathbf{p}) = S(\mathbf{p}) + R(\mathbf{p})$$

is expressed as the sum of consumers' surplus S and of profit R. Welfare $W(\mathbf{p})$ attains its maximum value at the first best solution $\mathbf{p}^*$. For the linear case, welfare is given as

$$W(\mathbf{p}) = -\mathbf{p}\mathbf{b} + (1/2)\mathbf{p}\mathbf{A}\mathbf{p} + \mathbf{p}\mathbf{b} - \mathbf{p}\mathbf{A}\mathbf{p} - f - \mathbf{c}\mathbf{b} + \mathbf{c}\mathbf{A}\mathbf{p}$$
$$= -(1/2)\mathbf{p}\mathbf{A}\mathbf{p} - f - \mathbf{c}\mathbf{b} + \mathbf{c}\mathbf{A}\mathbf{p}$$

At prices $\mathbf{p}$, the welfare loss as compared to the first best solution amounts to

$$L(\mathbf{p}) = W(\mathbf{c}) - W(\mathbf{p})$$
$$= (1/2)(\mathbf{p} - \mathbf{c})\mathbf{A}(\mathbf{p} - \mathbf{c})$$

Since

$$x(\mathbf{c}) - x(\mathbf{p}) = \mathbf{A}(\mathbf{p} - \mathbf{c})$$

the loss can also be written as

$$L(\mathbf{p}) = (1/2)(\mathbf{p} - \mathbf{c})\{x(\mathbf{c}) - \bar{x}(\mathbf{p})\} \qquad (4.9)$$

This formula for the loss function will be useful for the numerical analysis in the fifth section of this chapter.

COMPARING LINEAR AND CONVEX DEMAND FUNCTIONS

In this section it is assumed throughout that cross price elasticities of demand vanish. The linear demand functions $x^L(p)$ are then fully determined by the current price structure p^o, by current demand x^o and by the price elasticities of demand at current prices p^o. Demand at zero prices $x^L(0)$ as well as prices p' at which demand $x^L(p')$ disappears, can then be simply calculated. The assumption of linear demand functions, if applied to the telecommunication tariffs, leads to implausibly low values for $x^L(0)$ as well as for p'. The demand for local calls would be about 14.6×10^9 at zero prices. This seems rather low as compared to the 1979 demand of about 12.2×10^9 local calls at a price of DM 0.23. Similarly, for linear demand functions, demand for local calls would be zero at a price of DM 1.38 per call. Again, this value seems implausibly low. Taking this into account, it might be more reasonable to assume convex demand functions. Nevertheless, the numerical analysis (see the fifth section of this chapter) will be restricted to the case of linear demand functions. But in this section it is shown that the welfare loss of current prices relative to optimal prices must be even larger for convex demand functions. More precisely, the following result will be established. Let us assume that there are only two commodities, that is, $n = 2$, and that marginal costs c_1 and c_2 are constant. Suppose we are given a pair of linear and convex demand functions $x^L(p)$ and $x^C(p)$, respectively, such that, at current prices p^o

$$x^L(p^o) = x^C(p^o) = x^o$$

Cross price elasticities of x^L and x^C are assumed to vanish, whereas the own price elasticities of the linear and convex demand functions coincide at current prices p^o. Then it must be true that the welfare loss of current prices relative to prices which are optimal at current profits is higher for the convex than the linear demand functions. Therefore, the welfare loss estimated in the fifth section of this chapter under the assumption of linear demand would be even higher if actual demand functions were convex. This section is devoted to the proof of the above result.

Let ε_1^o and ε_2^o denote price elasticities of demand for commodities 1 and 2 at current prices. The level r^o of current profits is then

$$r^o = (p^o - c)x^o - f$$

If the Ramsey numbers α_1^o and α_2^o, defined by

$$\alpha_j^o = (p_j^o - c_j)\varepsilon_j^o/p_j^o$$

are different – without loss of generality we might assume that

$$\alpha_1^o > \alpha_2^o \tag{4.10}$$

holds – then consumers' surplus can be increased by a proper change in prices, leaving the level r^o of profits fixed. In this case the current situation cannot correspond to a Ramsey–Boiteux optimum (see the second section of this chapter).

Elasticities of demand $\varepsilon_j = \varepsilon_j(p_j)$ typically depend explicitly on prices and so do the Ramsey numbers

$$\alpha_j = \alpha_j(p_j) = (p_j - c_j)\varepsilon_j(p_j)/p_j \tag{4.11}$$

The price vector $\mathbf{p}^R$ which leads to a Ramsey–Boiteux optimum at profit level r^o is given as the solution of the following system of equations

$$\left. \begin{array}{l} \alpha_1(p_1^R) = \alpha_2(p_2^R) \\ (\mathbf{p}^R - \mathbf{c})\mathbf{x}(\mathbf{p}^R) - f = r^o \end{array} \right\} \tag{4.12}$$

The solution depends, of course, on the assumed structure of demand. In the following the solutions will be compared for the linear and convex demand functions $\mathbf{x}^L(\mathbf{p})$ and $\mathbf{x}^C(\mathbf{p})$ introduced above. By assumption, the Ramsey numbers of $\mathbf{x}^L$ and $\mathbf{x}^C$ coincide at current prices $\mathbf{p}^o$.

Let $\mathbf{p}^{LR}$ and $\mathbf{p}^{CR}$ denote the price vectors which lead to the Ramsey–Boiteux optimum at profit level r^o for the linear and convex demand functions, respectively. Furthermore, the following gains in welfare

$$g^L = W^L(\mathbf{p}^{LR}) - W^L(\mathbf{p}^o)$$

and

$$g^C = W^C(\mathbf{p}^{CR}) - W^C(\mathbf{p}^o)$$

which arise from replacing current prices by Ramsey–Boiteux prices at profit level r^o in the linear and convex case, respectively, are considered. It will be shown that

$$g^L < g^C \tag{4.13}$$

and, if (4.10) holds, that

$$p_2^{CR} < p_2^{LR} < p_2^o \tag{4.14}$$

and

$$p_1^o < p_1^{LR}, p_1^{CR} \tag{4.15}$$

In other words, the gain in welfare if evaluated for the convex demand functions exceeds the gain in the linear case. Moreover, the price of commodity 1 (2) has to be higher (lower) at the Ramsey–Boiteux optimum compared to current prices $\mathbf{p}^o$ for both cases. The price of commodity 2 at the Ramsey–Boiteux optimum must be lower for the convex than the linear demand functions. For commodity 1, no such general statement seems possible. The remaining part of this section is devoted to the proof of (4.13)–(4.15).

For a given demand function $\mathbf{x}(\mathbf{p}) = \{x_1(p_1), x_2(p_2)\}$, the profit function of the public enterprise can be written as $R(\mathbf{p}) = R_1(p_1) + R_2(p_2) - f$ where

$$R_j(p_j) = (p_j - c_j)x_j(p_j)$$

The gain in welfare at prices $\mathbf{p}$ relative to current prices $\mathbf{p}^o$ amounts to

$$G(\mathbf{p}) = G_1(p_1) + G_2(p_2)$$

where

$$G_j(p_j) = -\int_{p_j^o}^{p_j} x_j(\pi_j)d\pi_j + R_j(p_j) - R_j(p_j^o)$$

It follows that

$$R'_j(p_j) = \{1 + \alpha_j(p_j)\}x_j(p_j) \tag{4.16}$$

and

$$G'_j(p_j) = \alpha_j(p_j)x_j(p_j)$$

where α_j are the Ramsey numbers as defined by (4.11).

Ramsey numbers are negative where prices exceed marginal costs. There they decrease with an increase in price for a large class of demand functions. This class includes all concave, linear and constant elasticity demand functions. Only for very extreme cases of convex demand functions might Ramsey numbers change with prices in a non-monotonic way. Such extreme cases will be excluded from the following analysis. As a consequence, all profit functions R_j have to be single peaked. The price vector $\mathbf{p}^M = (p_1^M, p_2^M)$ which yields the highest profit (prices charged by a monopolist) can then be determined as the unique solution of

$$1 + \alpha_j(p_j^M) = 0; \quad j = 1, 2$$

Next, we point out that the price vector $\mathbf{p}^R$ leading to a Ramsey–Boiteux optimum (see (4.12)) has the property that

$$\mathbf{c} \leq \mathbf{p}^R \leq \mathbf{p}^M \tag{4.17}$$

If, say, $p_1^R > p_1^M$ then lowering p_1^R would increase, both, profit and consumers' surplus. Similarly, if $p_1^R < c_1$, then increasing p_1^R would lead to higher profits as well as higher social welfare because the Ramsey number had to be positive there. In both cases, prices would not be Ramsey–Boiteux optimal and, therefore, (4.17) is established.

It is assumed that current prices are between marginal costs and the prices charged by a monopolist, that is, that

$$-1 < \alpha_j^o < 0 \quad \text{for} \quad j = 1, 2$$

In the following, only prices above marginal costs are considered. We claim that

$$p_1^o < p_1^R \text{ and } p_2^o > p_2^R \tag{4.18}$$

if $\alpha_1^o > \alpha_2^o$ holds. Recall that the profit functions $R_j(p_j)$ increase with prices $p_j \leq p_j^M$ and that the Ramsey numbers $\alpha_j(p_j)$ decrease with prices p_j at least for $c_j \leq p_j \leq p_j^M$. Since Ramsey–Boiteux prices $\mathbf{p}^R$ are characterized as the solution of equations (4.12), (4.18) follows immediately. Equation (4.18) holds for convex as well as linear demand functions. Therefore, except for

$$p_2^{CR} < p_2^{LR} \tag{4.19}$$

inequalities (4.14) and (4.15) are established. We now come to compare the cases with linear and convex demand functions. First, we claim that the Ramsey number is higher (lower) for the linear than the convex demand function at prices below (above) current prices. Formally, this can be expressed as

$$\alpha_j^L(p_j) \gtreqless \alpha_j^C(p_j) \leftrightarrow p_j^o \gtreqless p_j \tag{4.20}$$

The proof is simple. We construct a linear demand function which, at price p_j, has the same slope and the same price elasticity as the convex demand function. All we now have to compare are the Ramsey numbers of two linear demand functions with different slopes. This can be done by a straightforward calculation which then leads to a proof of (4.20). No details are given here.

As a first application of (4.20) it is shown that

$$\mathbf{p^{LM}} < \mathbf{p^{CM}} \tag{4.21}$$

where $\mathbf{p^{LM}}$ ($\mathbf{p^{CM}}$) denotes the price vector charged by a monopolist facing linear (convex) demand function. To prove (4.21) recall that

$$1 + \alpha_j^L(p_j^{LM}) = 0 \quad \text{for} \quad j = 1, 2$$

It then follows from (4.20) that

$$1 + \alpha_j^C(p_j^{LM}) > 0$$

and, hence, from (4.16) that $p_j^{LM} < p_j^{RM}$ as was to be shown.

Next, (4.20) is applied to the Ramsey–Boiteux vector $\mathbf{p^{LR}}$ for linear demand at profit level r^o. The Ramsey numbers associated with linear demand have there to be equal, that is

$$\alpha_1^L(p_1^{LR}) = \alpha_2^L(p_2^{LR})$$

It follows from (4.18) and (4.20) that

$$\alpha_1^C > \alpha_1^L = \alpha_2^L > \alpha_2^C \tag{4.22}$$

where all these Ramsey numbers are evaluated at $\mathbf{p^{LR}}$. Moreover, since demand at $\mathbf{p^{LR}}$ is higher for the convex than the linear demand functions, it must be true that the profit at $\mathbf{p^{LR}}$

$$r^1 = R^C(\mathbf{p^{LR}}) > r^o$$

is higher for the convex demand functions too.

The same relationship holds for the gain in welfare at prices $\mathbf{p}^{LR}$ relative to current prices $\mathbf{p}^o$ as we now show. The gain from lowering the price of commodity 2 amounts to the area ABCD (ABcd) in Figure 4.1 for the convex (linear) demand function. The gain is higher for the convex than for the linear demand function. For commodity 1, the price must be raised. The loss in welfare is given by the area ABCD for the convex and by the area abCD for the linear demand function in Figure 4.2. Since the area abCD is larger than the area ABCD, the loss is higher for the linear than the convex case. Therefore we have shown that

$$g^1 = G^C(\mathbf{p}^{LR}) > G^L(\mathbf{p}^{LR}) \qquad (4.23)$$

and

$$r^1 = R^C(\mathbf{p}^{LR}) > R^L(\mathbf{p}^{LR}) = r^o$$

The price vector $\mathbf{p}^{LR}$ is now considered as a new starting point for the case of convex demand functions. It follows from (4.21) that $\mathbf{p}^{LR} < \mathbf{p}^{CM}$. We look for the price vector which leads to a Ramsey–Boiteux optimum at profit level r^1 for the convex demand functions. Since (4.22) holds at prices $\mathbf{p}^{LR}$, the price of commodity 2 has to be lowered and that of commodity 1 must be raised for the same reason as before. Thereby

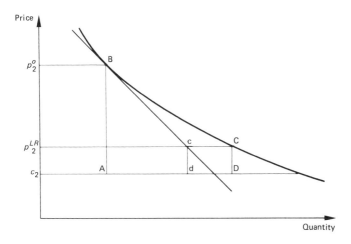

FIGURE 4.1   *The gain in welfare for commodity 2*

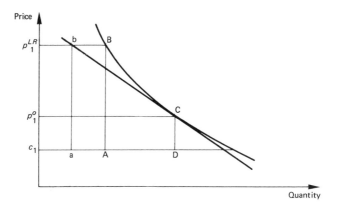

FIGURE 4.2   *The loss in welfare for commodity 1*

welfare increases, because prices are moving towards a Ramsey–Boiteux optimum. The Ramsey numbers (convex demand functions) are now equal whereas the profit level is still at r^1. Finally, both prices are lowered such that the Ramsey numbers remain equal, up to the point where the profit shrinks to the original level r^o. This movement brings prices closer to marginal costs and, hence, welfare increases further. Prices are now at $\mathbf{p}^{CR}$, that is, the Ramsey–Boiteux optimum at profit level r^o for the convex demand functions. Since the price of commodity 2 has never been raised, (4.19) is established. Welfare has never been lowered. Therefore, (4.13) follows from (4.23). Inequalities (4.13)–(4.15) are fully proven.

EMPIRICAL EVALUATION OF WELFARE EFFECTS

The tariff structure

As most other countries, the Federal Republic of Germany has two part telecommunication tariffs. The customer pays a fixed monthly charge for being connected to the network. In addition to that, tariffs are raised which depend on usage.

We have to distinguish between local and long distance calls. Tariffs for local calls depend on the number of calls but not on their duration, at least not before 1980. Since 1980, local calls have been charged on call duration as well. At the same time, local calling areas have been enlarged such that neighbouring exchanges are now included in these areas. The technical structure of the network is no longer reflected in the rate structure.

Long distance calls are divided into three distance bands. The rates increase with distance and are roughly proportional to the duration of calls within each distance band. Rates are different by time of day and day of week. They are lower during evenings and over weekends. Until 1979, there were three different rates; since then, only two remain.

For the following welfare analysis, the effects of changes in tariffs on the level of demand for connection to the network will be neglected. This can be justified as long as only changes in tariffs are considered which leave profits unchanged. Furthermore, network externalities will also be neglected (see Littlechild, 1975). The analysis of the optimal ratio of access charges and usage-dependent tariffs must be the subject of future research.

The data

For a full analysis of the telecommunication tariff structure, data on total revenue, number and duration of calls, price elasticities of demand and marginal costs for each distance and time-of-day category are required. Most of these data were not available. Therefore we had to work at an aggregate level and to introduce some rather restrictive assumptions. Most of the analysis takes place within the framework of a linear model (see the third section of this chapter). Cross price elasticities of demand are ignored throughout.

Our prior information on the cost structure of the telecommunication sector allows us to allocate total costs between the local and the long distance network. Therefore, only two services will be distinguished. Service 1 corresponds to a local call, service 2 to a long distance call of average duration and average distance. No distinction is made between day and night and between different distances. At this level of aggregation, the assumption that cross price elasticities vanish seems plausible. This would no longer be true if day and night calls appeared as different services (see Finsinger and Neumann, 1981, p. 21).

Demand for the two telecommunication services will be denoted by

$$\mathbf{x} = \mathbf{x}(\mathbf{p}) = \{x_1(p_1), x_2(p_2)\}$$

For the empirical analysis, the 'current' situation refers to 1979. Current prices for local and long distance calls are taken as

$$p_1^o = 0.23 \, (\text{DM}) \quad \text{and} \quad p_2^o = 1.62 \, (\text{DM})$$

These values correspond to average revenues per call. Current demand for local and long distance calls was

$$x_1^o = 12.2392 \quad \text{(billion calls)}$$
$$x_2^o = 7.0622 \quad \text{(billion calls)}$$

As for the price elasticities of demand, no reliable estimates are available (see the excellent survey by Taylor, 1980) though, of course, many empirical studies have been carried out. But at least, some qualitative results seem to emerge from all these studies. First, the price elasticity is smaller for local than for long distance calls (in absolute terms). Second, price elasticity for long distance calls increases with distance. Third, elasticity is smaller for business than for residence demand. Fourth, demand is more elastic during evenings and nights than during days. Fifth, elasticities are higher in the long run than in the short run.

Numerical estimates of price elasticities differ significantly among different studies. As for local calls, estimates of short run elasticities between -0.03 and -0.35, and of long run elasticities between -0.07 and -0.7 are reported. For long distance calls, elasticities are estimated at values between -0.1 and -1.7 (short run) and between -0.4 and -2.7 (long run). The German Bundespost used to work with a price elasticity of demand for long distance calls of -0.5 (see Socher, 1972). Since then, they have come to the conclusion that this value under-estimates the true elasticity (see Auer, 1981). Our own interpretation of the quantitative and qualitative results of all these empirical studies leads to the following values

$$\varepsilon_1^o = -0.2 \quad \text{and} \quad \varepsilon_2^o = -1.0$$

for the price elasticities of the demand for local and long distance calls at current prices $\mathbf{p}^0$. These are long run values for the demand aggregated over residence and business demand.

For simplicity and for lack of data, we have to work with a linear cost function (see the third section of this chapter)

$$k(\mathbf{x}) = f + c_1 x_1 + c_2 x_2$$

In this way only usage-dependent costs are included. To arrive at estimates of the three parameters of the cost function, information on total cost, on the allocation of investment costs to different cost components of the network and on the degree of economies of scale has been used.

Investment costs dominate all other costs for a telecommunication network. Plank (1980, p. 10) argues from an engineering viewpoint how total investment costs have to be allocated to the different cost components such as terminal equipment, switching and transmission. Usage dependent costs are defined as those costs of operating and installing equipment which are used jointly by many customers. For that reason, all costs caused by installation and maintenance of any particular customer's direct connection to the network have to be subtracted from total costs. It is fair to assume that this part of total costs is covered from fixed charges. The same holds true for special services. Finally, we point out that all payments to the government budget are listed as costs though, of course, they play the role of profits for an economic analysis. Taking all this into account we arrive at an estimate of

$$k(\mathbf{x}^o) = 9.2601 \quad \text{(billion DM)}$$

Due to economies of scale, not all of these costs can be attributed to the single services (see the third section of this chapter). No general agreement has been reached as to what extent economies of scale in telecommunications still exist. But recent empirical studies (for a survey we refer to John R. Meyer *et al.*, 1980) seem to suggest that economies of scale due to the intensity of use, have lost in importance. After evaluating different empirical studies, we came to use a value of 1.25 for the scale elasticity. This means that 80 per cent of usage dependent costs are attributable (see the third section of this chapter). Attributable costs were allocated to local and long distance calls in the same ratio as investment costs (see Plank, 1980, p. 10). Attributable costs for the two services were then divided by the number of the corresponding calls, leading to the following values for marginal costs

$$c_1 = 0.21 \text{ (DM)} \quad \text{and} \quad c_2 = 0.68 \text{ (DM)}$$

Therefore, the function expressing usage dependent costs can be written as

$$k(\mathbf{x}) = 1.852 \times 10^9 + 0.21x_1 + 0.68x_2$$

Empirical evaluation of marginal price changes

The theory of welfare effects caused by marginal price changes (see the second section of this chapter) is now applied to the above estimates of demand elasticities and cost functions. The Ramsey numbers at current prices $\mathbf{p}^o$ can be easily calculated from the estimates given in the preceding subsection as

$$\alpha_1^o = -0.0152 \quad \text{and} \quad \alpha_2^o = -0.5798$$

They are significantly different and, therefore, welfare can be increased even at the current profit level. For that, the price p_1 of local calls has to be increased and, to leave profits unchanged, the price p_2 of long distance calls must be lowered properly. Let us consider a change in prices given by

$$\mathrm{d}p_1 = 0.01 \quad \text{and} \quad \mathrm{d}p_2 = -0.04 \text{ (DM)}$$

It follows from (4.6) that the level of profit will not change whereas the level of welfare, according to (4.7), increases by 164×10^6 (DM). Even a small change in prices leads to substantial gains in welfare. The estimated value of these gains depends more heavily on the values of parameters corresponding to long distance calls (ε_2^o and c_2) than on those for local calls. A sensitivity analysis has been carried out, leading to the conclusion that gains are possible even at extreme values of marginal costs and demand elasticities.

Empirical evaluation of global welfare effects

The linear model developed in the third section of this chapter will now be used to arrive at estimates for prices which are optimal in the sense of Ramsey–Boiteux as well as for prices, proportional to marginal costs. In Table 4.1, values for six different cases denoted by $A - F$ are reported. The loss L in welfare is evaluated relative to the first best solution where prices are equal to marginal costs (see equation (4.9)). Demand and cost functions are assumed linear. We now discuss the different cases.

Case A

This is the first best solution. Prices are equal to marginal costs and, due to the above convention, no loss in welfare occurs.

TABLE 4.1   *Estimated values of prices, demand and welfare losses relative to the first best solution*

Case	L (billion DM)	p_1 (DM)	p_2 (DM)	x_1 (billion calls)	x_2 (billion calls)
A	0	0.21	0.68	14.426	11.157
B	1.9248	0.23	1.62	12.2392	7.0622
C	0.8461	0.44	1.19	9.9628	8.9454
D	0.8871	0.39	1.25	10.5214	8.6573
E	0.036	0.27	0.80	11.8674	10.6543
F	0.045	0.25	0.81	11.9972	10.5942

A: first best solution.
B: current situation (1979).
C: Ramsey–Boiteux optimum at profit r^o.
D: cost based pricing at profit r^o.
E: Ramsey–Boiteux optimum at zero profit.
F: Cost based pricing at zero profit.

Case B

This corresponds to the 'current' situation which, for our analysis, was taken as the values for 1979. The reported loss in welfare is due to the large current profits and to distortions caused by the structure of prices. Its value would not much be affected by using different values of ε_1^o, while it would be nearly proportional to changes in the estimated value of ε_2^o.

Case C

Current profits of the telecommunication sector amount to $r^o = 4.9957$ (billion DM). Case C corresponds to the Ramsey–Boiteux optimum, leaving profits unchanged at r^o. The gain in welfare relative to the current situation amounts to 1.0787 (billion DM). If demand functions were convex, this gain would be even larger (see the previous section in this chapter).

Case D

Knieps, Müller and Weizsäcker (1981) propose to use prices which are proportional to marginal costs (cost based pricing)

$$p_i = dc_i \quad \text{for} \quad i = 1, 2$$

These authors argue that, while Ramsey–Boiteux pricing is obviously superior to cost based pricing from the static viewpoint, for dynamic efficiency it is the other way round. Under case *D*, the loss in welfare is reported for cost based prices leading to the current profit level r^o. Compared to Ramsey–Boiteux pricing (see case *C*), the loss is not much higher (41 million DM). If compared with current prices, both pricing rules require changes into the same direction.

This result depends, of course, on the assumed form of demand and cost functions as well as on the values of current parameters. If, instead of linear demand functions, it was assumed that price elasticities of demand were constant, then prices and welfare under cost based and Ramsey–Boiteux pricing would differ to a greater extent.

Case E

The profits arising from the telecommunication sector are used to cover deficits of postal services as well as to contribute to the governmental budget. Under case *E*, prices are calculated which lead to zero profits (cost covering tariffs). The reported value of the welfare loss does not take into account that the government must now raise the sum r^o in an alternative way. If, for instance, the sum was raised by taxation, some new distortions would occur.

Case F

The reported values refer to cost based pricing at zero profit level. Under cost covering tariffs, losses in welfare are significantly lower than at current profits because prices can now be set closer to marginal costs.

CONCLUSION

We have shown that substantial losses in welfare arise from the structure and level of current (1979) telecommunication tariffs in the Federal Republic of Germany. To arrive at numerical estimates, a lot of simplifying assumptions had to be imposed. Accuracy could be improved if data would be available on a more disaggregate level. But we believe that, in this case, losses might turn out to be even higher. There would be plenty of room for more distortions.

First, costs arising with long distance transmission have been declining recently. So far, the rate structure has not been adapted. A second distortion arises from the current peak load pricing practice. The substantial growth of residence demand and the attractive tariffs during evenings have led to a shift of the user peak to evenings where rates are low. The Bundespost responds by investing large sums to remove bottlenecks occurring at low rate periods, thus adding further distortions. Third, uniform prices apply to agglomeration and rural areas though, of course, marginal costs are lower in agglomeration than in rural areas.

Our welfare analysis does not take account of these distortions. Therefore a more detailed study based on better data might lead to the conclusion that even larger welfare losses are involved with the current telecommunication tariff structure of the Federal Republic of Germany.

REFERENCES

Auer, E. (1981) 'Vom Mondscheintarif zum Billigtarif', *Vorabdruck aus dem Jahrbuch der Deutschen Bundespost*, vol. 81 (Bad Windesheim).

Finsinger, J. and K.-H. Neumann (1981) 'Wirtschaftspolitische Maßnahmen und die Opposition der Verlierer', discussion paper IIM/IP 81–9, Berlin, April.

Guesnerie, R. (1977) 'On the direction of tax reform', *Journal of Public Economics*, vol. 7, pp. 179–202.

Knieps, G., J. Müller and C. C. von Weizsäcker (1981) Die Rolle des Wettbewerbs im Fernmeldebereich, (Baden-Baden: Nomos Verlag).

Littlechild, St.-C. (1975) 'Two-Part Tariffs and Consumption Externalities'. *The Bell Journal of Economics*, vol. 6 (1975), pp. 661–70.

Meyer, John R. *et al.* (1980) *The Economics of Competition in the Tele-communications Industry* (Cambridge, Mass.: Oelgeschlager Gunn and Hain).

Plank, K.-L. (1980) 'Neue Entwicklungen im Fernmeldewesen', *Fachberichte der Telefonbau und Normalzeit*, (Frankfurt: Heft 1).

Schön, H. (1973) 'Ein weiterer Schritt im Aufbau der neuen Fernmeldeordnung', *Jahrbuch des elektrischen Fernmeldewesens*, vol. 24 (Bad Windesheim) pp. 42–143.

Socher, J. (1972) 'Die Elastizität des öffentlichen Fernsprechverkehrs gegenüber Gebührenänderungen (unter besonderer Berücksichtigung des künftigen Nahdienstes)' *Jahrbuch des elektrischen Fernmeldewesens*, vol. 23 (Bad Windesheim) pp. 159–217.

Taylor, L. P. (1980) *Telecommunications Demand: A Survey and Critique*, (Cambridge, Mass: Ballinger).

Willig, R. D. and E. E. Bailey (1979) 'The Economic Gradient Method', *American Economic Review*, vol. 69 pp. 96–101.

5 Public Interest Firms as Leaders in Oligopolistic Industries

INGO VOGELSANG

INTRODUCTION

In the German institutional economic literature firms with the attribute 'gemeinwirtschaftlich' have played a major role over the past hundred years. The term 'gemeinwirtschaftlich' has no obvious English translation and no unique meaning in German (for a discussion in English see Landauer, 1976). Today there is some agreement among authors that in order to earn this attribute firms have to pursue a public interest besides benefiting their shareholders. In this chapter they are called public interest firms (PIFs). Public enterprises, humanitarian institutions like the Red Cross, non-profit hospitals or homes for the aged are quite unanimously considered as PIFs in the literature. The most discussed borderline case concerns consumer and producer cooperatives. Their status as PIFs is doubtful because they are meant to serve their members' interest. The group most noisy about their status as PIFs are also a borderline case. They are the enterprises belonging to the German trade unions. Among others, trade unions control the largest German housing firm Neue Heimat (NH), the second largest life insurance company Volksfürsorge (VF), the sizeable Bank für Gemeinwirtschaft (BfG) and the largest consumer cooperative Coop Zentrale AG (Coop).

Whereas there is no doubt that these quite successful and respected companies serve the interests of the trade unions well, they themselves really like to be considered as serving the public interest. In the 1960s, therefore, Walter Hesselbach, then chief executive of the BfG and supervisory board chairman of most of the other trade union companies, started to advocate the position that all the trade union firms are PIFs because each of them purposefully acts like a 'pike in the fishpond' by promoting competition in sticky oligopolistic markets (Hesselbach, 1966). Subsequently this view has been emphasized in 1972 and 1978 trade unions' declarations on their enterprises.

The claimed function of promoting competition parallels that attributed to some public enterprises such as Volkswagen in its old days and some of the state owned banks (Landesbanken). One rationale given by politicians and economists for the public ownership of these enterprises was, and is, that they shall promote competition in narrow oligopolistic markets. In this chapter we show that on a conceptual level, trade-union firms may be close substitutes for public enterprises in this respect. It has been hard, however, to prove empirically that enterprises actually fulfil such a procompetitive role. The most extensive work on this matter has been a study by Röper (1976) on three of the trade union firms (NH, BfG and VF). This study suffered from several shortcomings. First, there was no theoretical model on how, and to what extent, a single firm can promote competition in an oligopolistic market. Röper believed that, if successful, the firm promoting competition would force the other firms in the market to behave competitively as well. Therefore one could not single out its effect, and the pike would look just like the other fish in the pond. This is a nirvana view of the potential success. As shown in this chapter, a firm promoting competition will have to behave differently from its competitors in order to be successful.

Second, there was no model of trade union firms based on plausible objectives. In this paper we treat trade union firms as tools of trade unions to pursue their objectives. These again are derived from the fact that trade unions are large-membership organizations.

Third, there was a lack of empirical data. Although Röper and his colleagues did extensive field work, they were actually only able to collect anecdotal evidence of the following kind. NH offers special services for unmarried mothers or old-aged people connected with the apartments they rent. All tenants have practically unlimited tenure. VF is specialized on life insurance policies for low-income families, offering the possibility of interrupting payments on policies. BfG gives special attention to credits for low-income consumers who have difficulties getting loans from other banks and are therefore often exploited by dubious lenders charging exorbitant interest rates. These anecdotes tell something about the specialities of the trade union firms, but little about their competitive impact. Given the shortcomings mentioned, Röper had to conclude that he lacked strong empirical evidence that trade union firms do in fact promote competition. In this author's view, however, something more can be said. This chapter tries to answer several questions. Assuming that empirical evidence is hard to come by, what are the incentives and capabilities of trade union firms to promote competition in their respective markets? Can conditions be established under which such a policy is in the interest of the trade unions? Answering these questions involves the use of some simple oligopolistic models, which lead to different results depending on the behavioural and structural assumptions made. To take the analysis further, these results, which clearly show the pikes to behave differently from the other fish in the pond, would have to be tested empirically.

HOMOGENEOUS MARKET MODELS OF TRADE UNION FIRM BEHAVIOUR

Except for the BfG which has helped the unions to achieve some financial independence from the 'capitalist' financial institutions, essentially all German trade union companies have emerged historically from cooperatives. Trade unions are typically associations with a large membership. Furthermore, as consumers defined by status and income, these members form a rather homogeneous group. Thus, clearly there were considerable economies of scope to be realized by merging cooperatives with trade unions (in fact this may also be true for other large membership organizations such as automobile clubs and the like). Because we do not know to what extent they hold today, we neglect such real cost advantages of trade unions in this chapter. Furthermore, both trade unions and cooperatives have to overcome the free-rider problem of setting in motion collective action that also benefits non-participating individuals. We return to potential consequences of this free-rider problem at the end of the chapter. Until then it is assumed that membership of trade unions can be taken as fixed. Furthermore, we assume that union and union-firm management want to maximize welfare of union members. Applied to a particular trade union enterprise denoted by index 1, total member welfare is taken to be the sum of profits Π_1 and consumers' surplus accruing to members from the enterprise's products. It is a partial equilibrium setting. Income effects are assumed to be absent. In the case of a homogeneous product, total member welfare is

$$W_m = \Pi(x_1) + \int_{\bar{p}}^{\infty} x_m(p)\,\mathrm{d}p \qquad (5.1)$$

where the integral is the area under the aggregate demand curve of members above the price $\tilde{p}$ they pay, x_1 is the output of trade union firm 1 and x_m is the quantity bought by union members in the particular market, whether it is bought from firm 1 or not. There are assumed to be n firms operating in this market without further entry and exit. The $n-1$ non-union firms maximize profits. Union members hold no share in these firms. All n firms use quantities as their strategic variables. They recognize their mutual interdependence. Thus

$$\Pi(x_j) = p(x)x_j - C(x_j) \quad \text{for all} \quad j = 1, \ldots, n \qquad (5.2)$$

where $x = \sum_{k=1}^{n} x_k$, $p(x) =$ inverse demand function and $C(x_j) =$ cost function, which is assumed to be the same for all firms. In the following we assume oligopoly equilibria always to exist and second order conditions to hold. Now if firm 1 wants to maximize W_m with respect to x

$$dW_m/dx_1 = (dp/dx)(dx/dx_1)x_1 + p - C'_1 - x_m \cdot (dp/dx)(dx/dx_1)$$
$$= p - C'_1 + (dx/dx_1)(p/\varepsilon)(s_1 - s_m) = 0 \qquad (5.3)$$

where $C'_1 = dC/dx_1$, $s_1 = x_1/x$, $s_m = x_m/x$ and $\varepsilon =$ price elasticity of market demand. From the first part of equation (5.3) it can be seen that the trade union firm sets quantity such that marginal costs equal marginal revenue plus the marginal consumer surplus increase accruing to union members. Equation (5.3) can be rewritten in terms of the relative price distortion as

$$(p - C'_1)/p = -(dx/dx_1)(1/\varepsilon)(s_1 - s_m) \qquad (5.4)$$

Generally we expect $1 \geq dx/dx_1 > 0$. $dx/dx_1 > 1$ would mean retaliation by the other firms in case of price reduction and collusion in case of price increases. The equilibrium solution then would tend towards a collusive result. This is unlikely in the given environment.

Because $\varepsilon < 0$ equation (5.4) means that in maximizing W_m the trade union enterprise will sell its output below (above) marginal costs whenever its market share as a seller is smaller (larger) than the market share of trade union members as buyers. The weight given to profits is measured by s_1, whereas s_m measures the weight given to union members as consumers. If both weights are equal we get marginal cost pricing by the union firm, because then marginal profit sacrifices are just outweighed by marginal consumers' surplus increases, just as in total social surplus maximization by monopolistic firms. Otherwise ($s_1 \neq s_m$) one component outweighs the other and gives rise to deviations from marginal cost pricing. Compared to this behaviour the typical profit maximizing firm j in the market will sell at

$$(p - C'_j)p = -(\mathrm{d}x/\mathrm{d}x_j)(s_j/\varepsilon) \tag{5.5}$$

With the same cost function for all firms and with $\mathrm{d}x/\mathrm{d}x_1 = \mathrm{d}x/\mathrm{d}x_j$ for all firms j in equilibrium, (5.4) and (5.5) imply that the trade union firm will sell a larger output than the other firms in the market. In doing so it will reduce the market price and the profits of the other firms, and this is what benefits the union members as consumers. Clearly, with this policy of the trade union firm the union members in total are better off than if their firm had simply maximized profits. But how does it compare to a purely cooperative arrangement? Using the same objective function (5.1) as above and restricting the firm to selling to members only we see that at the optimum firm 1 will set $p_1 = C'_1$ and sell $x_1 = x_m(p_1)$. Now p_1 is not necessarily the market price p. Thus three possible cases emerge.

(1) $p_1 = C'_1$ at $x_1 = x_m(p_1)$ with $p_1 = p$. In this case the cooperative is just as good or bad for trade union members as if firm 1 had openly served the market, because then $s_1 = s_m$ implies $p = C'_1$ in equilibrium.

(2) $p_1 = C'_1$ at $x_1 = x_m(p_1)$ with $p_1 > p$. In this case trade union members would stop buying from their cooperative. Their purchases from firm 1 would be reduced until $p_1 = C'_1 = p$. In this case, which could only occur with upward sloping C'_1, members would again gain no advantage from buying at their cooperative. Because here $s_1 < s_m$, the cooperative should instead follow the policy of expanding output by selling below marginal cost.

(3) $p_1 = C'_1$ at $x_1 = x_m(p_1)$ with $p_1 < p$. In this case the cooperative clearly offers an advantage to the members over buying in the market. But is this situation better than if the trade union firm decided to sell in the open market and maximize W_m? Selling in the open market in this case means a higher price for the union members and a larger output for the union firm.[1] Thus in this case maximizing W_m implies $s_1 > s_m$ and thus $p > C'_1$. Therefore the extra output will be sold at a profit. Furthermore, due to the price increase the profit increase on the old output $x_m(p_1) = x_1$ has to be higher than the loss in consumer surplus experienced by the union members as buyers. Figure 5.1 illustrates these points for the case of an upward sloping marginal cost curve. There the switch from a cooperative to an open

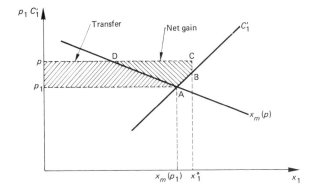

FIGURE 5.1 *Switch from cooperative to maximizing* W_m

market solution results in a change in output from $x_m(p_1)$ to x_1^*. Price is increased from p_1 to (the new equilibrium) market price p. Total increase of W_m is the shaded area ABCD.

Under the assumptions made, an open market policy by the trade union firms is never worse in terms of W_m than a closed shop cooperative. Now, within the context of the trade union firm maximizing W_m in the open market, let us discuss particular types of markets and behaviour.

Cournot Monopoly in Equilibrium

Suppose the trade union firm is a monopoly. This means $x_1 = x$. Then $dW_m/dx_1 = 0$ implies

$$(p - C_1')/p = -(1/\varepsilon)(1 - s_m) \tag{5.6}$$

We thus get the Cournot profit maximizing monopoly exactly when no one belongs to the union ($s_m = 0$) and the welfare maximizing marginal cost pricing when everyone belongs to the union ($s_m = 1$). Generally, within this model $s_m = 0$ defines the profit maximizing firm and $s_m = 1$ the public enterprise, giving zero weight to profits of other firms.

Cournot Oligopoly in Equilibrium

In this case all firms including firm 1 show Cournot behaviour. Thus $dx/dx_1 = 1$. Then $dW_m/dx_1 = 0$ implies

$$(p - C_1')/p = -(1/\varepsilon)(s_1 - s_m) \qquad (5.7)$$

whereas for the $n - 1$ profit maximizing firms

$$(p - C_j')/p = -(s_j/\varepsilon) \qquad (5.8)$$

holds. To elaborate on this textbook case of oligopoly theory, let us consider $C_1' = C_j' = $ constant. Because there is only one market price, p, the right hand sides of (5.7) and (5.8) have to be equal, implying

$$s_1 = s_m + s_j \qquad (5.9)$$

Furthermore, by definition of the market shares

$$(n - 1)s_j = 1 - s_1 \qquad (5.10)$$

(5.9) and (5.10) imply

$$s_1 = (1/n) + [(n - 1)/n]s_m \qquad (5.11)$$

In this case the trade union firm will always (except for $s_m = 1$) expand its output to a point where $s_1 > s_m$. Therefore the curiosity of pricing below marginal costs will never occur.

(5.11) and (5.7) imply

$$(p - C')/p = (1/n\varepsilon)(1 - s_m) \qquad (5.12)$$

If we had a Cournot oligopoly of n profit maximizers the relative price distortion would be

$$(p - C')/p = 1/n\varepsilon \qquad (5.13)$$

Thus it follows from (5.12) and (5.13) that through the presence of the trade union firm the price distortion is reduced in proportion to the share of trade union members as buyers. Taking the Harberger approach to measuring welfare losses we can approximate the dead weight welfare loss due to price distortion by

$$\Delta \approx \tfrac{1}{2} p x \varepsilon [(p - C')/p)]^2 \qquad (5.14)$$

The relative reduction in welfare loss due to maximizing W_m by the trade union firm 1 can now be expressed as

$$(\Delta - \Delta_1)/\Delta \approx 2s_m - s_m^2 \qquad (5.15)$$

Equation (5.15) is independent of the number of firms in the market, depending only on s_m. It describes a concave curve shown in Figure 5.2, showing that the marginal impact of s_m on welfare is greatest for small s_m.

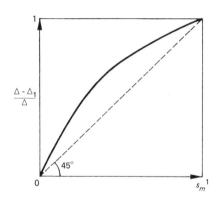

FIGURE 5.2 *Welfare improvement in the Cournot case with constant marginal cost*

Stackelberg Duopoly

Assuming an active role in its market may mean that the trade union firm 1 behaves as a Stackelberg leader. This can be treated in a straightforward fashion for the duopoly case. Here

$$\mathrm{d}x_j/\mathrm{d}x_1 = -[(p' + x_j p'')/(2p' + x_j p'' - C_j'')] \qquad (5.16)$$

(see, for example, Krelle, 1976).

Then $dW_m/dx_1 = 0$ implies

$$(p - C_1')/p = -(1/\varepsilon)(s_1 - s_m)[1 + (dx_j/dx_1)] \tag{5.17}$$

Again for simplification we assume $C_1' = C_j' = $ constant. Furthermore market demand is taken to be linear. Thus, for this simple case, (5.16) and (5.17) imply

$$(p - C')/p = -(1/2\varepsilon)(s_1 - s_m) \tag{5.18}$$

for the trade union firm as a Stackelberg leader and

$$(p - C')/p = s_j/\varepsilon \tag{5.19}$$

for the other duopolist as a Stackelberg follower. Thus

$$s_1 = 2/3 + s_m/3 \tag{5.20}$$

From (5.20) we may conjecture that extending this simple case to n oligopolists will lead to $s_1 = [n/(n+1)] + [s_m/(n+1)]$ and this will converge to the Cournot solution as n gets larger.

CONCLUSIONS AND EXTENSIONS

In the model discussed so far the trade union firm consistently increased output beyond the profit maximizing point. This results in a market price which is lower than under the ordinary oligopoly solution for the profit maximizing case. The policy of the trade union firm thus unambiguously benefits the consumers in these markets. Aggregate consumers' surplus is increased. The induced change in producers' surplus is less evident. Consider the following cases.

(1) *Constant marginal costs.* In this case total output in the market is increased at non-increasing average costs and thus social surplus is unambiguously increased as was shown above for the Cournot oligopoly case.

(2) *Always decreasing marginal costs.* This case implies a natural monopoly situation. Under pure profit maximization all n firms in the market could conceivably produce positive outputs in equilib-

rium. With the trade union firm maximizing W_m, however, either equation (5.4) or (5.5) will be violated, or $1 \geq dx/dx_1 > 0$ does not hold. This is so because the trade union firm expands its output such that price is closer to its marginal costs than for the profit maximizing firms. With decreasing marginal costs this will lead to a corner solution at which the profit maximizing firms do not produce at all. In this case it is not clear if the total quantity traded in the market will be increased over the pure profit maximizing oligopoly. With an increase in total quantity total surplus is unambiguously increased as well. If total quantity is decreased consumers' surplus and average costs both also decrease so that there is a welfare trade-off with no unique outcome.

(3) *Always increasing marginal costs.* In this case the outcome of the previous situation is reversed. The trade union firm produces a larger output at higher average costs and the other firms in the market produce smaller outputs at lower average costs than in the case of only profit maximizing oligopolists. A trade-off between average cost increase for the total output and consumers' surplus increase can occur. Generally this occurrence does not only depend on whether $s_m > s_1$ and thus $p < C_1'$ or $s_m < s_1$ and thus $p > C_1'$, although the first of these two cases obviously reveals a particular kind of cost inefficiency.

In order to see the welfare implications more clearly, let us consider an oligopolist denoted by subscript n trying to maximize total social surplus over x_n

$$\max_{x_n} W = \int_{\bar{p}}^{\infty} x(p)\,dp + \sum_{j=1}^{n} \Pi_j$$

This implies

$$dW/dx_n = -x\,(dp/dx)\,(dx/dx_n) + x\,(dp/dx)\,(dx/dx_n)$$

$$+ (dx/dx_n)p - C_n' - \sum_{l=1}^{n-1} C_l'(dx_l/dx) = 0 \qquad (5.21)$$

Assuming unified conjectural behaviour among the other firms in the market and the same cost function for all firms, we get the relative price distortion for the welfare maximizing oligopolist

$$(p - C'_n)/p = -(n-1)(dx_l/dx_n)[(p - C'_l)/p]$$
$$= [1 - (dx/dx_n)][(p - C'_l)/p] \qquad (5.22)$$

where $l \neq n$.

Generally we expect $1 - (dx/dx_n) \geq 0$ or $dx_l/dx_n \leq 0$, with equality holding in the case of Cournot oligopoly. This means that the welfare maximizing oligopolist will set quantity such that price equals marginal cost either if he holds the Cournot conjecture or if marginal costs are constant $(C'_n = C'_l)$.[2] Otherwise price will be above marginal costs. In these more sophisticated cases he expects that his output increase results in an output decrease by the profit maximizing firms because they face a decreased residual demand. Thus when he moves closer to marginal costs they move further away from marginal costs. This trade-off has its equilibrium at the point where the marginal quantity reduction by the other firms induced by the output increase of firm n equals the ratio of the relative price distortions for the two types of firms

$$(p - C'_n)/(p - C'_l) = -(n-1)(dx_l/dx_n) \qquad (5.23)$$

Thus, whereas the welfare maximizing oligopolist will increase his output beyond the profit maximizing point he will generally stop short of pricing below marginal costs.

In the oligopoly models we made a number of simplifying assumptions which need to be discussed before the results can be fully evaluated.

(1) We looked at homogeneous products only. This led to the use of quantities as the strategic variables. The analysis can readily be extended to the case of heterogeneous commodities and the use of price as the strategic variable. W_m then has to include consumers' surplus over more than one commodity. Thus for path independence the integrability conditions $\partial x_k/\partial p_l = \partial x_l/\partial x_k$ have to hold for all markets k and l. The results under this approach do not differ qualitatively from those discussed above. Again a possible outcome is that the trade union firm sets $p_1 < C'_1$.

(2) Maximizing W_m as described in the second section of this chapter may lead to losses by the trade union firm and/or its competitors. Should the competitors make losses due to the aggressive behaviour of the trade union firm they may want to leave the market, violating the

assumption that the number of firms in the market is fixed. Whereas this can be seen as the extreme case of firms selling zero output, it may introduce two problems. First, the resulting corner equilibrium means that the marginal conditions derived above do not necessarily hold any longer. This would not endanger the validity of our general argument. Second, monopolizing the market may be attractive for the management of trade union firms because it means increased sales, power and so on. This could distort our results. Should, on the other hand, the trade union firm make losses due to maximizing W_m, this could interfere with its ability to borrow outside capital and would necessitate subsidization through membership dues. Subsidies tend to have distortive effects (see, for example, Finsinger and Vogelsang, 1981, for some arguments). One may therefore want to introduce a balanced budget constraint $\Pi \geq 0$ for the trade union enterprises. If this constraint is binding it will weaken the aggressiveness of a trade union firm i in its market, but not basically change our results. The larger the trade union membership, the larger the chances are that the constraint will be binding.

(3) We have assumed that trade union membership is not influenced by the policy of the trade union firm to maximize W_m by competing in the open market. There may be offsetting influences that such a policy could have on union membership. On one hand, sacrificing profits means increased membership dues to maintain the same level of trade union services proper. The benefits of such profit sacrifices, however, are equally shared by all buyers in the respective markets independent of trade union membership. Suppose one can order union members by their willingness to pay membership dues. Define a marginal trade union member to be one whose membership benefits just outweigh the costs to him/her in terms of membership dues. Such a marginal member may leave the union if the union firms' profits decrease due to maximizing W_m. This is a marginal argument and therefore independent of whether the trade union firm does better than break even or not. Incidentally, it is even consistent for a marginal member to vote in favour of the trade union firm's policy to maximize W_m instead of Π_1, but then to leave the union after the vote has come through. Such a person is indifferent to being a member at current dues. If they have to be raised due to profit sacrifices he/she will leave the union without being worse off. On the other hand he/she gains as a consumer from the lower market prices. Maximizing profits in this scenario will be a membership maximizing strategy.

On the other hand, maximizing W_m may generate additional benefits for the trade union. The union can hope that the aggressive policy of its firm will benefit its public image, especially among potential new members. This alleged advertising effect parallels observations by Fischler (1980) on gratuitous services provided by private firms with high market power. Furthermore, the trade union's image definitely would be hurt by public knowledge of excess profits made by union firms. Thus, the union firm may have to find a way to dispose of some extra profits, and maximizing W_m may just be one of them. Last, but not least, the union firm may have to pay corporate taxes on its profits whereas the union members do not have to pay taxes on lower market prices (on the contrary, taxes are less).

(4) We have assumed that a policy of maximizing W_m can, and will, be implemented by the trade union firm's management. As indicated in the previous paragraph, such a policy may indeed be in the interest of the trade union as a membership organization. However, this does not assure that such a policy can be translated into concrete steps within the trade union firm. Some empirical hypotheses, however, can be derived, in order to test if such a policy is being followed.

First, we would expect such a policy from trade unions with large membership, not from trade unions like those in the UK, which vigorously compete with each other.

Second, we would expect trade union firms to operate in markets, where trade union members make up a comparatively large proportion of buyers.

Third, trade union firms should be large compared to other firms in their markets.

These crude hypotheses are not contradicted by the situation of trade union firms in Germany. However, there seems to be little evidence that trade union firms have grown beyond optimal size and no instances are reported where they in fact price below marginal costs.

NOTES

1. Note that in Germany cooperatives that choose to serve the general public are not allowed effectively to discriminate in favour of their customers. This is to prevent evasion of profit taxes.
2. Again always decreasing marginal costs imply that all other firms are competed out of the market and thus $p = C'_n$ in the welfare maximizing case.

REFERENCES

Finsinger, J. and I. Vogelsang (1981) 'Alternative Institutional Frameworks for Price Incentive Mechanisms', *Kyklos*, vol. 34, Fasc. 3, pp. 388–404.

Fischler, H. (1980) 'Monopolies, Market Interdependencies and the Logic of Collective Action: Some Critical Comments on Mancur Olson's Group Thesis', *Public Choice*, vol. 35, pp. 191–5.

Heidenheimer, A. J. (1980) 'Unions and Welfare State Development in Britain and Germany: An Interpretation of Metamorphoses in the Period 1910–1950', IIVG/dp/80–209 (Berlin, International Institute of Comparative Social Research).

Hesselbach, W. (1966) *Die gemeinwirtschaftlichen Unternehmen, Instrumente gewerkschaftlicher und genossenschaftlicher Struktur- und Wettbewerbspolitik, völlig überarbeitete Fassung 1971* (Frankfurt: Europa) (erste Fassung 1966).

Knieps, G. and I. Vogelsang (1982). 'The Sustainability Concept under Alternative Behavioural Assumptions', *Bell Journal of Economics*, vol. 13, no. 1, pp. 234–41.

Krelle, W. (1976) *Preistheorie 2. Auflage* (Tübingen: J. C. B. Mohr).

Landauer, C. (1976) 'Recent German Literature on Gemeinwirtschaft', *Social Research*, vol. 43, pp. 295–321.

Röper, B. (1976) *Theorie und Praxis der gemeinwirtschaftlichen Konzeption*, (Göttingen: Otto Schwartz).

Part III
Investment and Pricing

6 A Dynamic Analysis of Second-Best Pricing

RONALD R. BRAEUTIGAM

INTRODUCTION

The theory of second best for multiproduct firms has received much attention in the literature of economics over the past twenty-five years. Both regulators and economists have recognized that departures from marginal cost pricing will be necessary when there are economies of scale if the firm is to break even in the absence of nonlinear pricing schemes and direct subsidies to the firm.

The rudiments of this literature can be traced back to the treatment of the optimal taxation problem by a number of economists, including Ramsey (1927), Hicks (1947) and Boiteux (1956). Since the 1950s a number of papers have specifically addressed the setting of optimal prices (instead of taxes) for regulated multiproduct firms. Probably the most well known of these papers is by Baumol and Bradford (1970).

Virtually all of the work in this field has been in terms of static analysis. At one end of the spectrum one can view the problem in the long run, in which all factors of production can be set optimally at the same time that prices are determined. At the other hand one can address the problem of second best pricing in the short run, when some of the factors cannot be varied. One can specify a second best pricing rule in either case, where the rule maximizes economic efficiency subject to a static break-even constraint.

When we introduce time into the analysis, several additional interesting questions can be posed. Factors of production can be varied over time, though not costlessly. How would adjustment costs of this sort affect the selection of input levels? How would they affect the rules for second best pricing? Does a break-even constraint require that the firm avoid negative profits at each point in time, or that the present value of the profits should be non-negative? How does the choice of the break even constraint affect input selection and optimal pricing over time? These issues will provide the focus for this chapter.

THE STATIC PROBLEM

In order to compare the results from the time-varying problem with those in the static case, we briefly review the major results of the latter. The firm is assumed to have n products, indexed by $i = 1, \ldots, n$. The quantity of each output is denoted by x^i, and the vector of all outputs is $\mathbf{x}$. The inverse demand for output i is $p^i(\mathbf{x})$, so that demands may be interdependent in general.

We assume that the production of x involves the use of two types of factors. One of these types is fixed in the short run, and its level will be denoted by k. Its factor price is assumed to be a positive constant, r. The other type of factor is completely variable, even in the short run. Thus, when confronted with specified values of x and k, the efficient firm will choose the level of the variable input to minimize variable cost, which we denote by $V(\mathbf{x}, k, w)$, where w is the factor price of the variable input.

We also assume that $G(\mathbf{x})$ provides a measure of the gross (that is, not net of costs of production) benefit associated with the provision and consumption of $\mathbf{x}$. Then the net economic benefit associated with the provision of x, given k, is

$$T(\mathbf{x}, k, w) = G(\mathbf{x}) - V(\mathbf{x}, k, w) - rk \tag{6.1}$$

where we may interpret T as the sum of consumer and producer surplus, for example. We will assume that T is jointly concave in $\mathbf{x}$ and k.

$$\pi(\mathbf{x}, k, w) = \sum_i p^i(\mathbf{x}) x^i - V(\mathbf{x}, k, w) - rk \tag{6.2}$$

we will assume that π is jointly concave in $\mathbf{x}$ and k.

If no profit constraint is required or binding, then the economically efficient choices of x^i would be

$$T_{x^i} = p^i - V_{x^i} = 0, \; \forall i, \quad \text{when} \quad x^i > 0 \tag{6.3}$$

where the arguments of T, V and p are suppressed for convenience, and the subscripts denote partial derivatives (for example, $T_{x^i} \equiv \partial T / \partial x^i$).

In the long run, when k can be adjusted to an optimal level, in addition to (6.3) economic efficiency would require

$$T_k = -V_k - r = 0, \quad \text{when } k > 0 \tag{6.4}$$

These conditions are simply formal representations of first best.

If the firm can not break even at first best, then the notion of second best becomes relevant. We ask to characterize the choice of the x^i variables (and k in the long run) to maximize T subject to a constraint that $\pi > \pi^0$, where π^0 is a constant (usually zero in the second-best literature). Let μ be the Lagrange multiplier associated with the profit constraint. Then second best optimality, requires that

$$T_{x^i} + \mu\pi_{x^i} = 0, \quad \forall i, \quad \text{when } x^i > 0 \tag{6.5}$$

$$T_k = (1 + \mu)(-V_k - r) = 0, \quad \text{when } k > 0 \tag{6.6}$$

and

$$\pi \geq 0; \quad \mu\pi = 0; \quad \mu \geq 0. \tag{6.7}$$

Both (6.4) and (6.6) indicate that in the long run $[V(x, k, w) + rk]$ will correspond to the usual notion of a long run cost function $C(\mathbf{x}, r, w)$. In particular, in producing the vector $\mathbf{x}$, k will be chosen at a level such that the variable cost savings achieved with the marginal unit of $k(-V_k)$ will equal the cost of employing another unit of $k(r)$.

When $\pi \geq 0$ is a binding constraint, then (6.5) is one of the forms of the second best pricing rules reported by Baumol and Bradford. We note here that although Baumol and Bradford developed the rule for long run cost functions, its basic form remains valid in the short run as well. In the short run the relevant marginal costs are short run rather than long run.

TWO DYNAMIC PROBLEMS

A dynamic formulation will enable us to bridge the gap between the polar short and long run cases usually examined in discussions of second best.[1] We begin by distinguishing between the stock of capital a firm has on hand at time t, $k(t)$ and the gross rate of investment $I(t)$. Assume that capital depreciates at a constant rate, δ, so that the rate of change of capital stock $k'(t)$, where

$$k'(t) = I(t) - \delta[k(t)] \tag{6.8}$$

Further, there is a cost associated with the rate of investment $C[I(t)]$, and we assume that investment cost is a weakly convex function of the gross investment rate, so that $C'' \geq 0$. Thus, at any moment in time, the current value of net benefit is

$$T(\mathbf{x}, k, w, I) = G(\mathbf{x}) - V(\mathbf{x}, k, w) - rk - C(I) \tag{6.9}$$

where $\mathbf{x}$, k and I are all functions of t.

We will assume output levels (or their prices) are completely flexible. Output demand schedules, $p^i(\mathbf{x})$ are fixed. We seek to characterize the optimal choice of gross investment $I(t)$ and $\mathbf{x}(t)$ to maximize T in (6.9), subject to (6.8), and a break even constraint. The choice of a break even constraint is not unambiguous in a dynamic world. One possible choice is

$$\pi(\mathbf{x}, k, w, I) = \sum_i p^i(\mathbf{x}) x^i - V(\mathbf{x}, k, w) - rk - C(I) \geq 0 \tag{6.10}$$

so that profits must be non-negative at every time t. Still another possible specification is that the present value of profit should be positive over the time interval $[0, T]$. Let the discount rate s be a positive constant. Then this form of the constraint would require that

$$\int_0^T e^{-st} \pi \, dt \geq 0 \tag{6.11}$$

where the arguments of π are suppressed for convenience. We will examine the effects of both kinds of constraints.

It would be possible to construct a model which allowed the adjustment costs, $C(I)$, to be capitalized over time. The appendix to this chapter presents a formulation of such a model, which we do not analyze here. However, we note that the capitalization of adjustment costs will not affect the validity of the three propositions we present below, although it will alter the levels of efficient prices and investment over time.

In our analysis we will assume that gross investment is always non-negative, so that a formal constraint to that effect is met automatically. We will also assume that both T and π are jointly concave in $\mathbf{x}$, k, and I.

Model I.

Formally, then, one could characterize one model of second best as follows

$$\max_{(\mathbf{x},\,I)} \int_0^T e^{-st} T \, dt \tag{6.12}$$

subject to

$$k' = I - \delta k, \quad 0 \le t \le T, \quad K(0) = k_0 > 0 \tag{6.13}$$

$$e^{-st} \pi \ge 0, \quad 0 \le t \le T \tag{6.14}$$

Thus (6.12) represents the present value of net benefit which is to be maximized. Further (6.14) will be satisfied if and only if (6.10) is satisfied, and the formulation as in (6.14) will to some extent simplify the analysis.

Model II.

The formal representation of the second kind of second best problem will involve the isoperimetric constraint (6.11) instead of (6.14). Analytically it will be convenient to recognize that (6.11) can be rewritten as a differential equation with boundary conditions, as appears below in (6.17), (6.18) and (6.19).

$$\max_{(\mathbf{x},\,I)} \int_0^T e^{-st} T \, dt \tag{6.15}$$

subject to

$$k' = I - \delta k \tag{6.16}$$

$$y' = e^{-st} \pi \tag{6.17}$$

$$y(0) = 0 \tag{6.18}$$

$$y(T) \ge 0 \tag{6.19}$$

For both models, let $\hat{m}(t)$ be the costate variable associated with the state equation for k, and let $m(t) = e^{st}\hat{m}(t)$ be the current value of that multiplier.

For model I, let $\hat{\mu}(t)$ be the multiplier associated with (6.14), and let $\mu(t) = e^{st}\hat{\mu}(t)$ be the current value of that multiplier. For model II, let $\hat{\gamma}(t)$ be the costate variable associated with the state variable y, and let $\gamma(t) = e^{st}\hat{\gamma}(t)$ be the current value of that multiplier. Also, let z be the multiplier corresponding to the terminal constraint (6.19).

The necessary and sufficient conditions for optimality for both of these models are displayed in Table 6.1. For model I, the current value Hamiltonian appears in (6.20). Conditions (6.21)–(6.23) are derived from the usual optimal control necessary conditions derived from derivatives on the state, control, and costate variables. Equation (6.24) represents the first order condition on the variables x^i, (6.25) shows the conditions required by the break even constraint and (6.26) contains the required transversality condition since $k(T)$ is not specified.

For model II, the current value Hamiltonian is shown in (6.27). The relationships (6.28)–(6.30) reflect the optimal control necessary conditions derived from the derivatives on the state variable k, the control variable, and the costate variable associated with k. In (6.31) we have the first order conditions required if $\mathbf{x}$ is optimal. Relationship (6.32) reflects the fact that, since the Hamiltonian does not contain y, then the multiplier γ is a constant for all t. It also contains the information required by the transversality condition on γ, that $\gamma(T) = z$. Finally, (6.33) shows the conditions required by the terminal constraint (6.19),

TABLE 6.1   *Necessary and sufficient conditions*

Model I	$H = T + m(I - \delta k) + \mu\pi$	(6.20)
	$m' = (s + \delta)m - T_k(1 + \mu)$	(6.21)
	$T_I(1 + \mu) + m = 0$	(6.22)
	$k' = I - \delta k, \quad k(0) = k_o$	(6.23)
	$T_{x^i} + \mu\pi_x i = 0, \quad x^i > 0, \, \forall_i$	(6.24)
	$\mu(t) \geq 0, \, \mu(t)\pi = 0, \quad \pi \geq 0, \quad \text{for} \quad 0 \leq t \leq T$	(6.25)
	$m(T) = 0$	(6.26)
Model II	$H = T + m(I - \delta k) + \gamma\pi$	(6.27)
	$m' = (s + \delta)m - T_k(1 + \gamma)$	(6.28)
	$T_I(1 + \gamma) + m = 0$	(6.29)
	$k' = I - \delta k, \quad k(0) = k_0$	(6.30)
	$T_{x^i} + \gamma\pi_{x^i} = 0, \quad x^i > 0, \, \forall_i$	(6.31)
	$\gamma(t) = \gamma(T) = z$, a constant	(6.32)
	$z \geq 0, \, z\pi = 0, \, \pi \geq 0 \quad \text{at} \quad t = T$	(6.33)
	$m(T) = \pi_k \quad \text{at} \quad t = T$	(6.34)

and (6.34) represents the transversality condition imposed since $k(T)$ is not specified.

It turns out that these necessary conditions are also sufficient. In model I, T and π are both jointly concave in k and I by assumption, and the only state equation is linear in k and I. In model II, sufficiency is established since, T and π are concave in k, I and y, the state equation for k' is linear in k and I, the state equation for y' is jointly concave in I and k since π is jointly concave in those arguments, and the costate variable γ is positive for all t.

INSTANTANEOUS PRICING RULES

One of the immediate results that can be obtained from this analysis is that at any specified time t, with whatever level of capital, $k(t)$, is then in place, the optimal rules for pricing look very much the same for the dynamic case as they do for the static case. We state this formally as follows.

Proposition 1. At any time t, given $k(t)$ and a binding break even constraint for either model, efficient pricing requires that

$$(T_{x^i})/(\pi_{x^i}) = (T_{x^j})/(\pi_{x^j}), \Psi_{i,j} \tag{6.35}$$

The proof of this proposition follows directly from (6.24) for model I and from (6.31) for model II. This proposition indicates that the famous inverse elasticity rule derived in static models of second best carry through in the dynamic case.

We can relate this to the more conventional representation of so-called Ramsey optimal pricing, assuming independent demands, by rewriting (6.35) as

$$\left[(p^i - V_{x^i})/p^i\right]\varepsilon_i = R, \Psi_i \tag{6.36}$$

where ε_i represents the elasticity of demand in market i, and where $R\varepsilon$ $[-1, 0]$ is sometimes called a Ramsey number. In model I, $R = -\mu/(1 + \mu)$; in model II, $R = -\gamma/(1 + \gamma)$. Further, although R will generally vary across time in model I, we have the following results for model II.

Proposition 2. Along an optimal path for model II (in which the present value of profits is constrained to be non-negative), the Ramsey number R is not only equal in all markets, but is also constant over time.

The proof of this proposition follows directly from (6.32).

It is also perhaps worthwhile to note in passing that when the break-even constraint fails to be binding in either model, then, given $k(t)$, the optimal price in each market will be equal to short run marginal cost, just as in the static case.

EFFECTS OF ADJUSTMENT COSTS

To understand the effects of investment adjustment costs, it is instructive to consider what happens when the adjustment cost function is zero (or some constant not varying with the level of investment). In such a case, $T_I = 0$, so that $m - 0$ in (6.22) and (6.29). Therefore, in both cases the level of capital chosen in both models (using (6.21) and (6.28)) would satisfy $T_k = 0$. Recall from (6.4) that this is exactly the same rule that the static rules require for second best, in conjunction with the Ramsey rule (6.35) for setting prices. Thus, in the case for which $C' = 0$, the dynamic problem degenerates to a static one, and the optimal level of capital is chosen immediately.

Thus, the dynamic version of the problem becomes of interest only when $C' \neq 0$. The first level of interest would then be the case in which $C'' = 0$, but $C' > 0$. Recall from the definition of T in (6.9) that $T_I = -C'$.

For model I, when C' is a positive constant, the value of m (from (6.22)) will not necessarily be a constant. Thus, one would generally expect the value of m and k to adjust over time.

For model II, the story is quite different. When C' is a positive constant, then since γ is also a constant, m is a constant in (6.29). Therefore, m' is zero in (6.28), and the optimal level of capital for all time is chosen immediately.

When $C'' > 0$, then in neither model is there an immediate and complete adjustment to a level of capital that would be chosen for all time. In general, k' and m' will be non-zero over any finite time horizon.

Since the problem stated in terms of the current value Hamiltonian is autonomous (that is, not depending explicitly on t), it is possible to examine what would happen in both second best problems if the time horizon, T, were infinite. We can therefore characterize the nature of a steady state in this section. The steady state in these models will be defined by $k' = m' = 0$. For model I this will occur when

$$m' = (s + \delta)m - T_k(1 + \mu) = 0 \tag{6.37}$$

and

$$k' = I - \delta k = 0 \tag{6.38}$$

Since the general forms of (6.21) and (6.28) are the same, as are (6.23) and (6.30), the steady state characteristics of both models can be examined from (6.37) and (6.38). In addition we will use (6.22), which combined with (6.37) implies that

$$T_k = -T_I(s + \delta) > 0 \tag{6.39}$$

at a steady state. We contrast this with the capital selection rule in the static problem (see (6.4)) that requires $T_k = 0$. This leads to the following observation.

Proposition 3. The capital selection rules for the static and the steady state of the dynamic problems will coincide only when adjustment costs are constant, or when the discount and depreciation rates are both zero.

Thus, if the Ramsey pricing rule were satisfied in a static world, with no adjustment costs on capital, then capital would be chosen until the partial derivative of the total surplus function T with respect to capital were zero. But such a choice of capital would be too large to be benefit maximizing in the dynamic world with adjustment costs, at a steady state.

We should also note that this property is not unique to a second best world. In fact it also occurs at first best. This can be observed by noting that the comparative properties of T_k in proposition 3 are preserved when there is no binding profit constraint (that is, $\mu = 0$ in model I and $\gamma = 0$ in model II).

We can also pursue our analysis of the infinite horizon problem using phase plane analysis.[2] We perform that analysis here for model II, since the analysis is greatly facilitated in that case because we can take γ to be a constant in (6.28) and (6.29). To proceed, let us consider a redefinition of the net benefit function T, where the optimal **x** is optimized out. We will assume that $\bar{T}$ is jointly concave in k and I.[3] Then along a locus at which

$m' = 0$ in (6.28), we will have

$$m/(1+\gamma) = \overline{T}_k/(s+\delta) \tag{6.40}$$

Because $\overline{T}_k$ is assumed to be concave in k, then

$$d[m/(1+\gamma)] = \overline{T}_{kk}/(s+\delta) < 0 \tag{6.41}$$

So the $m' = 0$ locus can be depicted as in Figure 6.1, and has a downward slope as shown.

We can also graph the locus of $k' = 0$. From (6.30) we would have

$$I = \delta k \tag{6.42}$$

But from (6.29) we observe that

$$m/(1+\delta) = -T_I = C'(I) \tag{6.43}$$

and we may invert (6.43) to yield

$$g[m/(1+\gamma)] = I \tag{6.44}$$

where $g \equiv (C')^{-1}$. The properties of g can be established from those of C. Since $C'(0) = 0$, we have that $g(0) = 0$. Also, from (6.43) it follows that

$$d[m/(1+\gamma)] = C'' \, dI \tag{6.45}$$

and therefore,

$$\frac{dI}{d[m/(1+\gamma)]} = 1/C'' = g' > 0 \tag{6.46}$$

Thus (6.42) can be rewritten as

$$g[m/(1+\gamma)] = \delta k \tag{6.47}$$

Thus this locus passes through the origin and is upward sloping, as depicted in Figure 6.1. Thus Figure 6.1 illustrates typical paths generated by the differential equations. The figure also demonstrates the nature of the unique path leading to a steady state $\{[m/(1+\gamma)]^*, k^*\}$ in the infinite horizon problem. Thus, if $k_0 < k^*$, the steady state will be

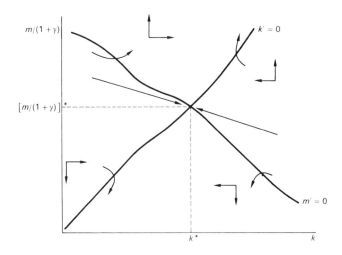

FIGURE 6.1   *Phase plane analysis*

approached monotonically, with $m/(1 + \gamma)$ falling. Since I and m are directly related, the investment rate also falls (rises) monotonically in this case when $k_0 < k^*$ ($k_0 > k^*$).

CONCLUSIONS

We have developed two rather simple dynamic characterizations of second best in this paper, and examined the rules for pricing and investment when there are investment adjustment costs. The analysis bridges the gap between the conventional short run and long run static models of second best. If prices (or output) can be adjusted instantaneously, then Ramsey-type rules will be appropriate for price setting in the dynamic world just as it is in the static world. The exact prices will differ depending on whether profit must be non-negative at every point in time, or whether the discounted profit must be non-negative over the planning horizon.

Adjustment costs generate capital choice rules in the dynamic world different from those in the static model when discounting and depreciation are introduced, even in the steady state that would be generated in an infinite planning horizon. The models we have presented could be extended to include systematic shifts in demand and technology, and the investment rules would be affected accordingly.

APPENDIX

The models discussed in this chapter can be formulated in a slightly different way with respect to the treatment of capital. In particular, if the adjustment costs, $C(I)$, incurred at time t are capitalized and depreciated, then the capitalized value of the adjustment costs can be represented by the state variable $\phi(t)$. Then $\phi(t)$ changes over time as follows

$$\phi'(t) = C[I(t)] - \delta\phi(t)$$

with an initial condition $\phi(0) = 0$, and a terminal condition $\phi(T) = \overline{\phi}$. If $\overline{\phi}$ were zero, for example, then by time T the adjustment costs would be entirely depreciated, with none remaining as capitalized.

So, for example, model II in this chapter can be written as

$$\max_{(\mathbf{x},I)} \int_0^T e^{-st} T dt$$

subject to:

$$k' = I - \delta k; \quad k(0) = k_0; \quad k(T) \text{ free}$$
$$\phi' = C - \delta\phi; \quad \phi(0) = 0; \quad \phi(T) = \overline{\phi}$$
$$y' = e^{-st}\pi; \quad y(0) = 0; \quad y(T) \geq 0$$

where

$$T = G - V - rk - C$$

and

$$\pi = R - V - rk - \phi r$$

In this formulation, the net benefit function T is constructed to recognize that the adjustment costs, C, are incurred at time t. However, the profit function, which may perhaps better be thought of as a cash flow requirement, allows for the adjustment costs to be spread over time through capitalization.

Model I could be written as

$$\max_{(\mathbf{x}, I)} \int_0^T e^{-st} T \, dt$$

subject to

$$k' = I - \delta k; \quad k(0) = k_0; \quad k(T) \text{ free}$$

$$\phi' = I - \delta \phi; \quad \phi(0) = 0; \quad \phi(T) = \overline{\phi}$$

$$e^{-st} \pi \geq 0; \quad 0 \leq t \leq T$$

The necessary conditions for optimality remain sufficient in both models (they are not presented here). Further, all three propositions developed in the paper remain valid for the modifications stated in this appendix.

NOTES

1. For an excellent summary of optimal control techniques, see Kamien and Schwartz (1981); see particularly, part II, chapters 1–8.
2. The general technique for handling the phase plane analysis for a problem of this type is unabashedly drawn from Kamien and Schwartz (1981), with some modification required for the problem at hand. See also Gould (1971).
3. The assumption that $\overline{T}$ is jointly concave in (k, I) is not innocuous. It is not implied by the original assumption that T is concave in ($\mathbf{x}$, k and I).

REFERENCES

Baumol, W. and D. Bradford (1970) 'Optimal Departures from Marginal Cost Pricing', *American Economic Review*, June 1970, pp. 265–83.

Boiteux, M. (1956) 'Sur la gestion des Monopoles Publics astreints a l'equilibre budgetaire', *Econometrica*, January 1956, pp. 22–40.

Gould, J. (1971) 'Diffusion Processes and Optimal Advertising Policy', in E. S. Phelps (ed.) *Microeconomic Foundations of Employment and Inflation Theory* (London: Macmillan) pp. 338–68.

Hicks, U. (1947) *Public Finance* (New York: Cambridge University Press) new edn, 1968.

Kamien, M. and N. Schwartz (1981) *Dynamic Optimization: The Calculus of*

Variations and Optimal Control in Economics and Management (Amsterdam: North-Holland).

Ramsey, F. (1927) 'A Contribution to the Theory of Taxation', *Economic Journal*, vol. 37 (1927) pp. 47–61.

7 R&D Cost Allocation with Endogenous Technology Adoption

ROBERT E. DANSBY[1]

INTRODUCTION

What are the welfare economic consequences of alternative methods of assigning research and development costs among technology producers and users?[2] We analyze this question, abstracting away from many of the institutional details which exist in a specific business environment and which may be important. Specifically, by means of a general theoretical model, we examine R&D cost assignments to a public utility and its customers which have the most favourable impact on aggregate welfare and consumer surplus.

Research and development costs possess properties of both fixed (for example, current variable cost of production is independent of current R&D expenditure) and joint cost (for example, a single R&D project may produce results which benefit more than one product). In a 'first best' world, optimal prices equal marginal cost and are unaffected by the assignment of fixed or joint costs; alternative assignments merely redistribute profits, by lump sum transfers, among products or producers without affecting aggregate profit or welfare. If product prices are determined by a 'second best' welfare optimum that constrains regulated firms to non-negative profits (Ramsey prices), then fixed costs are assigned according to the inverse price elasticity rule; products whose demand is less elastic bear a larger share of the fixed cost.[3] These results have led to an extensive literature on optimal taxation, (see the Bradford and Rosen, 1976 survey). A principal result is: in the absence of distributional considerations, taxes on final commodities are superior to taxes on intermediate products. The literature on the pricing of intermediate goods gives similar insights (see Feldstein, 1972, for example). A simple intuitive reason lies behind these results: taxation of intermediate products yields *input* factor price distortions and welfare losses that are avoided if final products are taxed instead.

A second relevant branch of economic literature concerns the pricing and *output* decisions of vertically integrated firms. Alternative R&D cost assignments may affect firms' pricing decisions regarding both intermediate and final products. The literature suggests that the price impact of cost assignments will depend on the market structure in upstream and downstream industries and, moreover, on the degree to which decisions in the vertically integrated firm are coordinated. These insights are gained from studies of price–cost margins for inter-industry transactions involving successive vertical industries, (see Waterson, 1980, for example).

Even though R&D costs have some characteristics of fixed costs, several properties distinguish them from ordinary fixed and other economic costs (see Dasgupta and Stiglitz, 1980). For example, the extensive literature on technology diffusion, (Rogers, 1962, Rosenberg, 1976) suggests that the profit motive dictates the eagerness with which firms adopt new innovations. Since R&D cost assignments affect the net profits resulting from use of alternative technologies, we expect them to influence firms' technology adoption decisions and hence the demand for current and future technology. Moreover, as shown by Carlton (1976), the incentive to adopt new production technology is greater for vertically integrated technology producers and users than for non-integrated firms.

These ideas suggest a fundamental tradeoff in the assignment of R&D cost among technology producers and users. Assigning more R&D cost to upstream technology producers, through a higher tax per unit of their output, may create an input price distortion that increases the deviation of intermediate product prices from marginal production cost. This intermediate product price distortion will cause downstream firms to make inefficient input factor usage decisions and may consequently lead to *higher* costs of final product production. Thus, the final product price may embody *both* the R&D costs and the costs caused by input distortions. On the other hand, reducing the R&D cost assigned to downstream technology users, through a lower tax per unit of their output, may increase their incentive to adopt the new technology, with consequent *lower* costs of final product production. These lower costs may more than offset the increased costs caused by input distortions.

The magnitude of these trade-offs, and the taxes which balance them, depend on the market structure and internal organization of the upstream technology producers and downstream technology users. Moreover their extent depends crucially on the economic factors which influence firms' technology adoption decisions, the deviation from marginal production cost of upstream prices, and on the impact of upstream prices on efficient factor usage by downstream firms. We are thus led to the Schumpeterian view that the sacrifice of some pricing efficiency may create an environment which promotes the introduction of socially beneficial innovations and consequent welfare gains.

This chapter examines the resolution of these trade-offs for three hypothetical market structure–internal organization scenarios. In each of the scenarios, we assumed R&D projects are undertaken by a central research organization,[4] which at some point in time, patents a new discovery that cost **R** dollars to make. The patent is made available, without discrimination, to technology producers who can use it to design and produce more efficient, technologically advanced equipment that reduces the cost of producing final outputs. The cost of the R&D is to be recovered by imposing a tax per unit of gross revenue on the upstream technology producers and downstream technology users, respectively, with the unit tax rate depending on the proportion of the total R&D cost assessed technology producers and technology users.[5] If the unit tax is uniform across all technology users, then a given user's share of R&D cost is proportional to his share of final output. If all R&D costs are assigned to technology producers, a user's share is proportional to his share of purchases of the producer's technology.[6]

The market scenario in the following section concerned with centralized corporate decisions assumes a vertically integrated monopoly firm consisting of a monopoly technology producer and several franchise monopolists that use the technology. Further, the overall corporate entity is assumed centrally to coordinate all decisions concerning input factor usage, technology adoption and pricing of the technology and final products. For this case it is argued that the public interest is likely to be served best if all R&D costs are allocated to downstream technology users. In the scenario in the following section describing vertical integration with decentralized control, the vertically integrated monopolists are assumed to operate at 'arms-length', that is, decisions regarding technology adoption, pricing and so on, are decentralized. In this case there are a variety of circumstances in which the interests of the corporation and of the public are best served if some or all of the R&D cost is assigned to the upstream technology producer. The final scenario shows that similar qualitative results hold if the technology producers are in a competitive industry and if there are several competitive downstream industries that might employ the new technology in production.

VERTICALLY INTEGRATED MONOPOLISTS

In this section we consider the allocation of R&D cost when the technology producer and technology users are vertically integrated. Specifically, it is assumed that there is a monopolist technology producer, and several franchise monopolists in the downstream technology using industry. Each of these downstream firms operates in geographically separated markets. The demand functions for each of the separate markets are identical. Moreover, the production process of each downstream firm is described by the same production function. However, each of the downstream firms may initially be using different technologies to produce their output. Thus, initially, each of the downstream firms may have different profit rates. The profit of the corporation equals the sum of the profit of the technology producer and the aggregate profits of the downstream final product producers. The corporation has a policy of allocating the R&D cost of a new technology only among the downstream firms that use the new technology in their production processes.

Let $\alpha^0(\theta)$ be the efficiency index of the technology initially employed in the production process of the θ downstream firm where $\partial\alpha^0/\partial\theta > 0$. A given firms' production function is $F(x, y, \alpha(\theta))$, where x is the amount of type α capital equipment, and y is the amount of numéraire input such as labour. The production process is such that output, from a given amount of factor usage, is larger the more efficient is the capital equipment input, that is, output increases with the efficiency index of the technology. Suppose ρ^0 is the R&D tax per unit of gross revenue imposed on downstream firms before discovery of the new technology. The profit rate initially earned by a θ type downstream firm is assumed to be $\pi^0(\alpha^0(\theta), \rho^0)$. It follows, from the assumptions, that π^0 increases with θ. If a θ type firm employed the new technology, having efficiency index α, in its production process then its profit rate would be

$$\pi(\alpha, \rho) = P(F)F(x, y, \alpha)(1-\rho) - \hat{P}x - ry \qquad (7.1)$$

where $P(F)$ is the final product demand function, ρ is the R&D tax per unit of gross revenue imposed on downstream firms when they adopt the new technology, $\hat{P}$ is the unit price of the new technology and r is the unit price of the numéraire input. A θ type downstream firm will adopt the new α technology, if

$$\pi(\alpha, \rho) \geq \pi^0(\alpha^0(\theta), \rho^0)$$

Downstream firms type $\overline{\theta}$ are indifferent between adopting the α type new technology and continuing to use the technology $\alpha^0(\overline{\theta})$, that is, for $\overline{\theta}$ type downstream firms

$$\pi(\alpha, \rho) = \pi^0(\alpha^0(\overline{\theta}), \rho^0) \tag{7.2}$$

Since π^0 is an increasing function of θ, it follows that all downstream firms with $\theta \leq \overline{\theta}$ would benefit from adopting the new α technology. The aggregate derived demand for the new technology is then

$$x \int_0^{\overline{\theta}} h(\theta)\,d\theta \equiv xH(\overline{\theta})$$

where x is the amount of the new technology[7] used by a particular firm and $h(\theta)$ is the population density, by type of technology initially used in production, of downstream firms. The corresponding cumulative density function is denoted by $H(\theta)$, with $0 \leq \theta \leq 1$.

The revenue, $\mathbf{R}(P, \hat{P})$, generated by the gross revenue tax imposed on the upstream technology producer, $\hat{\rho}$, and the gross revenue tax imposed on downstream firms, ρ, are selected to exactly recover the R&D cost R; hence

$$\mathbf{R}(P, \hat{P}) \equiv [\hat{\rho}\hat{P}x + \rho P(F)F]H(\overline{\theta}) = R \tag{7.3}$$

The profit earned by the technology producer is

$$\hat{\pi} = [\hat{P}(1 - \hat{\rho}) - c]xH(\overline{\theta}) \tag{7.4}$$

where c is the marginal cost of producing the new technology. The total profit earned by the vertically integrated corporation is then

$$\overline{\pi} = \hat{\pi}(\alpha, \hat{\rho}) + \pi(\alpha, \rho)H(\overline{\theta}) + \int_{\overline{\theta}}^1 \pi(\alpha^0(\theta), \rho^0)h(\theta)\,d\theta \tag{7.5a}$$

Because of the constraint imposed on the R&D tax rates, it follows that $\bar{\pi}$ depends on these tax rates only to the extent that they affect the number of firms that adopt the new technology.[8] Moreover, the technology price, $\hat{P}$, affects aggregate profits only through its effect on the number of firms adopting the new technology. These insights are clear once the aggregate profit function is written as

$$\bar{\pi} = [P(F)F - cx - ry]H(\bar{\theta}) + \int_{\bar{\theta}}^{1} \pi^0(\alpha^0(\theta), \rho^0)h(\theta)d\theta - R \quad (7.5b)$$

The number of firms that adopt the new technology is determined by the marginal adopter $\bar{\theta}$. The identity of the marginal adopter depends on the price of the new technology, $\hat{P}$, and the R&D tax imposed on downstream firms, ρ. All else being equal, an increase in the downstream R&D tax rate ρ, will reduce the number of firms that adopt the new technology since

$$\partial\bar{\theta}/\partial\rho = \{[\partial\pi(\alpha,\rho)/\partial\rho]\}/(\partial\pi^0/\partial\theta)$$
$$= -(P(F)F)/(\partial\pi^0/\partial\theta) < 0 \quad (7.6)$$

However, such an increase in the tax imposed on downstream firms may, because of the break-even R&D cost constraint (7.3), necessitate a decrease in the tax, $\hat{\rho}$, imposed on the upstream technology producer. If a decrease in $\hat{\rho}$ causes the price of the technology to fall, then there may be a net gain in the number of adopters since

$$\frac{\partial\theta}{\partial\hat{P}} = \frac{\partial\pi(\alpha,\rho)}{\partial\hat{p}} \bigg/ \frac{\partial\pi^0}{\partial\theta} = -x \bigg/ \frac{\partial\pi^0}{\partial\theta} < 0 \quad (7.6b)$$

and

$$d\bar{\theta} = \frac{\partial\bar{\theta}}{\partial\rho}d\rho + \frac{\partial\bar{\theta}}{\partial\hat{P}}d\hat{P} \quad (7.6c)$$

If changes in the downstream tax rate induce changes in the technology price that cause the number of technology adopters to increase, then aggregate profits of the corporation will increase, since

$$\partial\bar{\pi}/\partial(\bar{\theta}) = \{[P(F)F - cx - ry] - [\pi^0(\alpha^0(\bar{\theta}))]\}h(\bar{\theta})$$

which is positive by definition.

The number of technology adopters has similar affects on aggregate net consumer surplus of the corporation's customers. Customers who consume the final product of downstream firm θ will have a surplus of $S[\alpha^0(\theta)]$ if the firm uses technology α^0 and a surplus

$$S(\alpha) = \int_0^{F(x,y,\alpha)} P(z)\,dz - P(F)F \tag{7.7}$$

if the firm uses technology α. If output of a particular firm increases when the new technology is used in production, then $S(\alpha) > S[\alpha^0(\theta)]$. The aggregate net consumer surplus, resulting from consumption of the corporation's final output is then

$$\overline{S} = S(\alpha)H(\overline{\theta}) + \int_{\overline{\theta}}^1 S[\alpha^0(\theta)]h(\theta)\,d\theta \tag{7.8}$$

Therefore, if $F(x, y, \alpha) > F(\alpha^0)$ then changes in the allocation of R&D cost which induce an increase in the number of technology adopters will increase aggregate consumer surplus since

$$\frac{d\overline{S}}{d\overline{\theta}} = \{S(\alpha) - S[\alpha^0(\overline{\theta})]\}h(\overline{\theta})$$

Centralized Corporate Decisions

In what follows we examine the effect of alternative downstream R&D tax rates on the number of adopters, aggregate corporate profits and the aggregate surplus of final product consumers. We consider three possible objectives of the vertically integrated corporation: (1) monopoly profit maximization, (2) maximization of welfare subject to a profit constraint, and (3) maximization of profit subject to a rate-of-return constraint. The corporation is assumed to coordinate all decisions regarding the allocation of R&D cost, the adoption of new technology, factor input usage, price of a new technology and price of final outputs. For each of these objectives the vertically integrated, centralized corporation can coordinate the selection and administration of R&D tax rates and price of the new technology so that aggregate profits and consumer surplus are invariant to alternative R&D cost allocations. Consequently, for these circumstances, the choice of R&D cost allocation mechanism depends primarily on the cost and ease of its administration.

Profit Maximization

Suppose the vertically integrated, centralized corporation chooses factor inputs and the technology price to maximize profits of the corporation, that is

$$\text{Max } \bar{\pi}$$
$$x, y, \hat{P}$$

For a given value of ρ, let $\bar{\pi}^*$ denote the level of aggregate profits when the profit maximizing input combinations (x^*, y^*), and technology price, $\hat{P}^*$, are used. Then from first and second order conditions it is shown that[9]

$$d\hat{P}^*/d\rho = -[P(F^*)F^*]/x^*, \quad dx^*/d\rho = 0, \quad \text{and } dy^*/d\rho = 0$$

Hence it follows that $d\theta/d\rho = 0$ and $d\bar{\pi}^*/d\rho = 0$. Consequently:

> *The vertically integrated corporation which coordinates prices and factor usage so as to maximize profit, will be indifferent to alternative allocations of R&D cost among technology users and the technology producer.*

The intuitive reason for this is that any change in R&D cost allocation can be compensated for by an appropriate adjustment of the new technology price. These coordinated adjustments of the technology price, for different cost allocations, will not affect the aggregate derive demand for the new technology or the total profit of the corporation. Moreover:

> *The vertically integrated corporation which coordinates prices and factor usage so as to maximize profit, will find that its customers enjoy the same net surplus irrespective of the R&D cost allocation.*

That is, from the customers' point of view, it makes no difference how R&D costs are allocated among units of the vertically integrated, centralized corporation.[10]

Constrained Welfare Maximization

Similar results hold if the objective of the vertically integrated corporation is to maximize social welfare subject to profit constraints imposed separately on its operating units. In this case, the corporation's objective is

$$\underset{x,y,\hat{P}}{\text{Max}}\ \bar{W} = \left[\int_0^{F(x,y,\alpha)} P(z)\mathrm{d}z - cx - ry \right] H(\bar{\theta}) + \int_{\bar{\theta}}^1 (S^0 + \pi^0)h\mathrm{d}\theta - R$$

$$s.t. \quad \pi(\alpha, \rho) = P(F)F(1 - \rho) - \hat{P}x - ry \geq \beta \tag{7.9}$$

$$\hat{\pi} = \left[(\hat{P} - c)x + \rho P(F)F \right] H(\bar{\theta}) - R \geq \hat{\beta}$$

where equation (7.3) has been substituted into $\hat{\pi}$, and β and $\hat{\beta}$ are arbitrary constants. If the corporation directs its downstream subsidiaries to adopt the new technology if profit or surplus would be increased, then:

> *For any arbitrary R&D tax on downstream firms, the vertically integrated corporation can guarantee that the 'second-best' welfare optimum is achieved simply by using the optimal technology price.*[11]

In other words, the 'arbitrary' choice of R&D tax rate is guaranteed to be 'optimal' as long as the corresponding technology price is optimal. The centralized, vertically integrated firm can achieve this result by close coordination of the technology price selected when alternative R&D tax rates are used. Thus, the level of optimal aggregate welfare will be invariant with respect to alternative R&D tax rates. This qualitative result holds whether the corporation directs its subsidiaries to adopt the new technology on the basis of profit, that is, equation (7.2), or on the basis of the subsidiary's welfare. Of course, any adjustment in the R&D tax rate must be accompanied by a corresponding change in the technology price if this result is to hold. If zero profit constraints are imposed on the subsidiaries, that is, $\hat{\beta} = 0$ and $\beta = 0$, then obviously these cost allocation alternatives will have no impact on consumer surplus.

If positive profits are earned by the subsidiaries then optimal technology price decreases as the R&D tax rate on downstream firms, ρ, increases. This implies that even though aggregate welfare is invariant to changes in ρ, such adjustments will shift the relative benefits that accrue to the corporation and its customers. If the firm specific welfare criterion is used as a technology adoption criterion, the number of technology adopters $H(\overline{\theta})$ is dependent on $\hat{P}$, and ρ only through the factor inputs. But it is clear that a decrease in the technology price, $\hat{P}$, will increase the demand for this factor and consequently increase final output and aggregate consumer surplus. Since the optimal technology price decreases as the R&D tax on downstream firms increases, it follows that final product consumers are best off when all R&D cost is allocated to downstream firms.

Rate-of-Return Regulation

Suppose the corporation coordinates the choice of factor usage, technology price, and R&D cost allocation so as to maximize its profit subject to rate-of-return constraints on downstream firms. The profit, $\pi^0(\alpha^0(\theta), \rho^0)$, earned by downstream firms which continue to use their initial technology will satisfy the rate-of-return constraint imposed on them. If the R&D tax is only imposed on firms that adopt the new technology, then the corporation's objective is to

$$\underset{x, y, \hat{P}, \rho}{\text{Max}} \ \overline{\pi} \qquad\qquad (7.10)$$

$$\text{s.t.} \quad \pi(\alpha, \rho) \leq (s - i)\hat{P}x$$

where s is the rate-of-return on capital inputs allowed by regulators and i is the interest cost of capital. Here it is assumed that the equipment technology α is the only capital asset employed in the firm's production process. Note that only one constraint need be considered since all firms that adopt the new technology α will earn the profit $\pi(\alpha, \rho)$.

Under these circumstances, the vertically integrated corporation's optimal choice of technology price $\hat{P}$ will imply that the optimal downstream R&D tax rate equals zero,[12] hence it is optimal to assign all R&D cost to the upstream technology producer. However, the vertically integrated, centralized corporation can easily improve the situation by requiring that all its subsidiaries share in paying the R&D cost for the new technology, whether they use it or not.

If the R&D tax is imposed on all firms then the profit of a firm which does not adopt the new technology, that is, continues to use its initial technology, will decrease since $\pi^0(\alpha^0(\theta), \rho^0) > \pi^0[\alpha^0(\theta), \rho^0 + \rho]$. Consequently, each downstream firm is better off adopting the new technology if the R&D tax is imposed on all firms, since $\pi(\alpha, \rho^0 + \rho)$

$> \pi^0 [\alpha^0 (\theta), \rho^0 + \rho]$. The aggregate profit of the corporation would then be $\bar{\pi} = [P(F)F - cx - ry]H(1) - (R + R^0)$ where R^0 is the total R&D cost of the initial technologies and $H(1)$ is the total number of downstream subsidiaries. The optimal technology price and tax rate would then

$$\text{Max } \bar{\pi} \qquad (7.11)$$

$$\text{s.t.} \quad \pi \le (s - i)\hat{P}x$$

Since $\bar{\pi}$ is independent of $\hat{P}$ and ρ, the optimal $\hat{P}$ and ρ are related by $\pi = (s - i)\hat{P}x$. Consequently, any adjustment in the R&D tax rate must be exactly offset by a corresponding adjustment of the optimal technology price. Moreover, at the optimum technology price, $\hat{P}^* > 0$, the choice of the R&D tax is 'arbitrary'.[13] Hence, the corporation would be indifferent to alternative allocations of the R&D cost. In addition, aggregate consumer surplus is given by $S(\alpha)H(1)$. Since output of the corporation is invariant with respect to the R&D tax rate[14] it follows that consumers would also be indifferent to alternative allocations of the R&D cost. Therefore, we conclude that:

Under rate-of-return regulation, aggregate profit and consumer surplus are invariant to alternative R&D cost allocations among technology producers and users, if the vertically integrated corporation requires all downstream subsidiaries to pay the R&D tax and if technology prices are optimal.

The results of this section suggest that a vertically integrated centralized, corporation can coordinate its pricing policy for new technology so that the corporations' profits, before administration costs, and consumer surplus are invariant to alternative allocations of R&D cost. This was shown to be true for each of the objectives considered: profit maximization, Ramsey pricing and rate-of-return regulation. Therefore, except in this latter case, the vertically integrated, centralized corporation's choice of R&D cost allocation method should be based primarily on the cost of implementing and administering alternative R&D cost allocation mechanisms. If it is less costly and more convenient to recover the R&D cost as a per cent of downstream firms' gross revenue, then this is the method that should be used.

In the next section we show that these results depend crucially on the corporation's ability to coordinate all decisions regarding input factor usage, technology adoption, pricing the technology and allocation of

R&D cost. When the corporation's control of these decisions is decentralized, the implications for R&D cost allocation can be substantially different from the insights of the present section.

Vertical Integration with Decentralized Control

In this section it is assumed that the downstream subsidiaries have control of decisions regarding technology adoption and factor input usage, while the upstream subsidiary is responsible for setting the technology's price. The corporation takes account of the subsidiaries' decisions, in exercising its responsibility to select the relative allocation of R&D cost. Otherwise, the details of the models are similar to those discussed in the previous section. We first examine the consequences of the technology users' and technology producer's decisions, assuming their objective is profit maximization. These insights are then utilized to examine the corporation's choice of R&D cost allocation.

Technology Users

Each downstream subsidiary is assumed to adopt the new technology if its profit would be improved, given that the technology and numéraire input are used in the profit maximizing combination. In particular, if a type θ downstream subsidiary adopts technology α, the amounts used of the factor inputs will

$$\underset{x,y}{\text{Max}}\ \pi = P(F)F(1-\rho) - \hat{P}x - ry \qquad (7.12)$$

where the R&D tax rate ρ and the technology price $\hat{P}$ are taken to be given parameters.[15] The derived demands, x^* and y^*, for the factor inputs will then depend on $\hat{P}$ and ρ, that is, $x^*(\hat{P},\rho)$ and $y^*(\hat{P},\rho)$. It follows from routine comparative statics that[16]

$$\mathrm{d}x^*/\mathrm{d}\hat{P} = \pi_{yy}/M \quad \text{and } \mathrm{d}x^*/\mathrm{d}\rho = MF \cdot F_x - (\pi_{xy} \cdot MR \cdot F_y/M) \quad (7.13)$$

where $M = [\pi_{xx}\pi_{yy} - (\pi_{xy})^2]$ and is positive by second order conditions. Moreover

$$\mathrm{d}y^*/\mathrm{d}\hat{P} = -\pi_{yx}/M \quad \text{and} \quad \mathrm{d}y^*/\mathrm{d}\rho = (\mathrm{d}y^*/\mathrm{d}\hat{P})MR \cdot F_x$$
$$+ [\pi_{xx}MR \cdot F_y/M] \qquad (7.14)$$

The optimal profit rate earned by a firm that adopts the new technology is then

$$\pi^*(\hat{P}, \rho) = P(F^*)F^*(1-\rho) - \hat{P}x^* - ry^* \qquad (7.15)$$

where $F^* = F(x^*, y^*, \alpha)$. The downstream subsidiaries, whose profits would increase as a result of adopting the new technology, are those for which $\theta < \overline{\theta}$, where $\pi^*(\hat{P}, \rho) = \pi^0(\alpha^0(\overline{\theta}))$, that is

$$\theta < \overline{\theta} \equiv G[\pi^*(\hat{P}, \rho)] \qquad (7.16)$$

with

$$G'(\cdot) > 0 \quad \text{and} \quad \pi^0\{\alpha^0[G(\pi^*)]\} = \pi^*$$

Increases in $\hat{P}$ and ρ will reduce the optimal profit rate π^*, since[17]

$$d\pi^*/d\rho = -P(F^*)F^* \quad \text{and} \quad d\pi^*/d\hat{P} = -x^* \qquad (7.17a)$$

It also follows that the number of firms adopting the new technology declines as $\hat{P}$ or ρ increase

$$\partial\overline{\theta}/\partial\rho = -P(F^*)F^*G'(\cdot) \quad \text{and} \quad \partial\overline{\theta}/\partial\hat{\rho} = -x^*G'(\cdot) \quad (7.17b)$$

Therefore, alternative specifications of the R&D tax will have two important effects on the technology adoption and use decisions of downstream subsidiaries. First, a higher R&D tax levied on downstream subsidiaries will reduce their incentive to adopt the new technology. Secondly, the reduced net benefits of adoption will cause the number of firms adopting the technology to fall unless the upstream technology price falls enough to offset the effects of the increase in ρ.

Technology Producer

The extent of adjustment in the new technology's price, that would accompany changes in the R&D tax rate on downstream firms, is determined from the technology producer's pricing rule. It is assumed that the technology producer chooses the new technology price so as to maximize its profit, that is

$$\underset{\hat{P}}{\text{Max}} \ \hat{\pi} = [\hat{P}(1-\hat{\rho}) - c]x^*(\hat{P}, \rho)H(\overline{\theta}) \qquad (7.18)$$

where $x^*H(\bar{\theta})$ is the aggregate derived demand for the new technology by downstream subsidiaries and $\hat{\rho}$ is the R&D tax per unit of gross revenue, levied on the technology producer. The upstream firm's optimal technology price, $\hat{P}^*(\rho, \hat{\rho})$, then satisfies

$$\hat{\pi}_{\hat{P}} = [\hat{P}(1 - \hat{\rho}) - c][x^*h(\bar{\theta})(\partial\bar{\theta}/\partial\hat{P}) + H(\bar{\theta})(\partial x^*/\partial\hat{P})]$$

$$+ x^*H(\bar{\theta})(1 - \hat{\rho}) = 0 \qquad (7.19a)$$

yielding the optimum profit rate

$$\hat{\pi}^*(\rho, \hat{\rho}) = [\hat{P}^*(1 - \hat{\rho}) - c]x^*(\hat{P}^*, \rho)H[G(\pi^*)] \qquad (7.19b)$$

The effect on $\hat{P}^*$ of the R&D tax imposed on the technology producer, $\hat{\rho}$, is always positive,[18] that is

$$\partial\hat{P}^*/\partial\hat{\rho} = -\hat{\pi}_{\hat{P}\hat{\rho}}/\hat{\pi}_{\hat{P}\hat{P}} > 0 \qquad (7.20)$$

Consequently, raising the level of the upstream R&D tax, $\hat{\rho}$, will increase the optimal technology price, but has no direct effect on the number of technology adopters, that is, $\partial\bar{\theta}/\partial\hat{\rho} = 0$. On the other hand, raising the level of the downstream R&D tax, ρ, may either increase or decrease the optimal technology price. In particular

$$\partial\hat{P}^*/\partial\rho = -\frac{1}{\hat{\pi}_{\hat{P}\hat{P}}}\left\{[\hat{P}(1 - \hat{\rho}) - c]\frac{\partial^2[x^*H(\bar{\theta})]}{\partial\hat{P}\partial\rho} + (1 - \hat{\rho})\frac{\partial[x^*H(\bar{\theta})]}{\partial\rho}\right\}$$
$$(7.21a)$$

where the terms in brackets equals $\hat{\pi}_{\hat{P}\rho}$. Since $-\hat{\pi}_{\hat{P}\hat{P}} > 0$ it follows that

$$\sin(\partial\hat{P}^*/\partial\rho) = \sin\left\{[\hat{P}(1 - \hat{\rho}) - c]\frac{\partial^2[x^*H(\bar{\theta})]}{\partial\hat{P}\partial\rho} + (1 - \hat{\rho})\frac{\partial[x^*H(\bar{\theta})]}{\partial\rho}\right\}$$

Therefore, from first order conditions for $\hat{P}^*$, (see equation (7.19a)) it follows that

$$\{[\hat{P}(1 - \hat{\rho}) - c]/(1 - \hat{\rho})\} = -x^*H(\bar{\theta})/\{\partial[x^*H(\bar{\theta})]/\partial\hat{P}\} > 0$$

hence $1 - \hat{\rho} \geq 0$ implies that

$$\sin(\partial \hat{p}^*/\partial \rho) = \sin\left(\left\{\partial[x^*H(\overline{\theta})]/\partial \rho\right\} - x^*H(\overline{\theta})\right.$$
$$\left. \times \left\{\frac{\partial^2[x^*H(\theta)]}{\partial \hat{P}\, \partial \rho} \middle/ \frac{\partial[x^*H(\theta)]}{\partial \hat{P}}\right\}\right) \quad (7.21\mathrm{b})$$

hence $\partial \hat{P}^*/\partial \rho$ will be negative (positive) if aggregate technology demand, $x^*H(\overline{\theta})$, decreases (increases) with ρ and if the price derivative of aggregate technology demand decreases (increases) with respect to ρ.

Therefore, assigning more of the R&D cost to the upstream firm will increase the technology price but assigning more of the R&D cost to downstream firms may also increase the optimal technology price. If $\partial \hat{p}^*/\partial \rho > 0$ then the usual price distortion reasons for avoiding the assignment of fixed cost to intermediate factor producers would be less forceful, since intermediate price distortions would result from assignment of fixed cost to either the upstream or downstream firms. The relevant question would then be: which cost assignment creates the smallest price distortion?

Corporation's Decentralized Allocations

These countervailing forces are important because the corporation is presumed to recognize the diverse influence of its R&D cost allocation policy on the decentralized decisions of its subsidiaries. Given the decentralized decisions described in preceding subsections, we now examine the corporation's choice of R&D allocation among its subsidiaries when the corporation's objective is profit and constrained welfare maximization.

Profit Maximization

Suppose the corporation's objective is the maximization of its profit[19] subject to the constraint that all R&D cost is recovered, that is

$$\underset{\rho,\hat{\rho}}{\mathrm{Max}}\ \overline{\pi}^* = \hat{\pi}^*(\hat{\rho}, \rho) + \pi^*(\hat{P}^*, \rho)H(\overline{\theta}) + \int_{\theta}^{1} \pi^0[\alpha^0(\theta)]h(\theta)\mathrm{d}\theta$$

$$\text{s.t. } \mathbf{R}(\rho, \hat{\rho}) = \left[\hat{\rho}\hat{P}^*x^* + \rho P(F^*)F^*\right]H(\overline{\theta}) \geq R \quad (7.22)$$

where $\overline{\theta} \equiv G(\pi^*)$, π^* and $\hat{\pi}^*$ are defined in equations (7.15), (7.16) and (7.19b), respectively.

The Lagrangian for the problem in (7.22) is $L = \overline{\pi}^* + \lambda^0[\mathbf{R}(\rho, \hat{\rho}) - R]$, which has Kuhn–Tucker conditions

$$L_\rho = \overline{\pi}^*_{\hat{\rho}} + \lambda^0 \mathbf{R}_{\hat{\rho}} \leq 0; \qquad \hat{\rho}^* L_{\hat{\rho}} = 0$$

$$L_{\hat{\rho}} = \overline{\pi}^*_\rho + \lambda^0 \mathbf{R}_\rho \leq 0; \qquad \rho^* L_\rho^* = 0 \qquad (7.23)$$

$$L_{\lambda^0} = \mathbf{R}(\rho, \hat{\rho}) - R \geq 0; \qquad \lambda^{0*} L_{\lambda^0} = 0$$

From the properties of π^* and $\hat{\pi}^*$, it follows that[20]

$$\partial \overline{\pi}^*/\partial \hat{\rho} = -[\hat{P}^* + (\partial \hat{P}^*/\partial \hat{\rho})] x^* H(\overline{\theta})$$

and

$$\partial \overline{\pi}^*/\partial \rho = \{[\hat{P}^*(1 - \hat{\rho}) - c](\partial x^*/\partial \rho) - x^*(\partial \hat{P}^*/\partial \rho) - P(F^*)F^*\} H(\overline{\theta}). \tag{7.24}$$

The effect of alternative R&D cost allocations on the 'tax' revenue, $\mathbf{R}(\rho, \hat{\rho})$, is characterized by

$$\partial \mathbf{R}/\partial \hat{\rho} = \hat{P}^* x^* H(\overline{\theta}) - R(\rho, \hat{\rho})[h(\overline{\theta})/H(\overline{\theta})]G' x^* + H(\overline{\theta})$$
$$\times \{\hat{\rho}[x^* + \hat{P}^*(\partial x^*/\partial \hat{P}^*)] + \rho MR[F_x(\partial x^*/\partial \hat{P}^*) \qquad (7.25a)$$
$$+ F_y(\partial y^*/\partial \hat{P}^*)]\}\partial \hat{P}^*/\partial \hat{\rho}$$

and

$$\partial \mathbf{R}/\partial \rho = P(F^*)F^*(\overline{\theta}) - \mathbf{R}(\rho, \hat{\rho})[h(\overline{\theta})/H(\overline{\theta})]G'[x^*(\partial \hat{P}^*/\partial \rho) \\ + P(F^*)F^*]$$
$$+ H(\overline{\theta})\{\hat{\rho}[x^* + \hat{P}^*(\partial x^*/\partial \hat{P}^*)] + P \cdot MR[F_x(\partial x^*/\partial \hat{P}^*) \\ + F_y(\partial y^*/\partial \hat{P}^*)]\}(\partial \hat{P}^*/\partial \rho) + H(\overline{\theta})\{\hat{\rho}\hat{P}^*(\partial x^*/\partial \rho) \\ + \rho MR[F_x(\partial x^*/\partial \rho) + F_y(\partial y^*/\partial \rho)]\} \tag{7.25b}$$

where MR is marginal revenue.

Consequently, it is clear from these considerations that the optimum profit maximizing R&D cost allocation may prescribe a positive tax on the upstream technology producer. The corporation's profit maximizing upstream tax, $\hat{\rho}^*$, is positive only if $\partial \mathbf{R}/\partial \hat{\rho} > 0$, since $\partial \overline{\pi}^*/\partial \hat{\rho} < 0$. A set of sufficient conditions for a positive upstream tax is that

$$\partial x^*/\partial\rho < 0, \ \partial\hat{P}^*/\partial\rho > 0 \quad \text{and} \quad P(F^*)F^* + \rho MR\{(\partial F^*/\partial\rho)$$
$$+ [(\partial F^* \ \partial\hat{P}^*)/(\partial\hat{P} \ \partial\rho)]\} < 0 \quad (7.26)$$

These conditions imply that $L_\rho < 0$ and thus $\rho^* = 0$, therefore the constraint $\mathbf{R}(\rho, \hat{\rho}) \geq R$ implies that $\hat{\rho}^* > 0$. The first of these conditions merely states that the derived demand for technology, by a particular technology user, decreases as the downstream tax increases. It is obvious from equations (7.13) and (7.14), that this condition will be satisfied, for example, if the technology is a normal input and is complementary to the numéraire input. But the inequalities in (7.26) are also satisfied if the inputs are substitutes as long as $MR \cdot (\partial F^*/\partial\hat{\rho}) < 0$. The second condition requires that the optimum technology price increase with any increase in the downstream tax. This can happen if the technology price derivative of aggregate derived demand, $\partial[x^*H(\overline{\theta})]/\partial\hat{P}$, increases substantially as the downstream tax is increased. The third condition states that any increase in the downstream tax, ρ, reduces the 'tax' revenue from each downstream firm, that is, $\partial[\rho P(F^*)F^*]/\partial\rho < 0$. These conditions clearly may hold simultaneously and depend solely on properties of the aggregate derived demand for technology and the downstream production function.

A sufficient condition for the corporation's profit maximizing downstream tax, ρ, to be positive is that

$$\hat{P}^*x^* + \rho MR(\partial F^*/\partial\hat{P})(\partial\hat{\rho}^*/\partial\hat{\rho}) < 0 \quad (7.27)$$

which implies that $L\hat{\rho} < 0$ and $\hat{\rho}^* = 0$, therefore, $\rho^* > 0$ because of the 'tax' revenue constraint. This condition simply requires that any increase in the upstream R&D tax cause a decline in the upstream producer's 'tax' revenue per technology user, that is, $\partial(\hat{\rho}\hat{P}^*x^*)/\partial\hat{\rho} < 0$. The condition will be satisfied if derived factor demands are sufficiently elastic and if increases in $\hat{\rho}$ cause a sufficiently large increase in the optimal technology price.

More generally, we can expect that the characteristics of the underlying downstream production and final product demand functions will lead to derived demands which imply a positive R&D tax for both upstream and downstream firms. In these instances the corporation's profit maximizing R&D cost allocation, $(\rho^*, \hat{\rho}^*)$, must satisfy

$$\overline{\pi}^*_{\hat{\rho}}/\overline{\pi}^*_{\rho} = \mathbf{R}_{\hat{\rho}}/\mathbf{R}_\rho \quad (7.28a)$$

(see equations (7.24) and (7.25)). This condition says that in order to maximize corporate profit, given a tax revenue constraint, the upstream and downstream tax rates should be set so that the ratio of their marginal impact on profit equals the ratio of their marginal impact on R&D tax revenue. Let: (1) $\eta(\hat{\rho})$ and $\eta(\rho)$, respectively, equal the elasticity of the optimal technology price, $\hat{P}^*$, with respect to the upstream and downstream tax rates; (2) $E(\hat{\rho})$ equal the elasticity of aggregate derived demand, $x^*H(\overline{\theta})$, with respect to the technology prices $\hat{P}$; (3) $\varepsilon(\rho)$ equal the elasticity of derived demand, x^*, with respect to the downstream tax rate; and (4) $\tau(\hat{\rho})$ and $\tau(\rho)$, respectively, equal the elasticity of total R&D tax revenue with respect to the upstream and downstream tax rates. Then the optimal profit condition in equation (7.28) is equivalent to the requirement that[21]

$$\hat{\rho}^*/\rho^* = [\tau(\hat{\rho})/\tau(\rho)]([\eta(\rho)/\rho] + \{[P(F^*)F^*]/(\hat{P}^*x^*)\}$$
$$+ [(1-\hat{\rho})/\rho][\varepsilon(\rho)/E(\hat{P})]) \div \{1 + [\eta(\hat{\rho})/\hat{\rho}]\} \quad (7.28b)$$

These considerations lead us to conclude that

A vertically integrated, decentralized, profit maximizing corporation will not be indifferent to alternative allocations of R&D cost among technology users and producers. Properties of the upstream production cost, the downstream production function and the final product demand functions will dictate the optimum magnitudes of the tax rates ρ^* and $\hat{\rho}^*$. Generally, the optimal tax rates will be positive, that is, $\rho^* > 0$ and $\hat{\rho}^* > 0$, though either tax rate may be zero.

The effect of $\hat{\rho}$ and ρ on aggregate consumer surplus is given by

$$\partial\overline{S}/\partial\hat{\rho} = (\partial\hat{P}^*/\partial\hat{\rho})(P'(F^*)F^*(\partial F^*/\partial\hat{\rho})H(\overline{\theta})$$
$$+ x^*\{S(\alpha) - S[\alpha^0(\overline{\theta})]\}h(\overline{\theta})G' \quad (7.29a)$$

and

$$\partial\overline{S}/\partial\rho = (\partial\overline{S}/\partial\hat{\rho})[(\partial\hat{P}^*/\partial\rho)/(\partial\hat{P}^*/\partial\hat{\rho})] - (P'(F^*)F^*(\partial F^*/\partial\rho)H(\overline{\theta})$$
$$+ P(F^*)F^*\{S(\alpha) - S[\alpha^0(\overline{\theta})]\}h(\overline{\theta})G' \quad (7.29b)$$

Note that $S(\alpha) > S(\alpha^0(\overline{\theta}))$ and $G'(\cdot) > 0$, hence at the profit maximizing allocations $\partial\overline{S}/\partial\hat{\rho} < 0$ and $\partial\overline{S}/\partial\rho < 0$ if $\partial F^*/\partial\hat{\rho} < 0$, $\partial F^*/\partial\rho < 0$ and $\partial\hat{P}^*/\partial\rho > 0$. Therefore, even if the optimum upstream tax is zero, that is,

$\hat{\rho}* = 0$ and $\rho* > 0$, (see equation (7.27)), consumers would prefer that more of the R&D tax be allocated to the upstream technology producer if $\partial\overline{S}/\partial\hat{\rho} < \partial\overline{S}/\partial\rho$. Moreover, it follows from equation (7.29) that:

The R&D tax rates chosen by a profit maximizing, vertically integrated, decentralized corporation will be higher than the rates which maximize final product consumers' surplus, if $\partial\hat{P}/\partial\rho > 0$, $\partial F*/\partial\rho < 0$ and $\partial F*/\partial\hat{p} < 0$.

Second Best Welfare Optimum

If the corporation's objective, in the choice of R&D cost allocation, is maximization of welfare subject to constraints on corporation's profit and R&D cost coverage, then the corporation's decision problem is

$$\underset{\rho, \hat{\rho}}{\text{Max}} \ \overline{W} = \overline{\pi}* + \overline{S}*$$

$$\text{s.t. } \overline{\pi}* \geq \beta \tag{7.30}$$

$$RR(\rho, \hat{\rho}) \geq R$$

where $\overline{S}$ is aggregate consumer surplus (see equations (7.7) and (7.8)). Because we are examining the decentralized decision case, all functions are evaluated at $x = x*$, $y = y*$ and $\hat{P} = \hat{P}*$ (see equations (7.13), (7.14), and (7.19), respectively). The Lagrangian for the problem in (7.30) is $L = \overline{\pi}* + \overline{S}* + \lambda(\overline{\pi}* - \beta) + \lambda^0[\mathbf{R}(\rho, \hat{\rho}) - R]$ which has Kuhn–Tucker conditions

$$L_\rho = \overline{\pi}_\rho*(1 + \lambda) + \overline{S}_\rho* + \lambda^0\mathbf{R}_\rho \leq 0; \quad \rho*L_\rho = 0$$

$$L_{\hat{\rho}} = \overline{\pi}_{\hat{\rho}}*(1 + \lambda) + \overline{S}_\rho* + \lambda^0\mathbf{R}_{\hat{\rho}} \leq 0; \quad \hat{\rho}*L_{\hat{\rho}} = 0 \tag{7.31}$$

$$L_\lambda = \overline{\pi}* - \beta \geq 0, \quad \lambda*L_\lambda = 0 \quad \text{and} \quad L_{\lambda^0} = \mathbf{R} - R \geq 0; \quad \lambda^0*L_{\lambda^0} = 0$$

Since the marginal technology adopter $\overline{\theta}$ will produce more output using technology α than produced with technology α^0, it follows that $S(\alpha) - S(\alpha^0(\overline{\theta})) > 0$. Therefore, the conditions in (7.26) together with $\partial F/\partial\rho < 0$ and $\partial F/\partial\hat{\rho} < 0$ imply that the second best welfare optimal allocation is to have the upstream technology producer bear all R&D cost; that is these are sufficient conditions for $\rho* = 0$ and $\hat{\rho}* > 0$. Similarly, the conditions in (7.27) together with $\partial F/\partial\rho < 0$ and $\partial F/\partial\hat{\rho} < 0$ are sufficient to imply that the second best allocation is to have downstream firms bear all R&D costs; that is, these are sufficient conditions for $\hat{\rho}^* = 0$ and $\rho^* > 0$.

Therefore, if $\partial F/\partial \rho < 0$ and $\partial F/\partial \hat{\rho} < 0$, then final product consumers will prefer that all R&D costs be borne by the upstream technology producer if conditions (7.26) hold, but will prefer that the R&D cost be borne by downstream firms if the conditions in (7.27) apply. In general, however, we may expect that the second best welfare optimum will prescribe a positive R&D tax on both the upstream and downstream firms. The optimum tax rates will in these instances satisfy

$$[\bar{\pi}_{\hat{\rho}}^*(1 + \lambda) + \overline{S}_{\hat{\rho}}^*]/[\bar{\pi}_{\rho}^*(1 + \lambda) + \overline{S}_{\rho}^*] = \mathbf{R}_{\hat{\rho}}/\mathbf{R}_{\hat{\rho}} \qquad (7.32)$$

In this case however, there is no simple rule relating the optimal tax rates to a function of relevant elasticities. With explicit specification the production function F and final product demand function $P(F)$, explicit optimal tax rates can be derived. We leave such special cases for later discussion.

R&D COST ALLOCATION IN COMPETITIVE INDUSTRIES

In this section, the optimal allocation of R&D costs among competitive upstream technology producers and competitive downstream technology users is analyzed.[22] The upstream industry uses the results of R&D effort to produce a new technology, for example, a more efficient type of equipment. If used in the production processes of downstream firms the new equipment would allow production of final products at lower cost. The upstream firms are purely competitive in the market for equipment.

Suppose δ is the percentage of total R&D cost, R, allocated to upstream firms. The competitive price $\hat{P}$ for technology α must equal the minimum average variable cost of upstream production, c, plus the allocated share of the R&D cost per unit of upstream output, that is, $\delta R/X^S$, (where X^S is the output of technology α supplied by upstream firms).

All downstream firms are assumed to be employing an equipment technology type $\alpha^0(\theta)$ at the time upstream firms simultaneously introduce technology α on the market at the competitive price $\hat{P}$. All firms in a given downstream industry are identical, though different industries will differ by the type technology initially used, as indexed by $\alpha^0(\theta)$, where $\partial \alpha^0/\partial \theta > 0$. When the new technology is introduced, downstream firms must decide whether to continue using α^0 or to adopt the new technology. Firms that adopt the new technology must share in the payment of the R&D cost that led to the technology's development. A firm that decides to adopt technology α is required to pay a tax of ρ per unit of final output. Firms that do not adopt the new technology are required to pay the tax ρ. The competitive downstream firms then decide whether to adopt the technology α on the basis of a comparison of the production cost savings resulting from using technology α rather than α^0, and the final output tax ρ. The less efficient industries will gain the greatest cost savings from employing α rather than α^0. Consequently, for given value of ρ, there will exist an industry, $\overline{\theta}$, for which the production cost savings equals ρ. Firms in industry $\overline{\theta}$ will be indifferent between technologies α^0 and α. Firms having less efficient initial technologies, $\theta < \overline{\theta}$, will benefit in the short run from adopting technology α. Ultimately, the profits of these firms will again be driven to the zero profit competitive equilibrium. The real beneficiaries will be the consumers of industry θ's final product; their consumer surplus will increase as a result of the use of technology α. Firms in more efficient industries, $\theta > \overline{\theta}$, will not adopt the new technology. The total number of industries that adopt technology α decreases as the tax ρ rises.

This process of technology adoption leads to an aggregate derived demand, $X^D[\hat{P}, \alpha, \overline{\theta}(\rho)]$ for the new technology α. In equilibrium this downstream derived demand for technology α must equal the supply X^S produced by upstream firms. A further equilibrium condition is that price, P, in each downstream industry which adopts technology α must equal the minimum average variable cost of final production, $AVC(\hat{P}, P, \alpha)$, plus the output tax ρ. The average variable cost function, AVC, results from minimizing average factor cost with respect to use of the technology factor, a numéraire input factor, and the level of final output. At the final product price in industry θ, demand for the final product, $Q(P, \theta)$, must equal supply of the final product. The tax per unit of final output is set equal to the share, per unit of final output, of R&D cost allocated to downstream technology users.

Since firms in both the upstream and downstream industries earn zero profit in equilibrium, aggregate welfare will be equal to the surplus of final product consumers. The problem here is to determine an allocation of R&D costs which maximizes aggregate welfare. Properties of such an allocation are determined by exploring the technology adoption scenario outlined above and its implications for equilibrium, final product prices.

The considerations discussed above are precisely stated below in terms of equations which describe equilibrium prices and outputs in the upstream and downstream industries, for a given R&D cost allocation. The equilibrium price in the upstream technology producing industry is

$$\hat{P} = c + (\delta R/X^S) \tag{7.33}$$

where X^S is the aggregate supply of the new technology produced by firms in the upstream industry, c is the minimum average variable cost of producing the new technology and δR is the share of R&D cost allocated to upstream technology producers.

In equilibrium, the supply of the upstream industry must equal the derived demand for the technological equipment by downstream firms. The derived demand of a downstream firm, again because this industry is competitive, is determined by factor demand at minimum average total cost. If a downstream firm uses x amount of the upstream technology and y of a numéraire input factor in its production process, then the firm incurs a total cost of $\hat{P}x + ry$. Note that $\hat{P}$ is the price per unit of the equipment input obtained from the upstream industry and r is the price per unit of the numéraire input factor.

Downstream firms are classified according to the industries in which they operate. In particular, all firms in a given industry are assumed to be identical. However, the type of technology initially employed in production differs across industries. Output of a firm in a type θ industry is described by the production function $F(x, y, \alpha)$. The properties of the minimum average total cost function for a firm in industry θ are then deduced from the solution of

$$\underset{x,\,y}{\text{Min}} \left[(\hat{P}x + ry)/F \right] + \rho$$
$$\text{s.t. } F(x, y, \alpha) \geq Q(P, \theta) \tag{7.34}$$

where ρ is the tax per unit of final output and F is the final product output level of a firm in industry θ. From (7.34) we calculate the minimum average variable cost, derived demand for the upstream factor and competitive output level of a firm in the downstream industry. Suppose that $h(\theta)$ is the distribution of firms by industry, that is, $h(\theta)$ equals the number of firms in industry θ. Suppose that AVC^0 is the minimum average variable cost associated with use of the initial technology α^0. All the firms in industry type θ will adopt the new technology α if

$$\theta < \overline{\theta} \quad \text{where} \quad AVC(\hat{P}, P, \alpha) + \rho = AVC^0(\overline{\theta}), \; \partial AVC^0/\partial\theta < 0 \quad (7.35)$$

That is, firms in industry θ adopt the new technology if the resulting cost savings, $\Delta AVC \equiv AVC^0(\theta) - AVC(\hat{P}, P, \alpha)$, per unit of output are greater than the downstream R&D tax, ρ, per unit output. If $\overline{\theta}$ is defined as the θ for which $\Delta AVC = \rho$, then all firms in industries $\theta \le \overline{\theta}$ will adopt the new technology while firms in industries $\theta > \overline{\theta}$ will continue using the initial technology. Note that $\overline{\theta}$ is a function of $\hat{P}$, ρ, AVC^0 and α. The aggregate derived demand for the technology α, X^D, must equal the supply X^S,

$$X^S = X^D \equiv \int_0^{\overline{\theta}} x(\hat{P}, P, \alpha, \theta)h(\theta)\mathrm{d}\theta \equiv xH(\overline{\theta}) \qquad (7.36)$$

The equilibrium price of the final product of industry θ is

$$P = AVC(\hat{P}, P, \alpha) + \rho \qquad (7.37)$$

At this price the total demand for the final product of industry θ is $Q(P, \theta)$; in equilibrium this demand must equal the supply of the final product, that is

$$Q(P, \theta) = F(\hat{P}, P, \alpha)h(\theta) \qquad (7.38)$$

Finally, the R&D tax rate must raise sufficient revenue to cover the R&D cost allocated to downstream technology users, that is

$$\rho \int_0^{\overline{\theta}} Q(P, \theta)\mathrm{d}\theta = (1 - \delta)R \qquad (7.39)$$

Equations (7.33)–(7.39) then describe the equilibrium relationship among upstream technology price, final product prices and the R&D taxes imposed on technology producers and technology users. These equilibrium conditions reduce, after appropriate substitutions to the equilibrium system to:

$$\hat{P} = c + \left[\delta R \bigg/ \int_0^{\bar{\theta}} x(\hat{P}, P, \alpha) H(\theta) d\theta \right]$$

$$P = AVC(\hat{P}, \alpha) + \left[(1-\delta)R \bigg/ \int_0^{\bar{\theta}} Q(P, \theta) h(\theta) d\theta \right] \qquad (7.40)$$

$$AVC(\hat{P}, \alpha) + \left[(1-\delta)R \bigg/ \int_0^{\bar{\theta}} Q(P, \theta) h(\theta) d\theta \right] = AVC^0(\bar{\theta})$$

In these equations, the relative level of R&D cost allocated to upstream and downstream industries is represented by δ; $\delta = 0$ means that all R&D costs are borne by downstream industries, while $\delta = 1$ means that all R&D costs are allocated to upstream industries.

It is clear from equations (7.40) that changes in the R&D cost allocation will influence the number of industries that adopt the new technology and the final product prices in industries that use the new technology. The magnitude of these effects is deduced by totally differentiating equations (7.40) and solving for $dP/d\delta$ and $d\bar{\theta}/d\delta$, obtaining

$$d\theta/d\delta = (R/J) \bigg\{ (\partial AVC/\partial\hat{P}) \int_0^{\bar{\theta}} xh d\theta - \left[1 + \delta \int_0^{\bar{\theta}} (\partial x/\partial\hat{P}) h d\theta \right] \\ \times \left(R \bigg/ \int_0^{\bar{\theta}} Qh d\theta \right) \bigg\} \qquad (7.41)$$

and

$$dP/d\delta = (\partial AVC^0)/\partial\theta)(d\theta/d\delta)$$

where J is the Jacobian of the equations[23] in (7.40).

Since $\partial AVC^0/\partial\theta$ is assumed to be negative, it follows that changes in the R&D cost allocation which reduce the equilibrium final product price will increase the number of industries that adopt the new technology. However, it is clear from equation (7.40) that δ adjustments which reduce final prices may increase intermediate prices, since

$$\mathrm{d}\hat{P}/\mathrm{d}\delta = [(1 - \delta)B^2 + (\partial AVC^0/\partial\theta) + (1 - \delta)B^1(\partial AVC^0/\partial\theta)]$$

$$\times R \int_0^{\overline{\theta}} xh\mathrm{d}\theta + \delta[A^2 - A^3(\partial AVC^0/\partial\theta)]R/Q$$

where A^2, A^3, B^1, B^2 and $\overline{Q}$ are defined in the Notes.[23]

In this competitive market scenario the consumers' interests are served if consumer surplus is increased by adjustments in the R&D cost allocations. Aggregate consumer surplus is given by

$$S = \int_0^{\overline{\theta}} \int_P^{\infty} Q(z, \theta)\mathrm{d}z\mathrm{d}\theta + \int_{\overline{\theta}}^{1} \int_{AVC^0}^{\infty} Q(z, \theta)\,\mathrm{d}z\mathrm{d}\theta$$

since it is assumed that AVC^0 is the equilibrium final product price before introduction of the new technology. It is clear however that allocations which increase the number of technology adopters and/or reduce the final product price will be favoured by consumers, even if these allocations increase the intermediate product price.[24]

In competitive markets of technology producers and technology users, where x *and* $\overline{Q}$ *are elastic, allocating all R&D cost to downstream (upstream) industries maximizes the number of technology adopters and maximizes aggregate consumer surplus if*

$$\partial AVC/\partial\hat{P} < \left[1 + \delta \int_0^{\overline{\theta}} (\partial x/\partial\hat{p})h\mathrm{d}\theta\right] \Big/ (>) \left[\int_0^{\overline{\theta}} xh\mathrm{d}\theta \int_0^{\overline{\theta}} Qh\mathrm{d}\theta\right]$$

Hence, if the greater-than inequality holds strictly, then consumer surplus will be larger if all R&D cost is allocated to upstream technology producers, that is, $\delta^* = 1$. The allocation of R&D cost to the upstream industries will tend to increase the price of the technology. But because the surplus benefits that accrue to the customers of the additional adopters will generally be quite large, this sacrifice in efficiency may be warranted.

Optimal R&D cost allocations which distribute the R&D cost among technology producers and users must satisfy:

$$\delta^* = \left[(1/R)(\partial AVC/\partial \hat{P}) \int_0^{\bar{\theta}} xhd\theta \int_0^{\bar{\theta}} Qhd\theta - 1 \right] \div \int_0^{\bar{\theta}} (\partial x/\partial \hat{P})hd\theta$$

Hence there will be a tendency to assign some of the R&D costs to upstream firms when: (1) the R&D expenditure is small, (2) the derived demand for technology and final product demands are large, (3) the impact on derived technology demand of a change in technology price is small, or (4) the impact of technology price on the downstream firms' average variable cost of final production is large.

SUMMARY

In this chapter, we have used relatively simple static theoretical models to show that when technology adoption decisions are endogenous, vertically integrated, centralized firms should choose the allocation of R&D cost which is most convenient and least costly to administer since, in the centralized corporation prices can be coordinated so that profits and welfare are invariant to alternative cost allocations. However, in decentralized, vertically integrated corporations or in competitive markets, the optimal R&D cost allocation may require that some of these R&D costs be allocated to upstream technology producers. In these circumstances public interests may be best served by allocating some research cost to upstream firms. However the optimality rules also may dictate that product specific development costs be assigned to downstream firms.

There are a variety of assumptions made in this chapter which could usefully be relaxed. Of considerable interest is the problem of cost allocation when more than one new technology results from the R&D effort, especially if these technologies are discovered at different times. In these instances, considerations of intertemporal and stochastic phenomena will be important to the design of R&D allocation schemes. These subjects have not been treated in the literature and consequently are interesting topics for further research. Secondly, this chapter has focussed on the welfare consequences of a particularly simple allocation rule; one which distributes the R&D cost burden in proportion to a firm's output. However, we can envisage alternative allocation rules which afford considerably more flexibility. An important and interesting problem is the design of a general class of efficient and practically implementable allocation schemes.

Finally, this paper has focussed on the allocation of the cost of R&D results which are embodied in new technology, for example, new equipment. This covers a wide scope of types of R&D cost; for example all of the standard categories of R&D, such as basic research, fundamental development, product specific development and so on, may all produce results which are embodied in some new technology. However, certain types of R&D may produce results which are valuable but are never embodied in new technology. The remaining question is how the cost of these R&D projects should be allocated among technology producers and technology users. However, it should be rather intuitive that the optimal allocation of disembodied R&D will have properties that are qualitatively similar to the results derived in this chapter. A quite simple scenario that would yield these qualitative results follows. Suppose technology users employ technology input factors which are subject to economic depreciation. Even if these firms make use of R&D results which are pure public goods, they can subsequently be made to share in the cost of producing this public good if their use of it can be identified. For example, if the R&D producer also is a monopolistic producer of the technology inputs, the firm can recover the cost of the pure public R&D through the sale of replacement equipment. However, the size of the R&D cost share allocated to a particular technology purchaser will induce the same trade-offs that led to the results in this paper.

NOTES

1. The author, who accepts responsibility for any errors or omissions, has benefited from E. E. Zajac's comments on an earlier version of this chapter. The ideas expressed in this chapter are the author's and are not necessarily Bell System policy.
2. This paper examines fundamental trade-offs relevant to this policy issue. The models presented herein focus on static market considerations. However, it is recognized that ultimate resolution of the cited policy question must take account of the intertemporal considerations and problems of uncertainty that are basic to the overall question. A contribution along these lines is made by Dansby (1980) which examines R&D cost allocation in a market setting where potential technology users are differentiated so that their

technology adoption decisions lead to an intertemporal derived demand for the new technology.

3. The original arguments for these 'second best' cost allocations are in Ramsey (1927).

4. The specific character of the R&D organization is not of interest here. The model could be motivated by several alternative assumptions concerning the organization of the R&D effort. It is important that the level of R&D expenditure is regarded as exogenous to the model. Hence, upstream firms do not compete on the R&D dimension. The extensive literature on R&D and market structure provides a background for extending the model to competitive R&D and product markets (see Dasgupta and Stiglitz, 1980).

5. This paper may also be interpreted as treating the problem of selecting royalty rates for a royalty contract in which royalty payments are based on the licensee's total final output. The licensor revenue from the royalty payments equals the cost of the product, that is, the R&D cost of the invention. Obviously, this scenario places severe restrictions on the form of the royalty contract.

6. This is another intuitive reason that alternative R&D cost allocations can affect firms' incentives to adopt a given technology.

7. All firms that adopt the new technology will use the same amount of it since each of these firms face the same demand and production functions.

8. The number of firms that adopt the new technology is $H(\overline{\theta})$ which depends on the R&D cost allocation because $\overline{\theta}$ and $\pi(\alpha, \rho)$ do (see equations (7.1) and (7.2)).

9. The cited comparative static properties of the decision variables follow from the standard calculations. Since $d\hat{P}^*/d\rho = -[P(F^*)F^*]/x^*$, it follows from equation (7.6) that

$$d\overline{\theta}/d\rho = -\{[P(F^*)F^*]/\pi_\theta^0\} - (x^*/\pi_\theta^0)\{[-P(F^*)F^*]/x^*\} = 0$$

Moreover, from the envelop theorem it follows that

$$d\overline{\pi}^*/d\rho = \partial\overline{\pi}^*/\partial\rho = \partial\overline{\pi}^*/\partial\overline{\theta}\cdot d\overline{\theta}/d\rho = 0$$

10. Total differentiation of $\overline{S}$ in equation (7.8) yields

$$d\overline{S}/d\rho = \{S(\alpha) - S[\alpha^0(\overline{\theta})]\}h(\overline{\theta})(d\overline{\theta}/d\rho) + (\partial\overline{S}/\partial x)(dx^*/d\rho)$$
$$+ (\partial\overline{S}/\partial y)(dy^*/d\rho)$$

Since $d\overline{\theta}/d\rho = 0$, $dx^*/d\rho = 0$ and $dy^*/d\rho = 0$, it follows that $d\overline{S}/d\rho = 0$

11. The Lagrangian for the problem in equation (7.9) is

$$L = \overline{W} + \lambda[\pi(\alpha, \rho) - \beta] + \hat{\lambda}[\hat{\pi}(\alpha, \hat{\rho}) - \hat{\beta}]$$

For any arbitrary value of the R&D tax, the optimal technology price satisfies

$$\partial L/\partial\hat{P} = (\partial\overline{W}/\partial\hat{P}) + \lambda[\partial\pi(\alpha, \rho)/\partial\hat{P}] + \hat{\lambda}(\partial\hat{\pi}/\partial\hat{P}) = 0$$

Since

$$\partial\hat{\pi}/\partial\rho = (\partial\hat{\pi}/\partial\hat{P})[(\partial\overline{\theta}/\partial\rho)/(\partial\overline{\theta}/\partial\hat{P})]$$
$$= (\partial\hat{\pi}/\partial\hat{\rho})\{[P(F)F]/x\} \quad \text{and} \quad \partial\pi/\partial\rho$$
$$= (\partial\pi/\partial\hat{\rho})\{[P(F)F]/x\}$$

it follows that

$$\partial L/\partial\rho = (\partial L/\partial\hat{\rho})\{[P(F)F]/x\} = 0 \quad \text{at} \quad \hat{P} = \hat{P}*$$

Therefore, any 'arbitrary' ρ is optimal as long as the technology price is optimal.

12. The Lagrangian for (7.10) is $L = \overline{\pi} + \lambda[(s-i)\hat{P}x - \pi(\alpha,\rho)]$. The Kuhn–Tucker conditions for $\hat{P}$ and ρ are

$$\partial L/\partial\hat{P} = [\rho P(F)F + (\hat{P}-c)x]h(\overline{\theta})(\partial\overline{\theta}/\partial\hat{P}) + \lambda x(s-i-1) \le 0$$
$$\partial L/\partial\rho = [\rho P(F)F + (\hat{P}-c)x]h(\overline{\theta})(\partial\overline{\theta}/\partial\rho) + \lambda P(F)F \le 0$$
$$\hat{P}*(\partial L/\partial\hat{P}) = 0 \quad \text{and} \quad \rho*(\partial L/\partial\rho) = 0$$

If $\rho* > 0$ then $\partial L/\partial\rho$ must equal zero but this would imply that $\partial L/\partial\hat{P} > 0$, which is non-optimal, therefore a positive downstream R&D tax is not optimal. The optimal price of the technology will be positive, this implies that $\partial L/\partial\hat{P} = 0$ which in turn implies that $[\rho P(F)F + (\hat{P}-c)x]h(\overline{\theta}) = \lambda x [s-i-1]/(\partial\overline{\theta}/\partial\hat{P})$. When the latter expression is substituted into $\delta L/\delta\rho$ it is found that $\partial L/\partial\rho = -\lambda(s-i)$. If the rate-of-return constraint is 'effective' then $\lambda* > 0$. Since $(s-i) > 0$ by assumption, it follows that $\partial L/\partial\rho < 0$ and $\rho* = 0$ if $\hat{P}$ is chosen optimally.

13. The Lagrangian for (7.11) is $L = \overline{\overline{\pi}} + \lambda[(s-i)\hat{P}c - \pi(\alpha^0, \rho^0 + \rho)]$. The Kuhn–Tucker condition for $\hat{P}$ and ρ are

$$\partial L/\partial\hat{P} = \lambda x[(s-i)+1] = 0, \quad \text{and} \quad \partial L/\partial\rho = \lambda P(F)F \le 0\rho \ (\partial L/\partial\rho) = 0$$

Therefore, $\hat{P}* > 0$ implies that $\lambda* = 0$ when output is positive. Consequently, $\partial L/\partial\rho = 0$ for any arbitrary value of ρ.

14. To prove this result we obtain the first order conditions for x and y given the objective in Note 12. In particular

$$\partial L/\partial x = [MR \cdot F_x - c]H(1) + \lambda[(s-i)\hat{P} - \{MR \cdot F_x(1-\rho^0-\rho) - \hat{P}\}] = 0$$
$$\partial L/\partial y = [MR/F_y - r]H(1) - \lambda\{MR \cdot F_y(1-\rho^0-\rho) - r\} = 0$$

These are used in conjunction with $\partial L/\partial\hat{P} = 0$ to do the usual comparative statics which show that

$$dF/d\rho = F_x(dx/d\rho) + F_y(dy/d\rho) = -\lambda x[s-i+1]^2 T$$

where

$$T = L_{xx}MRF_2^2x - L_{yy}[P(F)F + xMRF_x]F_x - [\lambda P(F)FF_yL_{y\lambda}/x]$$
$$+ P(F)FF_yL_{yx} - 2\lambda MR(F_y)^2L_{x\lambda}$$

Since $d\bar{\bar{S}}/d\rho = -P'(F)F(dF/d\rho)$ it follows from the fact that $\lambda = 0$ (see Note 14), that $dF/d\rho = 0$ and $d\bar{\bar{S}}/d\rho = 0$.

15. The first order conditions are $\pi_x = MRF_x(1-\rho) - \hat{P} = 0$ and $\pi_y = MRF_y$ $(1-\rho) - r = 0$ where MR is marginal revenue and subscripted function indicate partial derivatives.

16. The comparative static results are determined from

$$\begin{vmatrix} \pi_{xx} & \pi_{xy} \\ \pi_{yx} & \pi_{yy} \end{vmatrix} * \begin{vmatrix} dx \\ dy \end{vmatrix} = \begin{vmatrix} -\pi_{x\hat{P}}d\hat{P} - \pi_{x\rho}d\rho \\ -\pi_{x\hat{P}}d\hat{P} - \pi_{y\rho}d\rho \end{vmatrix}$$

17. These results are obtained from equation (7.16) by noting that $d\pi^*/dx^* = 0$ and $d\pi^*/dy^* = 0$.

18. Note that $\hat{\pi}_{\hat{P}\hat{P}} < 0$ by second order conditions and that

$$\hat{\pi}_{\hat{P}\hat{P}} = -\hat{P}[x^*h(\bar{\theta})(\partial\bar{\theta}/\partial\hat{P}) + H(\bar{\theta})(\partial x^*/\partial\hat{P})] - x^*H(\bar{\theta})$$

It follows from the first order condition $\hat{\pi}_{\hat{P}} = 0$ that $\hat{\pi}_{\hat{P}\hat{P}} = -c[x^*h(\bar{\theta})$ $(\partial\bar{\theta}/\partial\hat{P}) + H(\bar{\theta})(\partial x^*/\partial\hat{P})]/(1-\hat{\rho})$. Since $\partial\bar{\theta}/\partial\hat{P} < 0$ and $\partial x^*/\partial\hat{P} < 0$ it follows that $\hat{\pi}_{\hat{P}\hat{P}} > 0$.

19. In general, the corporation's aggregate profit will be a percentage of the upstream subsidiary's profit plus a percentage of the downstream subsidiary's profit. Here it is assumed that these percentages are equal.

20. To get these results take the usual partial derivatives noting that $x^*(\hat{P}^*, \rho)$, $y^*(\hat{P}^*, Y)$, $\hat{P}(\rho, \hat{\rho})$ and $\bar{\theta} = G(\pi^*)$. Apply the envelop theorem and note that $\pi^* = \pi^0(\alpha^0(\bar{\theta}))$ by definition.

21. Equation (7.28b) is derived from equation (7.28a) by simple algebraic manipulation. The cited elasticities are defined precisely as

$$\eta(\rho) = (\rho/\hat{\rho}^*)(\partial\hat{P}^*/\partial\rho), \quad \eta(\hat{\rho}) = (\hat{\rho}/\hat{P}^*)(\partial\hat{P}^*/\partial\hat{\rho})$$
$$E(\hat{P}) = \{\hat{P}/[x^*H(\bar{\theta})]\}\{\partial[x^*H(\bar{\theta})]/\delta\hat{P}\}, \quad \varepsilon(\rho) = (P/x^*)(\delta x^*/\delta\rho)$$
$$\tau(\rho) = (\rho/R)(\partial\mathbf{R}/\partial\rho) \quad \text{and} \quad \tau(\hat{\rho}) = (\hat{\rho}/R)(\partial\mathbf{R}/\partial\hat{\rho})$$

22. Panzar (1980) examines the allocation of R&D cost in a competitive model with identical firms and free entry. The model presented in this section differs from Panzar's model since account is taken of the effect of R&D cost allocation on firms' incentive to adopt new innovations.

23. The Jacobian is given by

$$J = (1-\delta A^1)\{[1+(1-\delta)B^1](\partial AVC^0/\partial\theta) + (1-\delta)B^2\}$$
$$+ \delta A^2(\partial AVC/\partial\hat{P}) + \delta A^3(\partial AVC/\partial\hat{P})(\partial AVC^0/\partial\theta)$$

where

$$A^1 = R \int_0^{\overline{\theta}} (\partial x / \partial \hat{P}) h \mathrm{d}\theta; \quad A^2 = x(\hat{P}, P, \alpha) h(\overline{\theta})$$

$$A^3 = R \int_0^{\overline{\theta}} (\partial x / \partial P) h \mathrm{d}\theta / \overline{Q}; \quad \overline{Q} = \int_0^{\overline{\theta}} x h \mathrm{d}\theta$$

$$B^1 = (1 - \delta) R \int_0^{\overline{\theta}} (\partial \overline{Q} / \partial P) h \mathrm{d}\theta / \overline{Q}^2 \quad \text{and}$$

$$B^2 = (1 - \delta) R Q - \delta) R Q(P, \overline{\theta}) h(\overline{\theta}) / \overline{Q}^2$$

24. Since we assume that $\partial AVC^0 / \partial\theta < 0$, and since $A^1 < 0$, $A^2 > 0$, $A^3 < 0$, $B^1 < 0$ and $B^2 > 0$, it follows that the Jacobian is always positive if the derived technology demand and final product demand are elastic. The cited conditions then imply that $\mathrm{d}\overline{\theta}/\mathrm{d}\delta < 0$ for all δ; hence $\delta = 0$ must maximize aggregate surplus.

REFERENCES

Bradford, D. F. and H. S. Rosen (1976) 'The Optimal Taxation of Commodities and Income', *American Economic Review*, vol. 66, no. 2 (May), pp. 94–101.

Carlton, D. W. (1976) 'Vertical Integration in Competitive Markets under Uncertainty', University of Chicago, Working Paper No. 174, April.

Dansby, R. E. (1980) 'Intertemporal Technology Diffusion and R&D Expenditures', 4th World Congress Econometric Society, August.

Dasgupta, P. and J. Stiglitz, (1980) 'Uncertainty, Industrial Structure, and the Speed of R&D', *The Bell Journal of Economics*, vol. 11, no. 1, (Spring), pp. 1–28.

Feldstein, M. S. (1972) 'The Pricing of Public Intermediate Goods', *Journal of Public Economics*, vol. 1, no. 1, (April), pp. 45–72.

Jones, R. W. (1971) 'Distortions in Factor Markets and the General Equilibrium Model of Production', *Journal of Political Economy*, vol. 79, no. 3, (May), pp. 437–59.

Panzar, J. C. (1980) 'Vertical Integration, Public Inputs, and Market Structure', paper presented at 4th World Congress, Econometric Society, August.

Ramsey, F. P. (1927) 'A Contribution to the Theory of Taxation', *Economic Journal*, vol. 37, pp. 47–61.

Rogers, E. (1962) *Diffusion of Innovation* (New York, The Free Press of Glencoe).

Rosenberg, N. (1976) 'On Technological Expectations', *The Economic Journal*, vol. 86 (Sept.), pp. 523–35.

Waterson, M. (1980) 'Price-Cost Margins and Successive Market Power', *Quarterly Journal of Economics*, vol. 94, no. 1, (February), pp. 135–50.

Part IV
Public Decision-Making

8 The Contribution of Public Choice to Public Utility Economics – a Survey

CHARLES B. BLANKART[1]

PUBLIC CHOICE IN PUBLIC UTILITY REGULATION

Public choice is an economic approach to collective decision making. This means that the emergence of collective decisions is explained by the axioms of individuals' self-interest and rational choice. The logic of the market behaviour is thus extended to the behaviour in politics. In this paper it is shown, how specific kinds of political decisions, those on the regulation of markets, can be explained by the tools of public choice.

I should like to distinguish four branches of collective decision making in the field of regulation (see Figure 8.1).

First, who decides on whether a market transaction has to be regulated or to be left to the free play of demand and supply, and how are such decisions made?

Second, when regulation has been adopted, how does it work? Especially, what forces determine prices when they are shielded from direct influences of the market forces? In short: is there a positive theory of price formation in regulated industries?

Third, in some of these regulated markets the means of production are publicly owned, in others privately (for example, post offices *versus* most auto insurance companies). Why do we observe these differences? Is there an economic reason behind this choice in the sense that the least cost organization of public utilities is realized, or are there political interests at work, which try to realize distributive advantages?

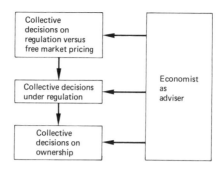

FIGURE 8.1   *Public choices within public policy on regulation*

A *fourth* question relates to all three fields together. Since the purpose of all economic analysis – and especially that of public utilities – is to find results which are useful suggestions to public policy, the problem arises; what is an economist's appropriate contribution to politics? What sort of advice should he provide to collective decision makers? Should he actively promote a policy oriented on efficiency or should he only react to demands for economic advice on the part of politicians?

Before we start our survey a note of caution is appropriate: Our procedure of grouping all public choice questions of public utility economics in four separate bundles of issues clearly means a simplification, since decisions made in one set of issues are not independent from decisions made in another one – for example, the question of *whether* to regulate at all is not independent from how regulation is expected to work. But because theories can only explain a part of the real world, such a concession seems legitimate. Yet, in order to take partial account of this problem, we concentrate on those theories which are relatively *general* and exclude theories on specific problems.

THE PUBLIC INTEREST IN UTILITIES

Why is it that prices are regulated in some markets and not in others? What issues are so substantial that regulation is considered necessary? Usually economists refer to economies of scale and their inherent tendency to establish natural monopolies. Under these conditions an efficient level of output may not be achieved. This view is, however, too narrow, since there exists a large number of regulations beyond natural monopoly situations, (see Blankart, 1979) such as food and drug regulation, school regulation and services of liberal professions (physicians, lawyers, opticians and so on). Regulations in these fields are due to political decisions. It therefore seems necessary to explore the reasons behind these political decisions.

From a public choice point of view, regulations are made on the constitutional level of a society as well as in the ongoing political process. Basic regulations securing private property and freedom of contract are usually assigned to the *constitutional level*. Their purpose is to guarantee an efficient use of scarce resources through free market exchange and to avoid externalities which would arise in an anarchic war of all against all. Conceptually these basic rules are adopted unanimously in the constitutional contract (Buchanan, 1975). Historically, however, some exogenous force or tradition has, mostly, established the rules of free markets.

The institutions of free markets do, however, not yet allow the provision of public goods, and they will not avoid all externalities. In order to cope with these problems, decisions in the *on-going political* process are needed. For saving transactions costs, such decisions are mostly made under less than unanimity rules, for example, simple majority rule. Under such rules it is feasible to decide on the provision of public goods and on the correction of externalities, because the free rider problem and strategic behaviour can be avoided. But less than unanimity rules allow for a much broader scope of political decisions beyond those on public goods and externalities. They make departures from free market pricing to regulated pricing feasible, even if the good in question is not public or characterized by externalities. Two examples may illustrate how this can happen.

Recently Owen and Braeutigam (1978) argued that individuals may not be willing to accept the procedure of the market mechanism because of its abrupt changes. Individuals may prefer the regulated procedure of the legal process which gives them the right to delay structural changes in the market and to defend the status quo. This theory helps to understand the emergence of regulation in such specific markets as postal services, railroads, telecommunications, airlines, bus transport and so on. It may also explain political movements towards regulation in the case of rapid price changes. Consumers will call for regulation when they are hurt by sharp price increases (of gasoline, rents, interests and the like) in order to preserve the status quo. Producer groups will press for market intervention when sudden price decreases occur (as in agriculture when the crop yields are extraordinarily high). Since large price changes will often happen in markets whose elasticities of demand and/or supply are absolutely low in respect to price, it can also be said that these figures are indicators of the political pressure for regulation (see Bernholz, 1966 and Blankart, 1981).

Another explanation of regulation under non-unanimity rules may be derived from distributive arguments. Spann (1974) investigates a polar case of regulation. He shows under what conditions a purely private good will be provided as if it were public; at a zero price and in equal quantities for every citizen. In a direct democracy, where log-rolling can be discounted because of high transactions costs, and under constant production costs, the majority always benefits from collective consumption of private goods if the elasticity of the tax shares is at least as progressive as in a Lindahl tax-sharing arrangement (which means under the equivalence principle) and if the income distribution is not skewed to the right.

The outcome is inefficient for two reasons. First, collective consumption of private goods implies that individual adjustment in quantities is not possible. Thus, even a Lindahl solution would be inferior to decentralized market provision. Second, the quantity decided upon collectively may be larger than under the Lindahl solution if demand is inelastic with respect to the tax price.

Spann's result is fairly general in the sense that it holds for demand and cost conditions which are shown to be not too restrictive. Yet, we would clearly expect different outcomes under alternative institutions of collective decision making. In a representative democracy, for example, log-rolling especially has to be taken into account, for the decision making group is smaller and transactions costs for bargains will be accordingly lower. Log-rolling facilitates the regulated public provision of private goods, because coalitions of minority interest groups can enforce their proper wants by spreading the tax burden over all citizens. This has been shown by Tullock (1959).

However, log-rolling outcomes are usually not stable. Bernholz (1974) shows that in general cyclical group preferences will always emerge whenever log-rolling is profitable for a group. Thus log-rolling implies the Arrow paradox. This leaves us in a state of indeterminateness about the long run development of regulation. We do not know whether regulation is a generally growing or declining phenomenon in politics. Most economists, however, believe that the number of regulations will grow over time. One reason is that log-rolling is combined with another institution: the right to vote upon an issue; in other words, the right to declare an issue as a common problem ('Kompetenzkompetenz' (Bernholz, 1979)). If all issues were private, no log-rolling would exist. Actually, however, nearly every issue can be brought before a parliamentary assembly and subjected to vote. Only a few human rights are excepted from collective decision making. These extended rights of parliamentary assemblies may promote the number of regulatory decisions. The number of regulated markets, however, does not necessarily grow, since counter-coalitions can enforce deregulations, or regulated markets may become irrelevant over time.

THEORIES OF COLLECTIVE PRICE FORMATION

Once an issue has been decided upon to be public, the next problem is, how does its collective regulation work? How much of the good will be provided and at what prices? These questions have to be answered in the context of a theory of collective price formation (in contrast to traditional microeconomics, which can be regarded as a theory of decentralized price formation).

Early attempts have been made by Buchanan (1968) in his paper 'A Public Choice Approach to Public Utility Pricing'. He analyzes public utility pricing in a very simple institutional framework of a one and two person economy. The purpose of his paper is therefore not to provide directly applicable results, but rather to set an alternative to the traditional benevolent-dictator approach to public utility pricing.

Buchanan's model disguises, of course, potential conflicts which arise when former decentralized decision making in markets is replaced by collective decision making in pluralistic societies. *Collectivization* of decision making leads to *bilateral* or *multilateral* monopoly situations with conflicts among the relevant political groups. According to traditional microeconomics, the outcome of such collective price formation processes is indeterminate. An important goal of public choice is therefore to formulate politico-economic interaction models leading to a solution of this monopoly problem. The main difficulty is that there are many *groups* participating in the political process of regulation – consumers, producers (capital owners and unions), governments, parliaments, regulatory commissions, managements, interest groups and so on. The task of formulating a model containing all these collective decision makers is therefore very difficult. Usually, in order to simplify the problem, only some outstanding *pairs* of collective decision making groups are selected and analyzed in a bilateral context. In this section we shall review successively three pairs of such interacting groups.

Consumers Versus Producers

First, we may look at public utilities as private enterprises regulated by consumers as a group. This institutional design may be typical for the USA and Canada, where many public utilities are privately owned, but collectively regulated for consumer protection.

There are several hypotheses of how the struggle of interests between consumers and producers will be resolved. Stigler (1971) finds that producer interests tend to dominate over consumer interests. This is the so-called capture theory, well known from the writings of Marxist economists (see Kolko, 1965). Stigler's result of a producer oriented regulation can be explained by Olson's theory (Olson, 1965) that small group interests of a few producers are easier to organize than large group interests of many consumers, because of the free rider problem. If this were the only truth, however, it would be hard to explain the recent rise in legislation for consumer protection. Even if these measures did not actually increase consumer welfare, they would generally not be in the interest of producers. It rather seems – according to Wagner (1966) – that political entrepreneurs find it profitable to protect the interests of formally unorganized consumers in order to obtain their votes in general elections. So the free rider problem in large groups may be overcome.

However the result of this extended model is again indeterminate. Only limiting solutions can be stated (Buchanan, 1975a). If producer protection prevails, the outcome is monopoly pricing with investors shifted out of equilibrium and seeking entry. If consumer protection predominates, there will be monopsony pricing with consumers in disequilibrium, as can be observed by shortages or rationing. There is no tendency in politics that the in-between solution results, with both parties in equilibrium.

Peltzman (1976) tried to find solutions between the two extremes by a closer analysis of a vote-maximizing regulator as an intermediary between consumers' and producers' interests. He suggests that regulation will be more producer-oriented in economic depressions than in expansions, that the regulatory lag will be stronger for demand than for cost changes, that elastic demand and economies of scale create regulation favourable for consumers and so on. There is considerable evidence that Peltzman's hypotheses apply in reality.

Government and Voters

Another polar relationship in the regulatory process is that between government and voters. This view of the regulation problem may be relevant when utilities are publicly owned, as is often the case in Europe, and the government is their hierarchical head. A selfish and unrestricted government would then try to behave like a monopolist in order to maximize revenues (see Brennan and Buchanan, 1980). Voters, on the other hand, as consumers of public services, may have a principal interest in low prices (at least, when the service is consumed by a majority). It may be argued that voters have also opposite interests in high prices, due to the fact that they are the legal owners of public enterprises in their capacity as citizens; but these interests are likely to be of less importance, for voters' property rights in public utilities are weak. They cannot elect (directly) the management of a particular utility, nor are they able to appropriate the dividends of a public enterprise making profits. Voters may only benefit from profits through other public expenditures or lower taxes. Since voters' influence on these decisions is also limited, they will discount the monetary value of profits from public utilities. The opposite may hold for deficits. Losses of public utilities may not be shifted to voters directly through higher taxes. Prices, on the other hand, affect directly voters' welfare. Prices will therefore have an impact on a governments' popularity and re-election probability, when the goods are consumed by a large part of the population.

However, voters' power to enforce a low price policy upon public enterprises is relatively small. It is only in elections that they can oblige the government to be responsive to their pricing goals. A selfish vote-maximizing government will therefore keep prices down before elections and increase them thereafter. Given this hypothesis, we should observe a cyclical fluctuation of public utility prices over an election cycle. Hubka and Oberman (1977) have been able to show that such a regularity does exist in post-war Austria. Similar results have also been found for postal services in the Federal Republic of Germany by Schmidtchen (1973). These findings are also in line with related studies on fiscal illusion by Schneider and Pommerehne (1980). Using Australian data the authors show that the government reduces strategically the burden of direct and indirect taxes before elections, when popularity is low. Since taxation can be seen as similar to regulation (Posner, 1971), this result confirms the argument above.

The ballot is, however, not the citizens' only base of power towards a monopolistic government; Hirschman (1970) shows that citizens may force government responsiveness vocally. The government, on the other hand, invests in loyalty or presents quasi-solutions (Bernholz, 1979) in order to appease voters' reactions.

Government and the Bureaucracy

A third bilateral monopoly situation may prevail between the *legislators and the government on the one hand and their bureaucracy* on the other. The latter must be understood in a broad sense, as ranging from public enterprises in the traditional sense to registration offices, schools, foreign affairs departments and so on; in short, all government organizations offering a service at a regulated price, including a zero price.

A *static* view of the interaction between governments and bureaucrats is given in the budget maximization model by Niskanen (1971). In this model the bureaucracy dominates the government. The government behaves passively because it has no information on the least-cost production of the bureaucracy. The bureaucracy is therefore able to exploit all producer and consumer rents. From the point of view of regulations, one of the most interesting extensions of the Niskanen model is its application to a public multi-product firm by Sherman (1980). He shows that budget maximization leads to the same price structure as that chosen by a welfare maximizing monopolist setting Ramsey prices. Moreover, this form of budget maximization is shown to imply a considerable degree of cross subsidization. The equivalence of budget maximizing and welfare maximizing price structures makes regulation very difficult, for an outside regulator can no more distinguish budget maximization from welfare maximization according to the Ramsey rule (see Blankart and Bongaerts, 1982).

An alternative view to the Niskanen model has been presented by Fiorina and Noll (1979). In their model the members of a parliament dominate the bureaucracy and use it as an instrument to facilitate service delivery for their local constituents. This view of interaction between bureaucracy and legislators is helpful in understanding the behaviour of the federal bureaucracy in the USA, where Congress members are elected under majority rule in single member districts. Other than in the Niskanen example the bureaucracy plays no autonomous role in the Fiorina–Noll model, but it nevertheless benefits from budget expansion as a supplier of public services.

A perhaps more important phenomenon than static budget maximization of the Niskanen type is the *dynamic* expansion of bureaucracies. The problem is, what are the reasons why bureaucracies expand (according to Parkinson's Law)? Frey and Pommerehne (1981) argue:

that bureaucrats show a considerably higher voting participation than persons working in the private sector;
that bureaucrats often vote for more public spending than voters employed in the private sector;
that bureaucrats may influence public sector growth in the preparatory phase of collective decision making on laws and spending decisions;
that bureaucrats form a large minority, and sometimes even a majority of deputies in parliament;
that bureaucrats are particularly well organized in unions.

Given these pressures, we would be pessimistic about the feasibility of plans to restrict the growth of bureaucracies. We would, rather, expect continuously rising costs for these institutions. Not due to a technically-given cost disease, but rather for behavioural reasons (see Schneider and Pommerchne, 1980). Prices of public services may or may not increase according to the possibilities of raising taxes or creating budget deficits in order to cover costs.

In apocalyptic visions of long run development it is predicted that the whole economy will eventually be taken over by bureaucracy. Then every domain of individual life will be regulated, and the range of personal freedom will approach zero. This development is, however, as Frey (1981) shows, not likely. For growing regulation creates its own incentives for individuals to move out of the legal economy into the shadow sector. Such a movement may be profitable because there is no regulation and no taxation. Empirical estimates show that the value added in the shadow economy has already reached 30 per cent of the Gross National Product (GNP) in some western countries (see Frey and Pommerehne, 1981). The bureaucracy, therefore, deprives itself of its tax base and will thus stabilize somewhere below a 100 per cent take-over of the economy. Regulation will reach its natural limits to growth.

THEORIES OF OWNERSHIP

A still unsolved question in public choice is, why are some public utilities publicly owned, whereas others are privately owned? Postal services, water provision and road maintenance are mostly made by public authorities; hospitals, schools and the like take both forms; pharmacies, physicians' services and, often, insurances are mostly held by private firms. Besides public and private utilities, there are a lot of intermediate institutions such as cooperatives and charitable non-profit organizations. However in this survey we shall investigate only the polar forms of public *versus* private firms. Since a definite explanation of the policy choice between public and private ownership of utilities cannot yet be given, we shall review three hypotheses representing the actual state of research. This will give us some insight into the desirable and real role of government in the field of public utilities.

The Lack of Entrepreneurship Hypothesis

This represents the conventional view on the contribution of the state to economic growth. According to this hypothesis, the government has growth targets which can only be realized on the basis of some social overhead capital or 'infrastructure'.[2] Due to a lack of private entrepreneurship generally, or specifically in this sector, the government actively creates the conditions and incentives for growth of the private economy by investing in social overhead capital. This view can be found in the traditional textbook literature of public finance and regulation (see Haller, 1972, Kahn, 1970), as well as in the theories of economic development (see Nurske, 1953, Hirschman, 1957, Jochimsen, 1966 and others). Such theories often do not clearly distinguish between what the government ought to do and what it actually does. However their relevance can only be judged according to their explanatory power.

A reference to *history* may help in judging the conventional wisdom on the role of the state in economic development. Growth-oriented government policies, based on the creation of social overhead capital, are often associated with the era of *mercantilism* and *cameralism*. In that time it was a prevalent goal of national sovereigns to have a positive balance of payments in order to increase the amount of gold in the country, and this required economic growth, among other things. But it seems that the growth target was attained mainly by an ordered budget and tax policy, and not so much by governments' own entrepreneurial involvement in the creation of a stock of social overhead capital. Such activities were limited to the proper needs of the army and of the court. Road building and maintenance, and manufactures with governmental participation are some examples. The latter, however, have mostly been laid off due to insufficient profitability, indicating that their contribution to economic growth was minor (see Heckscher, 1932, part 1, ch. 5; Kellenbenz, 1977, ch. 8).

In the 19th century, too, governments' contribution to the growth of social overhead capital, and thereby to overall economic growth, seems to have been modest. Pioneering achievements like railroads, electricity, gas, street cars and so on, were mostly due to private initiatives.[3] Governments were rather averse to risk with regard to these utilities. Only later on have these firms been taken over by governments. So the origin of many public enterprises in present day Europe is due to private initiative (see Gröner, 1975, for electricity, and Brunckhorst, 1978, for gas).[4]

Transactions Costs

Another hypothesis relies on the transactions costs for contracting public services with private firms. The government can be seen as a large multi-product firm, responsible for the provision of a number of services. It has to decide whether to *buy* these services from outside or to *make* them with its own means of production. This view of entrepreneurial policy choice is due to Coase (1937) and Williamson (1975). The authors stress that in the market place a firm will decide, by a comparison between the relative size of transactions costs *versus* monitoring costs, whether to have a good or service 'bought' or 'made'. Their main hypothesis is that outside purchase may be more costly than own-production for those services which are hard to specify, due to their intangible and long-term nature, and which imply monopolistic dependencies in the case of contract renewal.

At a first glance, government behaviour seems to be more or less in line with the transactions costs argument. Governments are not fully integrated firms. Physical inputs, for which contract negotiation and contract maintenance may be relatively easy, are often bought on the market place (for example, buildings, roads, raw materials); services which are by nature less tangible and which often have to be provided *over time*, such as defense and law enforcement, are mostly 'produced' within the government, because contracting out is difficult, due to the continuous need to enforce contracts (see Blankart, 1980).

There are, however, limitations in the application of the Coase–Williamson hypothesis on the organization of governments. The theory only holds for firms that are under permanent pressure of competition to find the least transactions *versus* monitoring cost arrangement and so the optimal degree of vertical integration. This may not hold for the government as a firm, because competition among governments is very limited; it is mostly confined to election time. We may infer that there are other forces at work, besides narrow economic calculations dictated by competition, when governments decide to produce a service by its own means, or to contract with private firms. Only an extended economic analysis including political factors is likely to shed light on why some utilities are publicly owned and others privately.

Theory of Nationalization

The question of ownership may therefore be better analyzed in a theory of nationalization. Nationalization can often be observed in times of social upheavals and revolutions. Governments then use the instrument of nationalization for redistribution and appeasement (see Fohlen, 1980). Nationalization may be popular and effective measures for this goal because they are spectacular and less costly for the treasury than redistribution programmes through taxes and public expenditure.

We may trace this argument one step further and ask: Why does it come to revolutions? Tullock (1971) argues that an individual calculates his expected benefits and costs when he decides to participate in a revolutionary movement. Since *public* benefits of revolutions are spread over the whole population, *private* benefits may play an important role in an individual's motivation. If private benefits consist in power of command over parts of the economy, nationalization may well result from revolutionary movements in order to reward active participants in revolutions.

Many take-overs of private utilities by the state, however, are not due to revolutions. They occur in settled times. So we observe numerous take-overs of local utilities providing gas, electricity, urban transport and so on, toward the end of the 19th century in Germany. It is not quite clear how these developments can be explained; for example, whether the transactions costs argument of Coase and Williamson applies (see Brunckhorst, 1978), or whether the interests of an expanding bureaucracy and the fiscal goals of governments cause these take-overs.

THE ROLE OF THE ECONOMIST AS ADVISER IN PUBLIC UTILITY REGULATION

Public utility economics is applied economics. Its task is to elaborate concepts for public policy. In this sense, economists working in the field of public utility economics are *advisers* to politicians. Due to their subject of investigation, they all contribute to the collective decision making process on public utilities, independently of whether they are officially appointed consultants of governments, or researchers in universities. Thus, there arises the question of what is the appropriate contribution of an economist studying public utility economics for public policy. The interesting point is that the 'established school' of *public utility economics*, which may be characterized by the works of Steiner (1957), Boiteux (1956), Kahn (1970/71), Turvey (1971), Rees (1976), Crew and Kleindorfer (1979), Bös (1981) and others, has quite a different view of an economist's appropriate contribution to public policy, from the *public choice* school. Therefore, it is worth while to compare the two opinions in this survey. (There are clearly many intermediate positions; but it is useful to have both end points distinctly compared.)

In the view of public utility economics of the established school, a researcher should find out what are the prices and quantities a public utility *should* set. Thus, his advice to politicians should consist not only in furnishing the right solutions for the supply policies of public utilities, but also directly in presenting recipes for their implementation. Politicians should primarily be provided with information on superior solutions. Given this information it is assumed that politicians can be persuaded to enforce these policies.

The criterion for the 'right solution' is mostly that of the maximization of consumers' and producers' surpluses or, equivalently, that of economic efficiency. This implies that any change in the status quo is regarded as desirable when compensation is possible, or whenever overall benefits are larger than overall costs. Then a policy measure is worth executing, independently of whether compensation is actually paid or not. Some economists (for example, Feldstein, 1972) use other welfare criteria. But this does not alter their basic approach to the problem of advice in public utility regulation. In their view, a better *understanding* of pricing according to efficiency or other criteria will help to implement these concepts.

In contrast the school of *public choice economists* shows no such optimism. Public choice economists emphasize the importance of the political process and would not agree that this mechanism can be disregarded in the context of economic advice to politicians. The economist's contribution to public policy should therefore not only consist of a maximization of a social welfare function, but also take account of the fact that social welfare is the result of a process of choice made by free individuals, and not by a hypothetical dictator. We may cite Buchanan (1975c, p. 255) to clarify this point of view:

> The object for economists' research is 'the economy', which is by definition a social organization, an interaction among separate choosing entities. . . . . The inference must be . . . that there exists no one person, no single chooser who maximizes *for* the economy, *for* the polity.

The main criticisms of the public choice school can be summarized in three points. The established approach to public utility economics may be *rational* in the sense that desirable solutions are logically derived from given targets, but it is *undemocratic* (because the targets are exogenous), and therefore it is *not* likely to be *relevant* in a democracy.

Public choice economists have developed quite different views of economic advice, compared to those of public utility economics. Two methodological approaches can be distinguished. One in which the economic adviser is *exogenous* to the political process, and another in which he is *endogenous*. The first approach can be sub-divided into *strong* and *weak* versions.

The *strong version* of the theory of economic advice with the economist standing *outside* the political process is due to Buchanan (1959). He sees the task of the advising economist as the elaboration of political exchange solutions embodying benefits for all participants. The economist is a middleman who arranges trades between different groups within the polity. Efficiency, which is often the goal in public utility economics, is not an end *per se*, but rather a starting point for finding politico-economic arrangements of mutual benefits. The search of such arrangements is seen to be the only proper task of the economist, because economics is a science of exchange, and the relative professional advantage of the economist is simply his finding ways and means for the benefit of every participant. The arrangements found by the economist can, however, never be imposed, as this would imply a utility measurement. The only test of whether a proposed arrangement is advantageous for all participants is its *unanimous approval*.

The contribution of the economic adviser to politics consists therefore only in the elaboration of informations, but of informations which go beyond those of the school of public utility economics, because they are aimed at an enforcement by unanimous approval. The probability that unanimity can be reached in a world of opposing political interests is, however, only limited, for incentives for strategic behaviour are very distinct under the unanimity rule. Therefore, Buchanan stresses the importance of constitutional choice. On the constitutional level, it may be possible to agree to the *rules of the game* to be applied later, due to the fact that future relative wealth positions are not yet defined. From this point of view, the economist should not propose *measures* such as peak load pricing, or Ramsey prices, because such advice will rarely be adopted unanimously. He should rather find out procedures or *rules* for determining prices which are *ex ante* advantageous for all participants.

One may criticize this approach as still too narrow, since the proportion of issues which can practically be solved by proposing alternative rules may be very small. On all other issues the economic adviser has to be silent. Buchanan's approach is therefore said to involve a large bias towards the status quo. Samuels criticizes that this bias is not a very convincing value judgement for there is no reason that continuity should be weighted *a priori* more than change (see Buchanan and Samuels, 1975). This argument does, however, not necessarily hold when there are majority coalitions opposing changes of the environment. As pointed out in the second section of this chapter, such groups may be interested in preserving historical prices or, at least, in delaying price changes through regulation. When they succeed in enforcing their goals, majority rule takes on a conservative role. In this situation an economist following Buchanan's approach and proposing an arrangement which is acceptable to all parties will be progressive because political change now becomes feasible.

Nevertheless, it can be argued that an economic adviser should be allowed to propose measures (not only rules) in order to be able to set alternatives when coalitions of interest groups enforce goals which are likely to be inefficient, and if commonly acceptable rules cannot be readily found. The economist will then formulate his proposals in such a way that at least a (counter) majority coalition will accept them. This is a 'weak version' of the previous theory of advice. It does not rely on the unanimity requirement, but nevertheless respects the institutions of the political process. It is thus more relevant than the approach of public utility economics which abstracts from the procedures of collective decision making. It also relies on the rules of collective decision making agreed upon in the constitution (for example, simple majority rule). In this sense its underlying value judgements may be acceptable (see Blankart, 1981).

Although this approach is more flexible than that of Buchanan, some criticisms remain. First, the stability of the coalitions arranged by the economist may be questioned, and therefore, also his contribution to politics. Second, it may not be evident whether a policy leads to efficient results or to inefficient ones, when the unanimity test is made. Third, economists' incentives to engage in this form of economic advice may be too weak to make this concept relevant.[5]

This latter criticism serves as a starting point of a third theory of advice. Frey (1978, 1981) argues that the economist is not an individual standing outside the self-interests of political groups. He is a utility maximizer too, and will serve the interests of those demanding his advice, especially of the government and the opposition.[6] Thus, Frey establishes a *positive theory of advice* by endogenizing the economic adviser. He argues that competition between the government and the opposition, as well as competition among advisers, will further general welfare as a by-product of the individualistic self-interested behaviour of politicians and advisers. Clearly, there may be some doubts as to whether the political process, as described by Frey, is realistic. First, competition between government and opposition may be imperfect, so the incentives to choose the best advisers for winning the elections may be weak. Second, imperfect competition may prevail among advisers, for the good supplied by advisers is information, which is by definition unknown *ex ante*. Therefore, rational selection of advisers by governments may be difficult. One would rather suppose a form of limited competition in the market for economic advisers leaving them some degree of discretion to provide that information which conforms to their personal views and to their schools of thought.[7]

However let us suppose perfect competition in the political sector. The resulting advice will not necessarily be rational, for even a perfectly competitive political process will be susceptible to the Arrow paradox, which may induce demands for, and supplies of, advice which is inconsistent.

The *conclusion* drawn from these different approaches to economic advice is that of a *dilemma*. The school of public utility economics gives priority to *rationality*, that is, to a consistent deduction of measures from given goals, at the cost of democracy, since the underlying goals are exogenously given. Frey's approach is *democratic*, but *advice* induced by the demand of competing governments is not necessarily *rational*. Only *unanimously* adopted proposals would satisfy both rationality and democracy. But the unanimity requirement may be of little help because of its conservative bias.

If one rejects the unanimity approach, the corollary is that one has to live with the dilemma that rational advice is not democratic, and democratic advice may not be rational. A broader view shows that this dilemma is inherent in the theories of economic policy and of public choice generally. This has been shown by Gäfgen (1976) and Homann (1981). The former author suggests that both approaches should be used in economics, in order to attain a division of labour between analytical and practical uses of economics in politics. Even in a public choice framework, where economic advisers are endogenous, demand for advice may not be so detailed that there remains no room for suggestions according to efficiency criteria. Moreover, it may be useful to analyze some programmes and proposals without linking them immediately to the problem of implementation in politics, and to leave this latter problem to more policy-oriented advisers. Nevertheless, the problem of collaboration between theoretical analysts and political economists remains to be settled.

NOTES

1. The author is indebted for helpful comments to Roger G. Noll, Dieter Bös, Ronald R. Braeutigam, Dennis Mueller, Jörg Finsinger, Bruno S. Frey and Monika Faber.
2. For a general critique of this view see Borchardt (1971).
3. A famous exception is the railway system of the Grand Duchy of Baden, which was built and run by the state (Fischer, 1963).
4. Extended inquiries by researchers of the historical school can be found in *Schriften des Vereins für Socialpolitik*, vols 128–30, 132 (Leipzig: Duncker and Humblot, 1908–1910).
5. The first and the third point of this critique hold also for the strong version.
6. Another area of advice seen by Frey refers to the constitutional level. There, the problems of advice are similar to those proposed by Buchanan (1959), and need not be treated here.
7. From a practical point of view see Park (1973).

REFERENCES

Bernholz, P. (1966) 'Economic Policies in a Democracy', *Kyklos*, vol. 19, fasc. 1, pp. 48–80.
Bernholz, P. (1979) *Grundlagen der Politischen Ökonomie*, vol. 3, *Kapitalistische und sozialistische Marktwirtschaft*, (Tübingen: Mohr).
Bernholz, P. (1974) 'Logrolling, Arrow-Paradox and Decision Rules: A Generalization', *Kyklos*, vol. 27, fasc. 1, pp. 49–62.
Blankart, Ch. B. (1979) 'Die wirtschaftspolitische Bedeutung von Skalenerträgen öffentlicher Unternehmen', *Zeitschrift für öffentliche und gemeinwirtschaftliche Unternehmen*, vol. 2, no. 1, pp. 1–25.
Blankart, Ch. B. (1981) 'Towards an Economic Theory of Advice and its

Application to the Deregulation Issue', *Kyklos*, vol. 34, fasc. 1, pp. 95–105.

Blankart, Ch. B. (1980) 'Über die relative Effizienz von Markt und Bürokratie aus der Sicht der Vertragstheoie', in E. Boettcher, Ph. Herder-Dorneich and K. E. Schenk (eds), *Neue Politische Ökonomie als Ordnungstheorie*, (Tübingen: Mohr) pp. 200–6.

Blankart, Ch. B. and J. C. Bongaerts (1982) 'On the Political Economy of Optimal Taxation', Munich, University of the German Armed Forces and University of Leyden, mimeo.

Boiteux, M. (1956) 'Sur la gestion des monopoles publics astreints à l'équilibre budgétaire', *Econometrica*, vol. 24, pp. 22–40; English version, 'On the Management of Public Monopolies Subject to Budgetary Constraints', *Journal of Economic Theory*, vol. 3, 1971, pp. 219–40.

Borchardt, K. (1971) 'Die Bedeutung der Infrastruktur für die sozialökonomische Entwicklung', in H. Arndt and D. Swatek (eds), *Grundfragen der Infrastrukturplanung für wachsende Wirtschaften*, (Berlin: Duncker and Humbolt) pp. 11–30.

Bös, D. (1981) *Economic Theory of Public Enterprise*, (Heidelberg: Springer).

Brennan, G. and J. M. Buchanan (1980) *The Power to Tax. Analytical Foundations of a Fiscal Constitution*, (Cambridge University Press).

Brunckhorst, H. D. (1978) *Kommunalisierung im 19. Jahrhundert*, dargestellt am Beispiel der Gaswirtschaft in Deutschland (München: Tuduv-Verlagsgesellschaft).

Buchanan, J. M. (1975a) 'Consumerism and Public Utility Regulation', in Ch. F. Phillips, Jr. (ed.), *Telecommunications, Regulation, and Public Choice*, (Lexington: Washington and Lee University) pp. 1–22.

Buchanan, J. M. (1975b) 'A Contractarian Paradigm for Applying Economic Theory', *American Economic Review*, vol. 65, no. 2, Papers and Proceedings, 1975, pp. 225–30.

Buchanan, J. M. (1975c) *Limits to Liberty*, (University of Chicago Press).

Buchanan, J. M. (1968) 'A Public Choice Approach to Public Utility Pricing', *Public Choice*, vol. 5, fall, pp. 1–18.

Buchanan, J. M. (1959) 'Positive Economics, Welfare Economics, and Political Economy', *Journal of Law and Economics*, vol. 2, October, pp. 124–38.

Buchanan, J. M. and W. J. Samuels (1975) 'On Some Fundamental Issues in Political Economy: An Exchange of Correspondence', *Journal of Economic Issues*, vol. 9, no. 1, pp. 15–38.

Coase, R. H. (1937) 'The Nature of the Firm', *Economica*, vol. 4, November, pp. 386–405.

Crew, M. A. and P. R. Kleindorfer (1979) *Public Utility Economics* (London: Macmillan).

Feldstein, M. S. (1972) 'Distributional Equity and the Optimal Structure of Public Prices', *American Economic Review*, vol. 62, no. 1, pp. 32–6.

Fiorina, M. P. and R. G. Noll (1979) 'Majority Rule Models and Legislative Elections', *Journal of Politics*, vol. 41, no. 4, pp. 1081–1104.

Fischer, W. (1963) 'Government Activity and Industrialization in Germany (1815–1870)', in W. W. Rostow (ed.), *The Economics of Takeoff into Sustained Growth* (London: Macmillan) pp. 83–94.

Fohlen, C. (1980) 'Frankreich 1920–1970', in C. M. Cipolla and K. Borchardt (eds), *Europäische Wirtschaftsgeschichte* (*The Fontana Economic History of*

Europe), *Die Europäischen Volswirtschaften im zwanzigsten Jahrhundert*, (Stuttgart: Gustav Fischer) pp. 101–37.

Frey, B. S. 'A Macro-Theory of Bureaucracy' in H. Hanusch (ed), *Anatomy of Government Deficiencies*, 1982.

Frey, B. S. (1978) 'Eine Theorie demokratischer Wirtschaftspolitik', *Kyklos*, vol. 31, fasc. 2, pp. 208–34.

Frey, B. S. (1981) *Theorie demokratischer Wirtschaftspolitik*, (München: Vahlen).

Frey, B. S. and W. W. Pommerehne (1981) 'How Powerful are Bureaucrats?' University of Zurich, mimeo.

Gäfgen, G. (1976) 'Politische Ökonomie und Lehre von der Wirtschaftspolitik: Zur Realisierbarkeit wirtschaftspolitischer Vorschläge', in H. Körner, P. Meyer-Dohm and E. Tuchtfeld (eds), *Wirtschaftspolitik und Wissenschaft, Festschrift zum 65. Geburstag von Karl Schiller*, (Bern, Stuttgart: Haupt) pp. 67–83.

Gröner, H. (1975) *Die Ordnung der deutschen Elektrizitätswirtschaft* (Baden-Baden: Nomos).

Haller, H. (1972) *Finanzpolitik, Grundlagen und Hauptprobleme* (Tübingen: Mohr).

Heckscher, E. F. (1932) *Der Merkantilismus*, vols. 1, 2, (Jena: Fischer).

Hirschman, A. O. (1957) *The Strategy of Economic Development*, (New Haven, Yale University Press).

Hirschman, A. O. (1970) *Exit, Voice and Loyalty* (Cambridge, Mass: Harvard University Press).

Homann, K. (1981) 'Zum Problem rationaler Politik in demokratischen Gesellschaften', in E. Boettcher, Ph. Herder-Dorneich and K. E. Schenk (eds), *Neue Politische Ökonomie als Vergleich von Ordnungen* (Tübingen: Mohr).

Hubka, B. and G. Oberman (1977) 'Zur Wahltaktik wirtschaftspolitischer Maßnahmen. Ein empirischer Test der Stimmenmaximierungshypothese', *Empirica*, no. 1, 1977, pp. 57–83.

Jochimsen, R. (1966) *Theorie der Infrastruktur. Grundlagen der marktwirtschaftlichen Entwicklung*, (Tübingen: Mohr).

Kahn, A. E. (1970, 1971) *The Economics of Regulation: Principles and Institutions*, Vols 1, 2 (New York: Wiley).

Kellenbenz, H. (1977) *Deutsche Wirtschaftsgeschichte* (München: Beck).

Kolko, G. (1965) *Railroads and Regulation, 1877–1916*, (New York: Norton).

Lindbeck, A. (1971) *The Political Economy of the New Left*, (New York: Harper and Row) 2nd edn, 1977.

Niskanen, W. A. (1971) *Bureaucracy and Representative Government*, (Chicago and New York: Aldine).

Nurske, R. (1953) *Problems of Capital Formation in Under-developed Countries* (Oxford).

Olson, M. (1965) *The Logic of Collective Action*, (Cambridge, Mass: Harvard University Press).

Owen, B. M. and R. Braeutigam (1978) *The Regulation Game. Strategic Use of the Administrative Process* (Cambridge, Mass: Ballinger).

Park, R. E. (1973) (ed), *The Role of Analysis in Regulatory Decision-making. The Case of Cable Television*, (Lexington: Heath).

Peltzman, S. (1976) 'Toward a More General Theory of Regulation', *Journal of Law and Economics*, vol. 19, August, pp. 211–40.

Posner, R. A. (1971) 'Taxation by Regulation', *Bell Journal of Economics and Management Science*, vol. 2, no. 1, pp. 22–50.

Rees, R. (1976) *Public Enterprise Economics* (London: Weidenfeld and Nicolson).

Sherman, R. (1980) 'Pricing Policies of the U.S. Postal Service', in B. M. Mitchell and P. R. Kleindorfer (eds), *Regulated Industries and Public Enterprises*, (Lexington: Lexington Books).

Schmidtchen, D. (1973) *Politische Ökonomie staatlicher Preisinterventionen. Dargestellt am Beispiel der 'politischen Preise' im Nachrichtenverkehr* (Berlin: Duncker and Humblot).

Schneider, F. and W. W. Pommerehne (1980) 'Illusions in Fiscal Policy, A Case Study' *The Swedish Journal of Political Science*, vol. 5, pp. 349–365.

Spann, R. M. (1974) 'Collective Consumption of Private Goods', *Public Choice*, vol. 20, Winter 1974, pp. 63–81.

Steiner, P. O. (1957) 'Peak Loads and Efficient Pricing', *Quarterly Journal of Economics*, vol. 71, no. 4, pp. 585–610.

Stigler, G. (1971) 'The Theory of Economic Regulation', *Bell Journal of Economics and Management Science*, vol. 2, no. 1, pp. 3–21.

Tullock, G. (1959) 'Problems of Majority Voting', *Journal of Political Economy*, vol. 65, no. 6, pp. 571–9.

Tullock, G. (1971) 'The Paradox of Revolution', *Public Choice*, vol. 11, Fall, pp. 89–99.

Turvey, R. (1971) *Economic Analysis and Public Enterprises*, (London: Allen and Unwin).

Wagner, R. E. (1966) 'Pressure Groups and Political Entrepreneurs: A Review Article', in *Papers on Market Decision Making (Public Choice)*, vol. 1, pp. 161–70.

Williamson, O. E. (1975) *Markets and Hierarchies: Analysis and Antitrust Implications* (New York and London: Free Press and Collier Macmillan).

9 Public Pricing with Distributional Objectives

DIETER BÖS[1]

INTRODUCTION

Unit prices of publicly provided goods often differ for social reasons. Examples range from cheaper railway or local bus tickets for retired people, students or scholars, to lower basic fees for the telephones of lower income people; from different prices for 1st and 2nd class railway tickets to lower hospital or school fees for lower income people.

These examples show the difficulties we are confronted with in defining the subject of this chapter. Public pricing with distributional objectives ('*social tariffs*') may mean cases of differentiation:

(1) between *lower income* and *higher income* people (for example, the recipient may have to prove that his income falls below a particular threshold value in order to be granted a lower price);
(2) between *goods* that typically are demanded by lower income and higher income groups, respectively, although this is not necessarily valid (for example, distinguishing between 2nd and 1st class railway or hospital services);
(3) between different *classes* or *groups* of people which typically differ with respect to their income, although this is also not necessarily valid (for example, retired and non-retired, students and non-students and so on).

In my opinion the most usual purpose of social tariffs is to help poorer people, which directly leads to differentiation according to (1) above. Types (2) and (3) are in my opinion only proxies for (1): differentiation between goods or between classes takes place to favour lower income

171

people, but avoid the compromising need for a means test and reduce the administrative costs of implementing a system of social tariffs.

As differentiation with respect to individual *incomes* is the most important background idea, my favourite model (in the second section of this chapter) differentiates explicitly with respect to incomes. And as social tariffs are determined politically to a very large extent, I have chosen a public choice model that describes the behaviour of a politician whose concern is with the majority's opinion regarding his decision.

However, the most usual approach in the theoretical literature on the topic (Feldstein 1972a, b, c; Roberts 1979) differentiates with respect to *goods*, distinguishing necessities versus non-necessities as mainly demanded by lower and higher income groups, respectively. I will show in the third section of this chapter how the use of proxies instead of the relevant 'income' variable causes difficulties and may well lead to socially undesirable results.

In the last part of this chapter we take a short look at differentiation with respect to *social groups*. We ask whether the basic ideas which underlie differentiation with respect to groups differ from those with respect to incomes.

DIFFERENTIATION WITH RESPECT TO INCOMES: A POLITICAL MODEL OF SOCIAL TARIFFS

Pricing of public utilities tends to be one of the major determinants of the political climate in local communities. Local politicians try to postpone price increases for local public transportation, for gas and for electricity until after the next election. The popularity of any local politician seems to be at stake if local public utilities work inefficiently or if prices have to be increased, if the interests of particular social groups are concerned. I recall sombre rumours in my own city, in Bonn, when the cheap transit tickets for students were abolished in January 1981.

Let us therefore assume that a local politician always considers public opinion and tries to follow a policy that is backed by, say, at least 50 per cent of the population. This does not mean that he holds referenda on each and every public utility decision (although referenda on local transportation are to be found comparatively often). It means that the politician is interested, at any point in time, in knowing the opinion of the majority. Thus the following model can be seen as the description of a referendum or as the description of a demoscopic opinion poll.[2]

Uniform Versus Non-Uniform Prices of a Public Utility

We regard a particular public utility, producing the quantity x_1 of some good. For the sake of simplicity all other goods of the economy are aggregated to a representative good x_2. We assume that both goods are produced at constant average costs c_i, $i = 1, 2$.[3]

The consumers $h = 1, \ldots, m$ demand quantities x_{ih}, $i = 1, 2$.[4] Supply is always assumed to cover total demand

$$x_i = \sum_h x_{ih} \quad i = 1, 2 \tag{9.1}$$

We ask every consumer in the local community whether he prefers:

(1) to buy quantities x_{1h} at uniform prices p_1 which are equal for everybody, *or*
(2) to buy quantities x_{1h} at non-uniform prices p_{1h} which differ with respect to the exogenously given individual incomes y_h.

Let p_{1h} be a *social tariff*

$$p_{1h} = \tilde{p}_1 + \tau_h \quad h = 1, \ldots, m \tag{9.2}$$

consisting of a flat part $\tilde{p}_1$ which is equal for all individuals and a differentiated surcharge τ_h.

The flat part $\tilde{p}_1$ falls short of the constant average costs c_1

$$\tilde{p}_1 = \beta c_1 \quad 0 \leqslant \beta < 1 \tag{9.3}$$

In terms of consumer expenditures we may denote

$$ac_h = \beta c_1 x_{1h}^* \tag{9.4}$$

as the allocational contribution of the consumer, where $x_{1h}^*(p_{1h}, y_h)$ is the optimal quantity that follows from the consumers utility maximization given the social tariff.

For the purpose of our simple presentation, we will assume that the surcharge $\tau_h > 0$ is chosen by the politician in such a way that it increases with increasing income[5]

$$\partial \tau_h / \partial y_h > 0 \tag{9.5}$$

and we denote

$$dc_h = \tau_h x_{1h}^* \tag{9.6}$$

as the distributional contribution of the consumer.

To present a fair basis of comparison between the uniform price p_1 and the non-uniform price p_{1h} we assume that public utility's pricing is always *cost-covering*.

Therefore the uniform price (case (1) above) equals

$$p_1 = c_1 \tag{9.7}$$

In case (2), however, cost-covering implies the following revenue–cost constraint

$$\sum_h p_{1h} x_{1h} = c_1 x_1 \tag{9.8}$$

which can be transformed using (9.2) and (9.3)

$$\sum \tau_h x_{1h} - (1 \quad \beta)c_1 x_1 \tag{9.9}$$

The Voting Decision of a Rational Consumer

All m consumers participate in voting on uniform versus non-uniform ('social') pricing for the good of the public utility. Everybody votes in favour of that alternative that yields the higher utility for him.

The consumer's valuation in the case of uniform pricing can be described by his indirect utility function

$$v_h(p_1, p_2, y_h) = \max_{x_{1h}, x_{2h}} u_h(x_{1h}, x_{2h}) \quad \text{s.t.} \ (p_1 x_{1h} + p_2 x_{2h} = y_h) \tag{9.10}$$

where the individual utility functions u_h are continuous, increasing and strictly quasi-concave in their arguments. Note that $p_1 = c_1$, according to (9.7), leading to

$$v_h(p_1, p_2, y_h) = v_h(c_1, p_2, y_h) \tag{9.11}$$

In the case of a social tariff, on the other hand, the consumer's indirect utility function is as follows

$$v_h(p_{1h}, p_2, y_h) = \max_{x_{1h}, x_{2h}} u_h(x_{1h}, x_{2h}) \quad \text{s.t.} \ (p_{1h} x_{1h} + p_2 x_{2h} = y_h) \tag{9.12}$$

As the consumer decides according to his utility, he will vote in favour of the social tariff if

$$v_h(p_{1h}, p_2, y_h) > v_h(c_1, p_2, y_h) \quad h = 1, \ldots, m \tag{9.13}$$

As the indirect utility functions *ceteris paribus* are strictly decreasing in any price, this comparison can be reduced to

$$p_{1h} < c_1 \tag{9.14}$$

and using (9.2), (9.3) and (9.9) this inequality can be transformed into

$$\tau_h < \bar{\tau} \quad h = 1, \ldots, m \tag{9.15}$$

where

$$\bar{\tau} = \sum_{k=1}^{m} \tau_k \cdot \left[x_{1k}^* \Big/ \left(\sum_{g=1}^{m} x_{1g}^* \right) \right] \tag{9.16}$$

$\bar{\tau}$ is a weighted average of the individual surcharges τ_h, each consumer's surcharge weighted by that consumer's consumption share of good 1.

As τ_h is increasing with income, the 'truly needy' will always favour the social tariff. And as $\bar{\tau}$ is a weighted average of the individual surcharges, the truly unneedy will always vote against the social tariff. And because τ_h is a well-behaving increasing function of y_h there exists one, and only one, income y_A for which $\tau_A = \bar{\tau}$. All consumers, whose income falls short of y_A vote in favour of the social tariff, and all consumers whose income exceeds y_A vote against it. (A plausible example is shown in Figure 9.1.)

The Politician's Decision

A particular social tariff will only be approved by a majority if (9.15) is fulfilled for more than 50 per cent of the voters.

This involves an important restriction of social price discrimination: socially discriminating policy in favour of poor minorities will not stand the above mentioned test and the majority-conscious politician will therefore decide not to help these minorities. (This is, of course, a natural result of majority rule; it is, however, of great importance for a theory of social tariffs.)

According to our assumptions it depends on the decision of the median income earner whether the social tariff will be approved of or not. But this result does not help us very much in understanding social

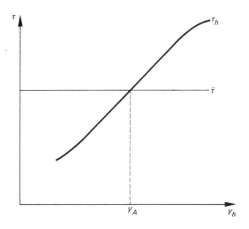

FIGURE 9.1

tariffs unless we exactly specify the utility functions, the personal income distribution and the social tariff function.

However, it is possible to find some further results at the fairly general level of analysis we started with. According to (9.15) it depends on the relation between the individual surcharge τ_h and the threshold $\bar{\tau}$ how many consumers approve the social tariff. And the threshold $\bar{\tau}$ depends not only on the individual surcharges τ_h, but also on the consumption pattern (x_{1h}^*), which itself depends on the consumer preferences, on the production costs and on the fiscal policy instruments β and τ_h, respectively.[6] In fixing the instruments β and τ_h the majority-conscious politician has, therefore, always to regard the individual reactions to his policy. This can best be seen, if we interpret the voting decision (9.15) in terms of individual expenditures. Inserting (9.6) into (9.15) we realize that a consumer votes in favour of the social tariff if

$$dc_h \bigg/ \sum_{k=1}^{m} dc_k < x_{1h}^* \bigg/ \sum_{k=1}^{m} x_{1k}^* \quad h = 1, \ldots, m \qquad (9.17)$$

Thus the social tariff is only approved by consumers whose individual share of distributional contribution falls short of their individual consumption share of good 1. This result is of importance as it reveals the dependency of the individual decision on the surcharge *and* on the preferences for the good in question, as revealed by the individual consumption share. Therefore, it is quite possible that somebody pays a comparatively low distributional contribution under the current schedule, but according to his preferences consumes a very low consumption share and therefore votes against the social tariff.

This result, of course, can also be shown in dependence on individual incomes. As (9.17) is a simple tautological transformation of (9.15), every consumer who favoured the social tariff according to (9.15) also favours it according to (9.17); everybody who was against the social tariff according to (9.15) is also against it according to (9.17). y_A is again the income that separates pro and contra voters.

A majority in favour of the social tariff will be found if the median voter's income is smaller than y_A. Whether this is the case or not depends on the rates of increase of the quotients involved in (9.17).[7, 8] Therefore the politician, in fixing the distributional contributions, should investigate the income elasticity of demand for the publicly supplied good. If this elasticity increases only slowly for incomes below the median, he must not increase the distributional contributions too quickly in this range if he is interested in a majority.

There is a further interesting interpretation of the consumer decision. The right hand side of (9.17) can easily be expanded by multiplying it by $\beta c_1 / \beta c_1 \; (= 1)$ which leads to the following condition

$$dc_h \left/ \sum_{k=1}^{m} dc_k < ac_h \right/ \sum_{k=1}^{m} ac_k \quad h = 1, \ldots, m \qquad (9.18)$$

Thus a consumer favours the social tariff only if his individual share of distributional contribution falls short of his individual share of allocational contribution. (The further discussion of this condition follows the same line as in the case of (9.17) and may therefore be left to the reader.)

The above-mentioned results imply that the politician in fixing his instruments has to consider the price elasticities and the income elasticities of demand for good 1 respectively. This implies that relatively *price-inelastic* goods are the better choice of social price differentiation. If demand is very elastic, the low income consumers will increase their demand drastically, the high income consumers will reduce their demand drastically and it may become impossible to have a majority-supported system of break-even social tariffs with any considerable extent of redistribution.

What about *income elasticities*? Let us assume good 1 alternatively to be a good that mainly is bought by higher income earners (a 'non-necessity') *or* a good that mainly is bought by lower income earners (a 'necessity'). Then the probability for a majority-support of social tariffs will usually be higher for the non-necessity case. The obvious reason for this paradoxical result is the following. According to our assumptions every consumer buys some quantity x_{1h}. In the case of the non-necessity therefore *many* lower income consumers buy small quantities x_{1h}. Therefore it is easy to favour many voters at low expense. (The individual 'expense' $(c_1 - p_{1h})x_{1h}$ is small because x_{1h} is small.)

In the case of the necessity, on the other hand, it is more complicated to find majority-supported social tariff schedules. If the quantities x_{1h} of lower income earners are comparatively large, an individual vote is 'costly'. The prices of higher income earners will have to be increased drastically which will drive them out of the market (in our model lead to very small quantities x_{1h} of the high income earners). In extreme cases this may even make it impossible to find a majority for a social tariff for a necessity that has any considerable extent of redistribution.

These paradoxical results are due to the differences of political and economic weights the individuals are given, the political one-man-one-vote principle confronted with the economic weights according to the quantities consumed.

Let us now combine the two above-mentioned approaches of price and of income elasticity. There may exist many cases of non-necessities with high price elasticities and vice versa. And in such cases the arguments mentioned above point into a different direction: necessities lend themselves to social tariff policy, because their demand typically is price inelastic; but they imply comparatively 'costly' votes. We have to conclude: the ideal candidate for a majority-supported social tariff is a demand-inelastic non-necessity. And this is a gravid restriction of the applicability of social pricing which follows the one-good approach.

Hence, our simple model is only a starting point for the explanation of social tariffs through political determination. The next important questions to be answered are the following:

(1) How far do interest groups influence the politicians in favour of social tariffs for their members? However, this effect is not as important as the above formulation. Take the typical examples of particular tariffs for retired people. They typically are not backed by a very strong pressure group, yet many social tariffs favour them. The reason is that they constitute many voters!

(2) May politicians favour a combination of 'minorities' so that their combined votes make up a majority? This may be regarded as a

straightforward extension of our model. Given the multiplicity of possible coalitions it becomes very complicated, however, to derive general rules for social tariffs from such models.

(3) May not the politician achieve his majority not by discriminating according to incomes, but according to goods typically demanded by lower and by higher income consumers? To deal with this interesting question we must first present this approach to public pricing and then interpret it from the point of view of a majority-conscious politician. This will be done in the next section.

DIFFERENTIATION WITH RESPECT TO GOODS: SOME PUZZLING FEATURES OF THE WELFARE MAXIMIZING APPROACH TOWARDS SOCIAL TARIFFS

Let us regard a politician who fixes prices for a public enterprise (either the management of the enterprise itself or some public authority outside of it). Without loss of generality we restrict ourselves to two goods:

good 1 (for example, 'first class') is a non-necessity. A comparatively high percentage of the quantity x_1 is bought by higher-income consumers. It has a numerically high price elasticity of demand because of easy substitutability and because lower-income consumers of this good are very sensitive to price increases;

good 2 (for example, 'second class') is a necessity. A comparatively high percentage of the quantity x_2 is bought by lower-income consumers. It has a numerically low price elasticity of demand.[9]

The politician will maximize *welfare*. Moreover, he tries to avoid extreme deficits in cases of increasing returns to scale, or extreme profits. Thus he maximizes welfare under a *revenue–cost constraint*.

Ramsey Pricing

An initial, appealing approach is to define welfare as the unweighted sum of individual consumer surpluses,[10] where the usual 'integrability conditions' hold for the individual surpluses as well as for the total surplus

$$W(p_1, p_2) = \sum_h s_h(p_1, p_2) = S(p_1, p_2); \quad \partial s_h/\partial p_i = -x_{ih}; \quad \partial S/\partial p_i = -x_i$$

(9.19)

$x_{ih}(p)$ and $x_i(p)$ are the individual and the total compensating demand functions for good i.[11]

If this welfare function is maximized under a revenue-cost constraint[12]

$$\max S(p_1, p_2) \quad \text{s.t.} \ [p_1 x_1 + p_2 x_2 = c(x_1, x_2)] \tag{9.20}$$

$c(\cdot)$ being the cost function, we obtain the following marginal conditions[13,14]

$$(p_i - c_i)/p_i = -[(1 + \lambda)/\lambda] \cdot [(\varepsilon_{jj} - \varepsilon_{ij})/D]; \quad i, j = 1, 2; \quad i \neq j \tag{9.21}$$

$c_i = \partial c/\partial x_i$; $i = 1, 2$, are the marginal costs. $\varepsilon_{ij} = \partial x_i/\partial p_j \cdot p_j/x_i$; $i, j = 1, 2$, are the compensating price inelasticities ($\varepsilon_{ii} < 0$ is therefore always valid). $D = \varepsilon_{11}\varepsilon_{22} - \varepsilon_{12}\varepsilon_{21}$ (we always assume $D > 0$). $\lambda < 0$ is the Lagrangian multiplier of the optimization approach (9.20). $(p_i - c_i)/p_i$ is denoted 'price-cost margin' below.

These marginal conditions imply the well known *Ramsey price structure*

$$\Delta P(R) = [(p_1 - c_1)/p_1]/[(p_2 - c_2)/p_2] = (\varepsilon_{22} - \varepsilon_{12})/(\varepsilon_{11} - \varepsilon_{21}) \tag{9.22}$$

This price structure is usually exposed to criticism because of its undesirable distributional results. Let prices exceed marginal costs and let the absolute values of the cross price elasticities be low compared with the absolute values of the direct ones. Then according to our assumptions the price–cost margin of the necessity has to exceed the price–cost margin of the non-necessity. But a price structure that burdens the necessity and favours the non-necessity is considered distributionally undesirable.

Feldstein Pricing

As a consequence of the above, Feldstein (1972 a, b, c) suggested an alternative welfare function that explicitly refers to the distributional concern of the politician

$$F(p_1, p_2, U'(y_h)) = \sum_h U'(y_h)s_h(p_1, p_2) \tag{9.23}$$

$U'(y_h) > 0$ is the social marginal utility of income and is assumed to decrease with increasing income $dU'(y_h)/dy_h < 0$. Thus the consumer surpluses of lower-income people are given a higher weight in the welfare function, which should shift the prices into the expected directions.

If this distributionally-weighted welfare function is maximized under a revenue–cost constraint

$$\max_{p_1 p_2} F(p_1, p_2, U'(y_h)) \quad \text{s.t.} \quad [p_1 x_1 + p_2 x_2 = c(x_1, x_2)] \quad (9.24)$$

the price–cost margins are as follows

$$(p_i - c_i)/p_i = -(1/\mu D)[\varepsilon_{jj}(\mu - F_i) - \varepsilon_{ij}(\mu - F_j)]; \quad i, j = 1, 2; \quad i \neq j \quad (9.25)$$

where $\mu < 0$ is the Lagrangian multiplier of the optimization approach (9.24) and F_i can be labelled as Feldstein's 'distributional characteristic'

$$F_i = (\partial F/\partial p_i)/x_i = -\sum_h \{[x_{ih} U'(y_h)]/\sum_k x_{ik}\}; \quad i = 1, 2 \quad (9.26)$$

The marginal conditions (9.25) imply the following Feldstein price structure

$$\Delta P(F) = [(p_1 - c_1)/p_1]/[(p_2 - c_2)/p_2]$$
$$= [\varepsilon_{22}(\mu - F_1) - \varepsilon_{12}(\mu - F_2)]/[\varepsilon_{11}(\mu - F_2) - \varepsilon_{21}(\mu - F_1)] \quad (9.27)$$

Comparing Ramsey and Feldstein Pricing

Needless to say that Feldstein pricing, by definition of the optimum according to (9.24), leads to a distributionally best result with respect to this objective function and the given constraint. However, how 'good' are these distributional results if they are compared with other price structures? Comparing the Ramsey and the Feldstein price structures, we may require that Feldstein prices favour necessities more than Ramsey prices. *Usually this will be the case.*[15]

However, there may exist perverse cases where the maximization of a distributionally-weighted consumer surplus leads to higher prices for necessities than the maximization of the unweighted consumer surplus under the same revenue–cost constraint. These possible perversities depend on the fact that favouring lower-income groups in this model does not differentiate between incomes but between goods.

Usually the shifts in the price–cost margins are used as proxies for the shifts in the prices. Let us for the moment accept this approximation. We regard only cases where both prices exceed marginal costs.[16] Then the necessity is favoured if

$$\Delta P(F) > \Delta P(R) \quad (9.28)$$

which implies (ε_{ij}^F and ε_{ij}^R referring to the Feldstein and the Ramsey optimums, respectively)

$$[\varepsilon_{22}^F(\mu - F_1) - \varepsilon_{12}^F(\mu - F_2)]/[\varepsilon_{11}^F(\mu - F_2) - \varepsilon_{21}^F(\mu - F_1)]$$

$$> [\varepsilon_{22}^R - \varepsilon_{12}^R]/[\varepsilon_{11}^R - \varepsilon_{21}^R] \qquad (9.29)$$

Let us for the moment assume that we can neglect the cross-price elasticities. Then (9.29) reduces to

$$(\varepsilon_{22}^F/\varepsilon_{11}^F) \cdot [(\mu - F_1)/(\mu - F_2)] > \varepsilon_{22}^R/\varepsilon_{11}^R \qquad (9.30)$$

The reader may be reminded that $\varepsilon_{ii} < 0; i = 1, 2$ is always valid because we have neglected income effects by choosing compensating elasticities. Moreover, as we restrict ourselves to prices above marginal costs, we learn from (9.25) that in such a case $(\mu - F_i) < 0$, which implies $\mu < F_i < 0; i = 1, 2$. Let us return to condition (9.30). Will it always hold? No, for the following reasons.

(1) *The direct price elasticities of demand ε_{ii} will usually change if the prices change*
The distributional objectives aim at a lower price of the necessity. This typically implies a numerically lower elasticity ε_{22}. And according to the allocative 'inverse elasticity structure' which is implied in the Feldstein rule as well, this means a tendency towards a price increase of the necessity. It can immediately be seen from (9.30) that such changes of the elasticities work against lower Feldstein prices of the necessity.

Usually this difficulty is overcome by the assumption that the elasticities are constant for the comparison (9.30). This assumption can be justified if we restrict ourselves to a politician who is unwilling to change prices abruptly for fear of political disturbances and therefore only compares Ramsey prices and Feldstein prices that are not far from each other. Needless to say there may exist a lot of cases where this does not hold and where the above mentioned change of elasticities may lead to unexpected results.

(2) *There may exist cases of a perverse ranking of the 'distributional characteristics'*
Let us assume constant elasticities ε_{ii}. Then (9.30) reduces to $F_2 < F_1 < 0$, which implies

$$\sum_h \{[x_{1h}U'(y_h)]/(\sum_k x_{1k})\} < \sum_h \{[x_{2h}U'(y_h)]/(\sum_k x_{2k})\} \qquad (9.31)$$

There will exist many cases where this condition holds, because we have assumed that the weights $U'(y_h)$ decrease with increasing income and that x_1 is mainly demanded by higher income people and x_2 mainly by lower income people. But we can easily think of combinations of the realizations of x_{ih} and $U'(y_h)$ that do not fulfil these conditions. The reader may be reminded that we only assumed that 'a comparatively high percentage' of total demand comes from higher (lower) income people. Therefore we have neither excluded purchases of necessities by higher income people nor purchases of non-necessities by lower income people. Moreover we have only assumed that $U'(y_h)$ is a decreasing function of incomes. We have not included any assumptions on $U''(y_h)$, on the sensitivity with respect to higher incomes or lower incomes and so on.

Moreover, if the *cross-price elasticities of demand* are taken into account (going back to inequality (9.29)), general conclusions are next to impossible.

A last objection may be added. Our comparison has not focussed on the prices themselves, but on the ratios of price–cost margins. But a lower price–cost margin may imply a higher price if the *marginal costs change* correspondingly. This can be a further reason why Feldstein prices of a necessity may exceed Ramsey prices.

Majority Rule and Feldstein Prices

Let us now regard Feldstein pricing from the point of view of a majority-conscious politician. We ask every consumer whether he/she prefers cost-covering Feldstein prices to cost-covering Ramsey prices. If more than 50 per cent do so, we have found a political explanation of why such a kind of pricing is applied.[17] Two additional assumptions seem to be necessary.

(1) The public opinion poll may be restricted to consumers of either good 1 or 2 only. Non-consumers are not asked. (This assumption is empirically sensible: polls on public transportation, for example, are usually taken by asking passengers of public transportation.)
(2) The voters consume either good 1 *or* good 2; not both.[18] (This is also sensible from the empirical point of view: if you are ill, you will not use first *and* second class hospitals at the same time.)

The *usual empirical evidence* of such cases proves that more than 50 per cent of all consumers buy the necessity and less than 50 per cent buy the non-necessity. First and second class railway or hospital facilities provide good examples. In such a case a pricing policy that favours the necessity will find a majority. And as Feldstein pricing usually favours the necessity, it will usually find a majority over Ramsey pricing.

However, there is *no theoretical proof* that this result must always occur.

(1) It is by no means guaranteed that more than 50 per cent of all consumers buy the necessity. We have only imposed the condition that it is mainly bought by lower income consumers, that is, that more than 50 per cent of its quantity is bought by consumers whose income is below average. But this definition does not exclude the possibility that such a necessity is bought by only 40, or even 20 per cent of all consumers. Good examples of such necessities are publicly supplied goods which in former times may have been bought by a majority of all consumers, but where the middle class consumers have changed to the 'non-necessity' substitute, and only the truly needy still buy the necessity.[19] In such cases the same problem arises as mentioned in the second section, above: policies that favour minorities do not find a majority.

(2) If more than 50 per cent of the voter–consumers buy the necessity, we can expect a majority in favour of Feldstein prices,[20] if they imply a lower price for the necessity and a higher price for the non-necessity as compared with the Ramsey prices. But, as we have shown above, there may well exist cases where the contrary is valid. And this may lead to a majority in favour of Ramsey prices.

For a majority-conscious politician it is, therefore, not sufficient simply to choose any function $U'(y_h)$ which is decreasing in income. He must also take into account the individual preferences which may lead to particular changes in the elasticities and to a particular demand pattern. And he must take into account how production costs change if demand changes. These allocational interdependencies may imply particular restrictions of the class of functions $U'(y_h)$ which lead to a majority.[21] Usually, however, Feldstein prices will find a majority.

DIFFERENTIATION WITH RESPECT TO GROUPS: DOES A WEAK EQUITY AXIOM HELP US TO UNDERSTAND SOCIAL TARIFFS?

If retired people, students, handicapped people and the like have to pay lower public utility prices than other groups of the population, the reason will most probably be that these groups are considered to be comparatively poor. However, this is probably not the only reason for a differentiation with respect to particular groups.[22]

A normative approach for a differentiation with respect to groups could perhaps be a *weak equity axiom*. Similar to Sen's definition of such an axiom[23] (which, however, refers to a distribution of a given total income among individuals only), we could define a weak equity axiom as follows. Let all people of a particular subset of consumers $a = 1, \ldots, m_a$ have a lower level of welfare than all people of another subset $b = 1, \ldots, m_b$ for each level of individual income. Then the optimal prices should be lower for the consumers of subset (a) than for those of subset (b).

The appealing feature of this axiom is that it is a very mild condition for public utility pricing and that, in fact, it could, for example, serve as a good normative basis for lower tariffs for the disabled. On the other hand the axiom does not give us any exact guidance on how to perform the interpersonal comparisons of utility that are involved. And it does not contain any guidance as to how much lower the prices of group (a) should be. Therefore its concrete application requires a lot of additional welfare judgments; thus the intuitive appeal of this axiom for public pricing disappears. Therefore I do not believe that the weak equity axiom furnishes an applicable basis for social tariffs.

CONCLUSION

This chapter deals with various different approaches to social tariffs. Since the political determination of social tariffs is quite important we first developed some conditions under which the political majority rule might refuse tariffs in favour of poor minorities and adopt tariff structures which favour a majority. We then turned to the usual welfare maximizing approach for social tariffs and showed some deficiencies which arise when a policy objective which is defined in terms of individual incomes is to be achieved by differentiation with respect to goods. The last section was devoted to some remarks on a 'weak equity axiom' and to difficulties of transforming it into an operational formula for social tariffs.

NOTES

1. I gratefully acknowledge discussions on an earlier draft of this paper by Martin S. Feldstein, Gabor Gyárfás, Richard A. Musgrave and by some members of the Boston Public Enterprise Group, mainly Leroy P. Jones and Ingo Vogelsang.
2. For similar models see Usher (1977) and Bös (1981a, pp. 118–23, 1981b).
3. As good 2 is simply a proxy for the rest of the economy it is convenient to assume constant returns to scale for x_2, which guarantees that its price p_2 does not change according to changing x_1 and makes the simple transition from inequality (9.13) to (9.14) possible. There exist cases where the assumption of constant returns to scale for x_1 can be given up.
4. We assume $\partial x_{ih}/\partial y_h > 0$ (no inferior goods).
5. It is not very complicated to extend the analysis to surcharge schedules which fix different surcharges for different income brackets in such a way that the surcharges never decrease with increasing income. The limiting case of such a schedule would be a two-part schedule, fixing a low surcharge for lower income people and a high surcharge for higher income people. If such a pricing scheme is to be applied discrete schedules will be chosen practically always because of their lower information and transaction costs. For the theoretical analysis, however, we restrict ourselves to (9.5).
6. The interpretation of (9.15) *a priori* seems to be easier, if one realizes that $\bar{\tau} = (1 - \beta)c_1$. However, because of (9.9), β and τ_h are not independent from each other; their relationship in the optimum depending on the consumption pattern (x_{1h}^*). Thus one is again back at the interpretation given in the text.
7. A technical note: $\partial x_{1h}^*/\partial y_h$ is used here as implying a change from the hth to the $h + 1$st consumer, thus leaving $\sum x_{1h}^*$ constant. The same is valid for $\partial dc_h/\partial y_h$.
8. Remember that our assumptions only imply $\partial x_{1h}^*/\partial y_h > 0$ and therefore also $\partial dc_h/\partial y_h > 0$. They do not imply $\partial dc_h/\partial y_h > \partial x_{1h}^*/\partial y_h$.
9. In practical applications of our theoretical model one should, however, always carefully check whether these assumptions are fulfilled. A good counter-example is London Transport (Grey, 1975, pp. 68, 107, 112–27; Fairhurst, 1975; Glaister–Collings, 1978). It produces two goods: the underground (rail) and the bus (road). The underground has the higher percentage of higher-income consumers but the numerically lower price elasticity of demand. One could argue that underground passengers prefer the greater comfort of London's tube and that they do not realize price increases as intensively as bus passengers, just because of their higher income. The difference between that aspect and our assumptions may depend on the fact that it cannot simply be argued that 'bus' is a necessity and 'underground' a non-necessity.
10. The standard reference for this approach is Baumol-Bradford (1970). However, the main lines of thought are already due to Ramsey (1927).
11. For more details see Bös (1981a).
12. For the sake of simplicity we restrict ourselves to cost-covering prices.
13. For the transformation note that $\delta x_i/\delta p_j = \delta x_j/\delta p_i$.
14. For a more extended interpretation of (9.21) see Bös (1981a), pp. 56–7.

15. For an extended interpretation see Feldstein (1972a), Bös (1981a, pp. 96–7, 100).
16. Other possible cases are dealt with in Bös (1981a, pp. 96–7, 100).
17. The additional reasons of the avoidance of the explicit revelation of one's income position and of lower administration costs have already been mentioned in the introduction.
18. A more rigorous treatment of the problems that arise in this case can be found in Bös (1981b).
19. Sometimes, the supply of such a necessity may be given up by the public utility. But sometimes it is still supplied because of social reasons or because of the influence of its cheaper price on the consumer price index.
20. Note that this includes the possibility that some higher income voters vote in favour of Feldstein pricing because it cheapens the necessity they are buying.
21. The reader may be reminded of equations (9.17) and (9.18) which also showed an interdependency of distributive and allocative determinants of the (local) politicians fiscal policy.
22. Sometimes this differentiation is combined with an off-peak regulation, that is, old-age retired people can travel at a cheaper price, but only at off-peak times.
23. Sen (1973), p. 18.

REFERENCES

Baumol, W. J. and D. F. Bradford (1970) 'Optimal Departures from Marginal Cost Pricing', *American Economic Review*, vol. 60, pp. 265–83.

Bös, D. (1981a) *Economic Theory of Public Enterprise, Lecture Notes in Economics and Mathematical Systems* (Berlin: Springer).

Bös, D. (1981b) 'Distributional Equity, Majority Voting and Public Pricing', Bonn, Mimeo.

Fairhurst, M. H. (1975) 'Variations in the Demand for Bus and Rail Travel in London up to 1974', *London Transport Economic Research Report, R 210* (London).

Feldstein, M. S. (1972a) 'Distributional Equity and the Optimal Structure of Public Prices', *American Economic Review*, vol. 62, pp. 32–6.

Feldstein, M. S. (1972b) 'Equity and Efficiency in Public Sector Pricing: The Optimal Two-Part Tariff', *Quarterly Journal of Economics*, vol. 86, pp. 175–87.

Feldstein, M. S. (1972c) 'The Pricing of Public Intermediate Goods', *Journal of Public Economics*, vol. 1, pp. 45–72.

Glaister, S. and J. J. Collings (1978) 'Maximisation of Passenger Miles in Theory and Practice', *Journal of Transport Economics and Policy*, vol. 12, pp. 304–12.

Grey, A. (1975) *Urban Fares Policy* (Lexington: Heath).

Le Grand, J. (1975) 'Public Price Discrimination and Aid to Low Income Groups', *Economica*, vol. 42, pp. 32–42.

Ramsey, F. (1927) 'A Contribution to the Theory of Taxation', *Economic Journal*, vol. 37, pp. 47–61.

Roberts, K. W. S. (1979) 'Welfare Considerations of Nonlinear Pricing', *Economic Journal*, vol. 89, pp. 66–83.

Sen, A. (1973) *On Economic Inequality* (London: Oxford University Press).

Usher, D. (1977) 'The Welfare Economics of the Socialization of Commodities', *Journal of Public Economics*, vol. 8, pp. 151–68.

10 The Feasibility of Marketable Emissions Permits in the United States

ROGER G. NOLL[1]

In the decade of the 1970s, the United States Government vigorously pursued a policy to reduce substantially the pollution of the nation's air and water. Beginning with the Clean Air Act in 1963, a series of laws were passed which expanded the role of the federal government in setting and enforcing environmental policy goals, set substantially more ambitious goals in terms of the purity of air and water, and increased dramatically the resources available for writing and enforcing pollution regulations. Although all the returns are not in and considerable disagreement about the exact figures remains, a reasonable estimate of the cost of environmental regulation is in the range of thirty to fifty billion dollars annually. In some industries, such as chemicals, electric power generation and mining, the cost of compliance with environmental regulation accounts for as much as ten per cent of investment expenditures, and five per cent of annual sales.[2]

Whether these expenditures are worthwhile depends, of course, on the benefits from environmental regulation. As with costs, there is some disagreement about the effect of environmental policies on pollution, but the consensus is that, while progress has been made, the nation is still a long way from attaining the stated goals of environmental policy.[3] Indeed, there is enough agreement on this point that all of the major groups in the environmental policy arena – business, environmental protection organizations, politicians, and regulatory authorities – now generally favour substantial reform of the regulatory process. And the most widely supported direction of reform is to introduce a greater measure of decentralized decision-making, guided by economic incentives, as a substitute for regulatory rules promulgated by government.

This chapter reviews one area of environmental policy – air pollution controls – in the USA, in which the transition to a more incentive-based regulatory mechanism has been underway since 1977, when amendments to the Clean Air Act enabled the Environmental Protection Agency (EPA) to adopt a more flexible approach to regulation than the traditional method of setting standards for each specific source of pollution. EPAs new approach is commonly called marketable (or tradable) emissions permits, whereby pollution sources can buy, sell or trade emissions of various pollutants as long as the overall objectives of environmental policy are not sacrificed. To understand fully how marketable permits are being implemented requires some knowledge of the details of the standard-setting process that is being replaced; hence the first section of the chapter describes the most important features of the old approach. This section is intended to summarize a vast literature on American regulatory institutions. The second section of the chapter discusses the advantages and problems associated with implementing more decentralized, market-oriented approaches to environmental regulation. Most of the important questions about implementation depend upon empirical, rather than theoretical, issues, and so the discussion in this section is in the context of a particular case study: the regulation of sulfur oxides emissions in the Los Angeles air shed. The third section of the paper describes the methods that EPA has adopted for making the transition to a marketable permits system, and evaluates the progress to date. This section also contains some conclusions about how best to implement this change.

AIR POLLUTION REGULATION IN THE UNITED STATES

The environmental legislation that was passed in the USA between the mid-1960s and late 1970s was but a part of a larger political change. For a number of reasons, the issue of preventive health and safety measures became of high importance to political leaders. At the same time that environmental laws were being written, so too were tough laws regarding consumer products and occupational health and safety. The environmental laws that were passed in this context were defended on the grounds that pollution represented a significant threat to public health.[4]

In this milieu, the principal objective of air pollution controls became to reduce emissions to the point that they produced no deleterious health effects. Federal regulators were charged with the responsibility of establishing *ambient air quality standards* – maximum limits on the concentrations of various pollutants in the atmosphere – that were low enough to guarantee the absence of hazards to health. This is, of course, a highly controversial policy objective, for it implies an infinite value to human health: *any* expense is justified to reduce air pollution as long as *any* adverse health effect, however minor, is observed. Moreover, if there is no threshold of pollution below which there are no health effects, the implication of the policy is zero emissions – a goal that probably is technically impossible to achieve in a modern, industrialized society. Because of the difficulty of determining the maximum concentration that produces no health effects, very few ambient air quality standards have yet been established. Nevertheless, the goal of zero adverse health effects remains the objective of air pollution regulation and the basis for ambient air quality standards.

Setting Source-Specific Standards

For regions that do not satisfy ambient air quality standards, the next step is to develop a plan for achieving compliance. For regions that do meet the standards, the next step is to adopt a policy for preventing significant deterioration of air quality.

In this phase the full complexity of the American federal system is apparent. The role of the federal government is essentially to define the characteristics of an acceptable plan, allowing the states to work out the details within the federal guidelines. The resulting state strategy for reducing pollution is called a State Implementation Plan (SIP), and it must be approved by EPA or else the latter can take over air quality regulation in the state.

For areas that are not in compliance with ambient air quality standards, the basic approach of the SIP is to specify abatement standards for each source of pollution, where a source is normally defined as a point at which emissions occur. Thus, a complicated production facility, such as an oil refinery or a steel mill, may have several points at which emissions are released, and hence be regulated as several different independent sources. Federal ground rules require that states identify the significant sources, develop regulations for controlling their emissions and adopt a timetable for bringing these sources into compliance.

A major problem in developing source-specific regulations is that the relationship between the amount and pattern of emissions and measured ambient air quality is often quite complex and poorly understood. In only a few parts of the USA has the relationship between emissions and air quality been estimated relatively well. In most areas, the basic data that are necessary to estimate such a relationship – long-term time series of emissions and air quality measurements – are either unavailable, unreliable, or have only been collected for a few years. As a result, the relationship between source-specific standards and the extent to which gains are made in achieving ambient air quality standards is highly uncertain. In response to this difficulty, EPA allows a state to adopt a SIP without direct reference to whether the resulting emissions will satisfy ambient air quality standards. If a region does not satisfy the ambient air quality standards, its plan is acceptable if it requires that sources adopt the best available control technology by a specified target date, usually in the mid to late 1980s. The presumption is that this will attain air quality objectives. If not, state regulators must later adopt more draconian measures, such as shutting down some polluting facilities or curtailing automobile travel; however, whether these measures will ever actually be imposed is a matter of uncertainty and disagreement.

Regardless of whether a region is in compliance with air quality standards, a plan must be developed by state and local authorities for preventing further substantial deterioration of air quality due to the entry or expansion of polluting facilities. This, too, in practice amounts to setting in place a process for writing source-specific standards. Although the definition of what constitutes substantial degradation varies among regions, in many cases the standards for new sources amount to a requirement that there be no net increase in emissions – that is, a net zero discharge requirement for new sources.

The SIP procedure gives state and local regulatory authorities the job of identifying the appropriate standards for each source, old and new, in their jurisdiction. Because the best abatement technology normally depends on specific technical features of a source, in most instances general standards for a broad class of sources are not attempted. With a few exceptions, state and local governments are free to identify the best abatement technology for each source, given its special characteristics. The few exceptions are standards for extremely important sources that the federal government has decided to set itself, such as emissions limits for automobiles and for newly constructed coal-burning electric generation facilities – although even in these cases the states can set their own standards as long as they set even more demanding regulations than the federal standards.

In principle, two kinds of source-specific standards can be set. *Input standards* specify the technical method to be adopted by the firm for reducing emissions. Examples are requiring facilities that burn coal or oil to install stack-gas scrubbers or specifying the maximum permissible amount of sulphur and other impurities that are allowed in fuel. *Performance standards* specify the maximum permissible emissions from a source, but allow the regulated entity to choose whatever control technology it prefers so long as the emissions ceiling is not exceeded.

In practice, source-specific standards as they have been developed in the USA are a hybrid of these two approaches. Regardless of how a standard is formally expressed, the method for developing it is to try to identify the best control technology and to establish the emissions that would result if that technology were used. Even if the standard is expressed in performance terms, a firm that prefers to use another method to achieve its allowed emissions level normally must obtain advance approval. The regulatory authorities will require proof that the alternative method is as effective as the one upon which the standard was based.

There are two reasons for a heavy reliance by regulators on specifying the abatement technology to be adopted by polluters. One is that the states must convince EPA that the SIP represents a good-faith effort to achieve air quality objectives. Because relatively few areas know the relationship between emissions and air quality and, therefore, can make reasonably accurate predictions of the air quality results of their SIP, the most effective strategy for demonstrating that a SIP is reasonable is to show that all of the sources will be required to use the best technology for reducing emissions. A second reason is that source-specific standards must be developed in a formal regulatory process according to a set of procedural standards.[5] An enormous body of law in the USA – constitutional, statutory and common – protects the private sector against arbitrary and unreasonable confiscation of wealth by the government. Decisions of a regulatory authority must be based upon the evidence submitted in a formal, public process in which anyone who is significantly affected by the decision has an opportunity to participate. The decisions must be reasonably and rationally based on the evidence, and must be clearly derived from the statutory responsibilities of the regulator. The regulatory authority bears the burden of proving that the regulation is not capricious and arbitrary (for example, that it is rationally based upon substantial evidence).

The decisions of the regulator can be appealed in the courts. To withstand these legal challenges, regulators must be able to prove the reasonableness of each standard. Normally this means that the regulator must show that the standard is feasible *and* that it will make progress towards reducing emissions. If the regulator fails to show that emissions will be substantially reduced (that is, a performance standard) by a specific, verifiable technique (that is, an input standard), the regulated firm and environmentalist groups have grounds on which to appeal the decision in the courts. In fact, appeals of standards are commonplace, in part because the evidentiary basis is often shaky, but also in part because firms can delay the imposition of a costly standard by exercising their full rights of appeal through the judicial system.

Problems of the Present Approach

The standard-setting regulatory process has proven to have a number of important shortcomings.[6]

First, the process is expensive and time-consuming, requiring numerous technical studies by all of the adversaries in a regulatory process, rebuttals of these studies and formal hearings. The costs and delays inherent in the process have made progress in developing SIPs much slower than was anticipated. Moreover, the attention on technical, source-specific standards has deflected attention – and resources – away from developing good data on emissions and air quality, and hence has inhibited air quality modelling. Thus, over a decade after having begun to regulate air quality seriously, most local and state regulators are still largely in the dark about the likely effects of the regulations that are being proposed and adopted.

Second, the process is economically inefficient in that vast differences emerge among firms in costs per unit of abated emissions. Some production processes are easier to understand than others, and the costs and efficacy of abatement techniques are known with differing degrees of certainty. As a result, the maximal feasible extent to which regulators can be successful in legally forcing abatement varies from firm to firm. These differences are especially great between old and new sources of emissions.[7]

Third, the policy erects entry barriers against new and expanding firms. These barriers are of two forms: the generally higher standards applied to new sources, and the requirement to go through a time-consuming process during which production plans are made a public record that is available to competitors. To the extent that entry is retarded, competition and technological change are inhibited.

Fourth, the process creates perverse incentives with respect to technological innovation in abatement methods.[8] Because of the repermitting process, the adoption of an innovation is delayed until regulatory approvals are obtained for each source that can use it. Moreover, the expense of the process detracts from the attraction of cost-reducing abatement technologies. And, while manufacturers of abatement equipment have an incentive to invent ways to increase the abatement of emissions, polluting firms have no incentive to reduce their emissions below their currently active standard. Consequently, the latter can be expected to resist *all* improvements in abatement technology that involve any additional expense. In addition, the incentives for improving abatement technology focus primarily on separable technical fixes – that is, specific pieces of equipment or other changes in input – as opposed to innovations in manufacturing processes because the formal regulatory process is better equipped to deal with the former.

As a practical matter, elimination of the quasi-judicial regulatory process is not possible in the USA, deriving as it does from Constitutional principles having widespread political support. But even if it were possible to simplify the process and make it more like European environmental regulatory processes,[9] some of the problems of standards remain. The absence of appropriate economic incentives to improve the methods of emissions control and the dependence on officials outside of polluting entities to make technical abatement decisions create situations in which inefficient results are likely. The delays and formal burden of proof in the American system contribute to these problems, but are not the only important cause of them.

ADVANTAGES AND PROBLEMS OF TRADABLE EMISSIONS PERMITS

Tradable emissions permits are one example of a general category of environmental regulatory methods that rely on market incentives, rather than source-specific regulations, to achieve policy objectives. The other leading examples are emissions taxes and abatement bounties.

Tradable emissions permits are somewhat related to the regulatory system currently (1981) in operation. Source-specific standards either state directly or imply a legal ceiling on emissions rates for each source. Thus, they can be interpreted as permits to release given amounts of emissions. A natural way to conceive of a tradable emissions permits system is as a modification of the present implicit emissions permits in which firms in a region can rearrange the pattern of emissions by exchanging their permits. Firms would report to regulators changes in their permit holdings in order to facilitate enforcement; however, they would not need advance approval for transactions.

Emissions taxes are a charge per unit of emissions that is levied on all sources in a region. An abatement bounty is like an emissions tax, except that firms are paid a subsidy in proportion to the emissions reductions that they achieve.

The underlying principle of all of these systems is the same. Polluters are given an incentive to reduce emissions, but the choice of the abatement technique is left to their discretion. And, because all polluters face the same set of incentives, rational decentralized responses will lead to the attainment of any given regional emissions target at minimum total costs.

A second advantage of incentive-based approaches is that they avoid a major part of the process costs of controlling pollution. With taxes, bounties or tradable permits, government need not be in the business of specifying the technology of abatement or setting the emissions limits for each specific source. The principal task of regulators under incentive-based systems is to define overall objectives in terms of environmental quality and total emissions, and to enforce compliance with the system that generates the incentives, including the measurement of performance by each source. Both of these responsibilities are, of course, features of the system of source-specific standards.

A third advantage of incentive-based approaches is that they do a better job of promoting advances in abatement technology. In all three systems, emissions are costly to a firm because they result in either taxes, the necessity to hold monetizable emissions permits or a foregone opportunity to collect a bounty for reducing them. Consequently, polluters have a continuing incentive to search for less costly, more effective abatement methods. Thus, a firm that invents a better abatement technique finds a willing market, rather than a source of opposition to the adoption of the new method.

Advantages of Tradable Permits

The special advantages – and problems – of tradable emissions permits have been widely discussed in general, theoretical terms in the economics literature.[10] Only a brief review will be presented here.

One advantage of tradable permits in comparison with taxes and bounties is that they do not necessarily require involvement in the fiscal processes of government. The source-specific standards approach gives away its implicit emissions permits, and so, too, can a system in which the permits are tradable. This avoids the political issues associated with either taxing or subsidizing industry. Indeed, literally any wealth effect of taxes or bounties can be reproduced by the choice of allocating permits: auctioning them is equivalent to an emissions tax, while granting permits equal to original emissions and then purchasing them is equivalent to an emissions-reduction bounty. Thus, the tradable permits approach allows a separation between the equity issues of who should pay and the efficiency issue of how to minimize the costs of achieving the policy objective.

A second characteristic – not necessarily an advantage or disadvantage – of tradable permits has to do with the ways in which the uncertainties of the regulatory process are distributed.[11] Like the system of source-specific standards, tradable emissions permits specify the total emissions of a given pollutant in a given geographic area. Unlike source-specific standards, the geographic distribution of emissions – and hence of pollution – is not specified. Consequently, in the absence of a good model for estimating the distribution of emissions that a market would produce and another good model for estimating the effects of this pattern of emissions on pollution, tradable emissions permits are somewhat more uncertain than source-specific standards in terms of the resulting quality of the environment. Similarly, in the absence of the same kind of modelling capability, a given tax on emissions or bounty on emissions reductions will produce uncertainty in the distribution of emissions – and on total emissions as well, since neither system imposes limits on total emissions. Hence, taxes and bounties are more uncertain than tradable permits in terms of their effects on environmental quality.

A similar story can be told on the cost side. In the American system of setting hybrid standards having both performance and input dimensions, compliance costs are estimated as part of the regulatory process. These estimates vary, sometimes dramatically, so they must be regarded as uncertain even after the standard is adopted. A tradable permits system in which the implicit permits in current standards are made marketable has greater cost uncertainty; however, because the permits are voluntarily exchanged, the greater uncertainty arises because polluters may find an amount of cost-reducing trades of permits that is unknown in advance. Hence the added uncertainty arises solely because of the possibility of lower costs.

In the case of taxes and bounties, a distinction must be made between resource costs and the expenditures on taxes or bounties. Because the amount of abatement resulting from any given tax or bounty is uncertain, so, too, is the resource cost of abatement. However, the total cost is bounded by the product of the tax (or bounty) and the initial amount of emissions. If firms do opt for zero discharge, it is because the cost of complete abatement is less than the maximum possible tax or bounty payment. A similar argument shows that the expenditures on taxes or bounties are also uncertain, but bounded in the same fashion.

From the standpoint of a firm, the sum of emissions taxes and abatement costs is likely to be less uncertain than the sum of abatement costs and the costs of obtaining permits in a system of marketable permits. The announcement of an emissions tax conveys more information about potential tax liabilities and abatement costs than is conveyed by the announcement of the tradability of emissions permits. The reason is that in the latter case the price of the permits must still be determined by the market and will always have some degree of random variability.

A third feature of tradable emissions permits is that they have advantages with respect to enforcement requirements. Taxes and bounties - at least in their most efficient forms – depend on total emissions. Hence the quantity of emissions must be measured in a manner that produces a legally enforceable measurement of total quantity. In some cases, direct and continuous measurement can be avoided, such as by making occasional spot checks of processes that produce a constant rate of emissions or by performing a mass balance analysis on inputs and outputs to the production process. But in most instances the measurement requirements for estimating total emissions are quite demanding.

Tradable permits do not require an estimate of total emissions, but a determination of whether the firm is releasing more or less emissions than are permitted. Spot checks, when backed by appropriately calculated non-compliance fines that make compliance an optimal strategy, are more likely to be feasible with tradable permits than the other incentive-based methods. Even if continuous monitoring is adopted, the technical requirements are easier, for all that need be measured is whether emissions are above or below a given limit. Mechanisms that are very simple, even simpler than the methods now in use – for example, optical scanning of stack emissions, chemical dosimeters like litmus paper or the radiation detectors worn by workers in areas that can be contaminated by radiation – can be used to detect whether a firm is in compliance without measuring the actual amount of emissions. In this way, tradable permits are comparable to any performance-based, source-specific emissions standard. And, like performance standards, tradable permits usually present more difficult enforcement problems than input standards because the latter require only an observation that a required technical fix is in place.

A fourth characteristic of tradable permits is that they can relatively easily accommodate economic growth. As economic expansion in a region proceeds, the optimal amount of emissions – and the optimal pattern of abatement among sources – is likely to change. A system of source-specific standards cannot readily accommodate this reality, because to do so requires rewriting the standards for every source in the region. Consequently, present procedures and policies impose far heavier burdens on new and expanding firms than on old sources, with deleterious effects on economic change as described above. Emissions taxes, too, must be adjusted as the economic structure of a region changes, for, if not, environmental quality will deteriorate in direct proportion to economic growth – a result that is not likely to be correct. If firms are allowed to enter before the tax is adjusted to their presence, legal problems can arise, not to mention political problems, if the new level of the tax makes the entrant economically unviable. In any case, the *ex ante* emissions tax gives false signals to potential entrants. Moreover, unless the emissions consequences of the entrant are examined fairly closely, as in the present source-specific standards, regulators do not know how the tax should be adjusted. Abatement bounties present similar problems, but in addition they actually encourage the entry of polluting industries into heavily polluted areas.[12] If a firm can expect its abatement costs to be subsidized, it will have diminished incentive to take into account the social costs of environmental degradation in selecting a location for a facility. Indeed, if the abatement bounty is high enough to produce voluntary abatement, investments to control emissions can enhance profitability by the maximal amount only in heavily polluted areas (where presumably the bounty is highest). As with taxes, the solution to the problem is *ex ante* review of entrants to decide through a regulatory process whether entry is desirable, thereby undermining the advantages of an incentive-based regulatory system.

Tradable emissions permits allow entry to occur without advance approval by the acquisition of permits in the market. Regulators may then, *ex post*, adjust the number of permits, or may even have a long-term plan for gradually changing the number of permits in order to accommodate growth.

In the context of existing regulatory policy in the USA, with ambient air quality standards based upon the goal of eliminating adverse health effects, environmental quality will not be allowed to deteriorate with economic growth, even though this might be the more efficient option. The advantages of a system of tradable permits in this case are even greater, for it is the only method that can accommodate entry without *ex ante* review of the emissions of the entrant. In order to prevent an increase in total emissions, taxes and bounties would have to be adjusted for all sources by an amount necessary to leave emissions unchanged. Thus, only tradable permits escape source-by-source regulatory review of each new or expanding polluting entity.

The preceding discussion suggests that the case for experimenting with tradable emissions permits is strong, justifying close examination of the implementation problems associated with such a system. Indeed, there are some aspects of a tradable permits approach that raise important design questions.

Design Problems for Tradable Permits

The main purpose of a tradable permits system is to convey to polluters – new and old – appropriate price signals about the social cost of emissions so that each can select a combination of capital investments, operating practices and emissions releases that minimize the sum of abatement costs and permits costs. The economic efficiency of the system depends on firms being able to buy and sell permits relatively easily, with incidental transactions costs, at competitive prices. The principal implementation problems associated with a tradable permits system are related to the question of whether these conditions for an efficient market can be satisfied.

One problem is the possibility of 'thin' markets – that is, markets in which transactions are rare, and in which few firms are willing to buy or sell. In such a situation, the transactions costs of trading permits can prevent the market from being much of an improvement over source-specific standards. If a firm that seeks to buy permits must invest substantial time and resources in finding a potential trading partner, and then engage in bilateral negotiations to determine a price, the ability of the permits market to find a cost-minimizing total cost of achieving ambient air quality standards is undermined. Moreover, infrequent trades arranged through negotiations are less likely to convey clear price signals to potential entrants, firms contemplating expansion or sources considering further abatement and the sale of some emissions permits.

A second problem is related to the structure of the permits market. In some air sheds, one or two firms can account for a very large share of emissions. Moreover, there is some tendency for regulators to require somewhat greater abatement efforts from the largest firms. In this situation, if a tradable permits system is initiated by making tradable the emissions permits that are implicit in current standards, it is conceivable that only one or two firms will be seeking to buy permits, with all other firms seeking to be sellers. If so, the market may not settle on the competitive equilibrium price, but a monopsonistic price instead. More generally, the degree to which a market diverges from the competitive ideal depends on the initial allocation of permits, and in any situation it is technically possible to pick an initial allocation that produces a monopoly or a monopsony.[13] Thus, a design problem for a tradable permits market is to avoid an initial allocation that has this property.

A third problem has to do with the definition of markets and permits. As discussed briefly above, the relationship between emissions and pollution is often very complex. Pollution at any given receptor point is the consequence of emissions from several locations, and often depends on their interactions as well. Similarly, every source of pollution has a unique pattern of polluting effects, which, because of interactions, may also depend on emissions from other sources. In general, to achieve theoretical efficiency (ignoring transactions costs and possible market imperfections) requires a separate market for each point where pollution damage occurs, and a separate transformation function for each source of pollution that maps its holdings in pollution permits at any source to its emissions allowances. Of course, this degree of complexity is impractical to implement. Hence, an important design problem is to make simplifications in the definition of permits and regions in which permits are valid that do not sacrifice too much in the way of the potential efficiencies of a market mechanism. At one extreme, a large geographic region can be treated as one market, with the implication that the region will be treated as one large mixing bowl in which emissions from all sources are uniformly spread across the region. As a description of reality, no pollution problem – not even emissions into standing bodies of water – has this fully mixed property; however, as a practical matter it may be a workable assumption. A somewhat more complicated strategy is to define a few receptor points at which pollution is measured and require firms to purchase emissions permits for pollution at each receptor point where their emissions cause pollution.

The best way to organize the market – the definition of a permit and the sources that must hold it – depends only in part on the physical aspects of the pollution problem. It also depends on the economic incentives operating upon sources. If abatement cost functions for all sources lead to more or less the same degree of abatement (that is, they are all reducing emissions by roughly the same proportion), a permits market that is defined crudely, even wildly incorrectly, as a mixing bowl may still be workable. In the worst case – in which each receptor point is polluted by only one source – the cost-minimizing distribution of emissions may still produce approximately the same amount of abatement at all sources.

In most regions, pollution problems exhibit both kinds of characteristics: localized, single-source pollution and effects from the combined emissions of many sources. A plume from a smokestack may be the primary cause of pollution on receptors a few miles downwind, but as distance from the stack increases its emissions will mingle with the releases from other facilities. To take an extreme example, the problem of acid rain in Canada, New York and New England is probably the cumulative effect of emissions from literally thousands of sources, some more than a thousand miles away. Whether a tradable permits market is workable, then, depends on the relative importance of the local *versus* long-distance effects, and on the likely pattern of abatement that will emerge from the market.

A fourth issue in the design of a tradable permits system is its flexibility with respect to changes in ambient air quality or total emissions targets. Because the relationship between emissions and air quality and the effect of air quality on health are not well understood, there is a good chance that new knowledge will cause regulators to want to change emissions levels. A decision to create more permits is relatively straightforward to deal with; regulators can give away or sell some net increment to the total emissions rights in an area. But a decision to reduce the number of permits raises potential difficulties. The heart of the issue is still another dimension of the definition of an emissions permit. Is its lifetime perpetual, or of fixed duration? Can it be redefined by fiat, or as an outcome of a regulatory process, or must changes in the number of permits be accomplished by purchase by the state? Obviously, the ease with which the number of permits can be changed depends on the answers to these questions. Moreover, a constraining factor on building into the permits system a mechanism for changing the number of permits is the effect of the mechanism on the willingness of firms to hold permits. If polluting entities are made to believe that the value of an emissions permit is subject to significant change at the whim of the state, abatement strategies – in terms of both the amount of abatement and its distribution between long-term capital investments and changes in operating methods – are likely to be affected.

Finally, some account needs to be taken of so-called air pollution episodes: periods when meteorological conditions are exceptionally unfavourable and so air pollution builds up over a number of days. To limit emissions to a level consistent with good air quality on these worst days is irrational; it is far less costly to curtail economic activity for a few days a year than to build in abatement capacity that would keep air quality high regardless of the weather. The current practice is to announce the degree of unfavourability of conditions a day in advance and to invoke special regulations when conditions look especially bad. To do something much more complicated than this is of dubious value, because the frequency and magnitude of air pollution episodes is not very high, and will be lower still as limits on emissions are lowered.

The tradable permits system could easily adopt the present approach to episodes, with the emissions permits applying only in the vast majority of days when there is no special condition. Alternatively, separate emissions permits markets could be implemented, one for normal conditions and one or more for episodes, with regulators announcing each day which permits apply tomorrow. Because this problem is relatively easy compared to the other four, it will be ignored for the remainder of this chapter.

Variants in System Design

The design features available to attack the first four problems are as follows.

(1) *Permit life.* Regulators could elect to make the durability of emissions permits uncertain by stating that they were valid until a formal regulatory procedure declared them to be invalid or changed the amount of emissions allowed by a single permit. Such a system would create incentives among firms to adopt production methods with some flexibility in emissions, and to hold more permits than were actually used. Alternatively, regulators could define the time period in which a permit is valid. At one extreme, permits could be perpetual, requiring regulators to buy them back to reduce total emissions. Or, regulators could assign a fixed life. If regulators decided to alter the number of permits, they could do so by allowing firms to trade in old permits for new at a specified exchange rate. Finally, regulators could have several different kinds of permits: some perpetual, some of a fixed, long-term duration and some with a

short life (for example, one year). Some periodic variability in the number of permits could be accomplished through the process of reissuing the permits with the short life; somewhat greater variability could be introduced as the intermediate-duration permits expired.

(2) *Market definition.* An emissions permit pertains to a particular geographic area. The size of the region and the variety of permits a source must hold for a given emissions allowance is a design feature of the system. Regulators could define emissions permits as freely tradable among all sources in a wide geographic area. Alternatively, a region could be subdivided into smaller areas, with trades between areas either barred or permitted according to some transformation of the value of a permit across area boundaries. Or, markets could be defined according to the location of receptors. In each area of the region, a coefficient would be estimated that related the effect of a unit of emissions on ambient air quality at a receptor point. Sources could then be required to hold permits to pollute at a receptor point equal to their quantity of emissions multiplied by the corresponding coefficient.

(3) *Market initialization.* Regulators must select a method for initially distributing the permits. One possibility is to give them away according to some rule. Examples of allocation rules are: in proportion to pre-control emissions, in proportion to emissions allowed under existing standards or equal to the expected equilibrium distribution of emissions if abatement costs were minimized. Alternatively, permits could be given to entities other than sources of pollution: the poor, schools and the like, presumably any of which would then elect to sell them. Or the government could allocate the permits by auctioning them. The latter two options suggest that sources of pollution would have to pay for permits; however, this is not necessarily the case for a state auction. Ownership of permits could be conferred on sources according to one of the rules for giving permits away, but sources could then be required to use an auction process to allocate the permits among themselves, with the revenues from the auction divided among the sources in proportion to their ownership shares.

(4) *Market operation.* Once an initial allocation has been made, provisions must also be adopted for later transactions. Government could leave the problem of organizing a continuing market to the private sector. Alternatively, given the record-keeping requirements of the government for purposes of enforcement, the government

could act as a marketplace by providing information about potential buyers and sellers to anyone requesting it. Or the government could be more than a passive marketing agent by actually requiring regular opportunities for reallocation of permits. This could be accomplished by forcing periodic re-auctioning (with proceeds re-distributed among the sources) of some fraction of the permits. A re-auctioning process fits naturally with a system in which permits have fixed durations, for then the replacement of old permits by new ones can be accomplished through an auction of the same sort as used to accomplish the initial allocation.

Solving the Design Problem: A Case Study

The importance of the first four potential problems of a tradable permits system depends on the empirical features of the emissions problem that the system is designed to solve. The following discussion uses a particular example – the control of sulphate particulates in Los Angeles – to illustrate how these issues can be assessed. This analysis is based upon relatively complete information about abatement costs, emissions inventories and the relationship between emissions and air quality throughout the region. Los Angeles probably has the most sophisticated regulatory system for air pollution in the world, in part because local agencies have been collecting emissions and air quality information for two decades and in part because these data have been extensively used by research scholars to study the Los Angeles air pollution problem. This information, of course, is especially helpful for illustrating the way that issues of designing a permits market might be resolved, and for designing a particular set of market institutions for this pollutant in this region. It is not necessary, however, to have all of this information in order to move towards a tradable permits system. Following the discussion of the Los Angeles sulphate problem, attention will be turned to methods of approaching the same design problems when the available information is less reliable.

The problem of sulphate particulates in Los Angeles is somewhat unusual in that the state, not the federal government, is solely responsible for its regulation. Sulphate particulates are suspected of being a health hazard and having other damaging effects, but the principal justification for controlling them in Los Angeles is that they account for a very large part – approximately one third – of the reduced visibility due to air pollution in Los Angeles. There is no federal ambient air quality standard for sulphate particulates; however, the state has adopted a standard of 25 micrograms per cubic metre, averaged over a 24 hour period.

Although sulphates are released directly into the atmosphere by some sources, by far the most important cause of sulphates is the release and subsequent atmospheric oxidation of sulphur dioxide, nearly all of which is associated with petroleum products that contain sulphur as an impurity. There is a federal ambient air quality standard for sulphur dioxide; however, Los Angeles is not in violation of it. Hence, the state standard for sulphates is the binding constraint on sulphur dioxide releases.

To control sulphate particulates in Los Angeles requires controlling emissions from about forty different categories of sources. The most important sources are electric utilities that burn oil to generate electricity, petroleum refiners, coke calciners, glass manufacturers, a steel mill, industries that are heavy fuel burners and mobile sources burning gasoline. A tradable emissions permit system must be designed to account for emissions from these major sources.

The tools with which to undertake an analysis of the design of a permits market in Los Angeles are a detailed model of the relationship between emissions and air quality, and estimates of the abatement cost functions for all major sources in the region. The abatement cost functions provide estimates of the costs to each source of various degrees of abatement of its sulphur oxide emissions. A firm seeking to minimize the sum of its expenditures on permits and its abatement costs would elect to abate up to the point at which the marginal cost of abatement equaled the market price of a permit; therefore, the abatement cost functions provide a means for predicting the quantity of permits that each source would seek to hold at any given permit price. When all of the abatement cost functions are combined, the relationship between abatement and permit prices for the entire region can be estimated. Thus, given a limit on total emissions for the entire region – that is, the number of permits to be issued – the abatement cost data yield a prediction about the price of a permit, the distribution of remaining emissions in the air shed and the expenditures on abatement (in total and by source).

The abatement cost information was gathered in the following manner.[14] First, public regulatory records and publications were searched to find cost estimates for various abatement methods for each source. Then, preliminary abatement cost functions were estimated and circulated among industry representatives and regulators for comments. The responses were then used to revise the cost estimates. For most sources, a few discrete abatement options were discovered, each with differing costs and levels of abatement. Thus, for most sources the abatement cost function is a step function.

The model relating emissions to air quality is based upon an analysis of detailed measurements of emissions and air quality.[15] Air quality estimates are made for each of the seventeen monitoring stations in the region, based upon meteorological conditions and the pattern of emissions among the sources in the area. The structure of the model is such that the geographical location of the sources and measuring stations is specified, so that the effects of changing geographical patterns of emissions can be estimated. Thus, the patterns of abatement and emissions predicted by the cost model under varying assumptions about the design of the permits market can be fed into the air quality model to predict the results in terms of the concentration of sulphate particulates at each of the measuring stations.

One important result of the cost and air quality studies is that mobile sources – autos and trucks – do not need to be dealt with directly in a permits system. Accurate air quality forecasts can be developed if mobile sources are redefined as fixed traffic sources along major arterial streets, using normal traffic densities and average auto emissions to calculate the emissions from these pseudo-fixed sources. Moreover, by far the least expensive method for reducing sulphur emissions from vehicles is to reduce the sulphur content of fuel. Consequently, it is feasible – with little loss of efficiency – to allocate responsibility for mobile source emissions to distributors of refined products. Indeed, because Los Angeles refines more fuel than is consumed locally, responsibility for mobile sources can be pushed even further back in the production process to refiners. This is an important advantage, for each automobile emits a tiny amount of sulphur. The transactions cost of forcing vehicle owners to purchase emissions permits in very small denominations are probably roughly equal to the price of the permit, for the latter is unlikely to be more than a few dollars a year. Moreover, to be efficient, the auto permits would have to be related to use of fuel, which creates a very difficult enforcement task. Thus, allocating responsibility for mobile sources to distributors or refiners greatly improves the performance of the permits markets. This result is true for sulphur emissions in any region; however, it is not necessarily true for controls on hydrocarbons and NO_x, the main components of photochemical smog. The reason is that in the latter case some cost-effective methods for reducing emissions are in the control of the vehicle owner. Thus, to place responsibility on others – for example, auto manufacturers – would entail some loss of efficiency. This would have to be balanced against the greater transactions costs for including in the market literally millions of holders of small amounts of permits.

The next issue to be attacked is the possibility of an imperfectly competitive market structure. The first step in attacking this issue is to stimulate the competitive allocation of permits. This is achieved by finding the minimum-cost allocation of abatement responsibilities among the sources that achieves a target level of total emissions. A permits market begins with some initial allocation rule. For each source, the difference between the initial allocation and the competitive allocation is the amount of permits it will buy or sell. By examining these differences, the structure of both the supply and demand sides of the market can be observed.

Although numerous market simulations have been made under varying assumptions about ambient air quality standards and the availability of substitutes for petroleum fuels, three examples will be presented here.[16] One assumes that the state's ambient air quality standards will be satisfied all of the time, the second assumes that the standard will be violated approximately two weeks per year and the third assumes that the emissions allowed under regulations now in place become freely tradable. All cases assume that the availability of natural gas as a fuel for industrial boilers and electric utility generation will be as it was in the early 1970s, which means neither freely available (as it would be under total deregulation of energy) nor severely curtailed (as it was about to be in the late 1970s before natural gas price regulation was eased). Under this assumption, the controls on sulphur oxides emissions that were established in 1977 would produce emissions of about 300 tons of sulphur dioxide equivalent per day in Los Angeles; to meet the standard all of the time requires that emissions be cut in half, but to meet it all but two weeks per year, on average, requires a further reduction of only about 50 tons per day. Thus, the three cases represent a major change, a minor reduction, and no change in currently enacted (but not yet fully in place) source-specific standards.

The single largest source of emissions is an electric utility. In 1973, prior to controls, this source accounted for approximately 28 per cent of emissions in Los Angeles. Table 10.1 shows the share of permits that this firm would be expected to hold under two simulated market structures for the cases described above.

The shares reported in Table 10.1 should not be taken too literally. Two important sources of error could have an important effect on these estimates. First, treating each source as having a few discrete choices of

TABLE 10.1   *Fraction of total emissions accounted for by largest permit holder in Los Angeles*

	(A) Competition (per cent)	(B) Monopsony (per cent)
(1) Make existing permits tradable with historical gas supplies	48	33
(2) Violate standard two weeks/year with historical gas supplies	43	40
(3) Satisfy standard all of the time with historical gas supplies	32	32

SOURCE: Robert W. Hahn, 'An Assessment of the Viability of Marketable Permits', Doctoral dissertation, California Institute of Technology, May 1981.

abatement methods and hence facing an abatement cost function that is a step function, creates only a handful of potential emissions equilibria that are feasible for a particular firm. In reality, the abatement cost functions are likely to be smoother than the functions used in the model. Second, the shares of permit holdings for the largest firm are likely to be underestimates. Among the major source categories in Los Angeles, abatement costs are best known – and least likely to be overestimated – for electric utilities. This means that even greater efficiency gains may be possible by substituting abatement elsewhere for the emissions reductions at utilities that are calculated from the existing cost data.

With these caveats in mind, the results in Table 10.1 illustrate the possibility of serious market imperfections, depending upon the selection of an emissions target and an initial allocation of the permits. Column (A) shows the cost-minimizing allocation of permits under the three emissions targets described above. This allocation is the competitive equilibrium. If the initial allocation process is an auction so that all firms are buyers, the share of the largest source is the share shown in column (A). Other initial allocations can raise this figure substantially. For example, suppose the allocation is designed to retain present emissions levels and is a proportion of pre-control emissions. In this case, the largest source, assuming the market were competitive, would seek to increase its share of holdings by 20 per cent of the total number of permits (the difference between 48 per cent on line (1), column (A) and the 28 per cent share of baseline emissions). This would make this source an almost complete monopsonist, that is, the only source of demand for permits at the competitive equilibrium price (almost all other firms would be sellers). The potential inefficiency of a monopsonist is that it will systematically understate its demand in order to force the price of permits down. This is achieved by engaging in excessive abatement, the extra costs of which are made up in the effects of pushing down permit prices.

Column (B) shows the results from the most extreme degree of monopsony that is possible for each of the three cases. Here it is assumed that the largest source has an initial allocation of no permits, and that all other firms are given permits in a manner that causes them to seek to be sellers at any price equal to or above the monopsony equilibrium. The discreteness in the options available to the utility strongly influences these numbers: the actual emissions produced in lines (1) and (2) of column (B) are identical, and in line (3) the monopsony and competitive equilibria are the same. Such extreme results should not be expected to emerge in the real world. Nevertheless, the pattern of the results – a greater divergence between competitive and monopsony shares for higher total limits on emissions – is likely to be robust for this particular case. The reason is that in the range of the competitive equilibrium for emissions limits around the most stringent standard, the supply of permits from other firms to the largest source is very elastic, even with discrete options in the abatement cost analysis. This undermines the opportunity of the monopsonist to take advantage of its high market share: over-abatement will not force much of a drop in permit prices and hence the gains from the latter will not generate much of an offset against the higher abatement costs that are necessary to allow the firm to reduce its demand for permits.

The tentative conclusion from this analysis is that for the particular case at hand, monopsony appears to be a serious design concern only if regulators do not conform to the existing ambient air quality standards. The actual allocation rule is certain to be less likely to cause monopsony than the extreme case analyzed here, yet even under this extreme assumption imperfections in the permit market appear relatively unimportant if the emissions limit is low. On the other hand, market imperfections could be important if existing permits were simply made tradable unless the initial allocation were designed to guard against it.

Multiple Permits Markets

Another important implementation issue is the degree of geographical resolution in the definition of an emissions permit. In the case of sulfates in Los Angeles, a permit could be defined as a license to emit a given amount of sulphur oxides anywhere in the air shed. Or, permits could have a varying value depending on the geographic location of the source holding them, with the relationship based upon estimates of the damage created by emissions from different sources. Finally, the permits could be defined in terms of the resulting pollution at each of the seventeen sites at which air quality has been measured, with an air quality model being used to calculate the number of permits a given source must hold at each receptor site for each unit of emissions that it releases. The last alternative is the most complicated to implement, for it requires that sources participate in seventeen markets and that the state be continuously available to run air quality simulations whenever any firm seeks to change its emissions. While such a system is difficult – perhaps impossible – to operate in the real world, its results can nevertheless be simulated. The differences between the first system (all emissions are treated equally) and the last system (each receptor is associated with a separate market) thus provides a measure of the potential gross gains from a fine-tuned method of defining the permits.

Table 10.2 presents some of the results of these simulations.[17]

The case analyzed here is one in which natural gas availability is low. This case is likely to produce the greatest differences in abatement costs among various methods for organizing the permits market. Given the

TABLE 10.2   *Comparison of universal and receptor-specific permits (costs in $ millions)*

	Annualized costs of competitive equilibrium abatement for:		
		Receptor-specific permits that produce:	
Baseline emissions target in tons/day sulphur dioxide equivalent	(A) *Universal permits*	(B) *Same air quality for each receptor*	(C) *Uniform air quality equal to worst receptor*
150	682	682	682
250	565	557	545
300	515	513	505

SOURCE: Robert W. Hahn, 'Data Base and Programming Methodology for Marketable Permits Study', Open File Report 80–8, Environmental Quality Laboratory, California Institute of Technology, 1981.

historically available gas supply to Los Angeles, abatement costs tend to be about 60 per cent of the costs if natural gas supplies are low. Column (A) shows the annualized expenditures on abatement costs in the Los Angeles area under the competitive equilibrium distribution of permits if there is no geographical resolution in the permit system. Column (B) shows the costs if firms are required to buy pollution permits for each of the seventeen measuring stations in the air shed, subject to the condition that the air quality results at each station will be the same as the outcome from the system reported in column (A). Thus, the difference between (A) and (B) is the gain, if any, arising solely from geographical relocation of permits in a system that takes account of the specific polluting effects of emissions from each location in the region.

Column (C) further relaxes the system, allowing pollution at all measuring stations to be constrained only by the air quality achieved at the most polluted station under the allocation corresponding to Column (A). Thus, emissions can be reallocated and total emissions increased as long as pollution does not increase at the location that is most polluted under the column (A) allocation. Again, the results are affected by the discreteness in abatement options assumed in the model; however, the general result from the analysis is that there is little to be gained from fine-tuning the definition of permits. The reasons are twofold: the simple market allocates emissions relatively evenly over the region, and leaves relatively little differences among measuring stations in terms of the air quality results. Hence, there is little opportunity for improving the efficiency of the allocation through adopting a more complicated market system.

While these results may not be generalizable to other pollutants in other areas, they nevertheless suggest an important lesson. In order for a tradable permits system to be able to capture significant gains from a fine-tuned, complicated definition of permits and their markets, it is *not* sufficient that different sources have a significantly different pattern of effects. It must also be the case that the equilibrium allocation of permits in a crude, simplified market be such that emissions would be concentrated in a particular location.

If the comparison is to be made between a simple tradable permits system and the existing regulatory arrangement, the issue is whether a tradable permits system increases or reduces the geographic concentration of emissions compared to the present pattern. Because the present source-specific standards system tends to force some activities to over-abate (for example, electric utilities), while leaving other sources virtually unregulated, it should not be surprising to find that a tradable permits system evens out the pattern of emissions in comparison to the present system, and therefore makes more even the geographical distribution of measured pollution within a region. Moreover, if most sources face relatively low abatement costs for a substantial fraction of their emissions, a market system will lead to substantial abatement from all sources. In such a case, it should not be surprising to find situations in which there is relatively little additional gain from moving from a simple to a complex system.

Thin Markets

The final major potential source of a failure in the permits market is that transactions will be too infrequent to convey meaningful price signals to polluting firms, to make relatively easy the acquisition of permits for entry and expansion of polluting facilities, and to allow a firm to avoid the expense of organizing the market and engaging in extensive bilateral negotiation every time it desires to make a trade. This is an especially difficult design problem to get a firm grip on in advance of operating the market, because the indicators of the extent of market transactions are so crude. One measure is the number of firms accounting for existing and expected emissions. In Los Angeles ten companies account for approximately 85 per cent of the sulphur oxides emissions under current standards, assuming mobile sources are assigned to the oil refiners operating in the air shed.[18] Most major industrial polluters emit relatively small amounts of sulfur, so that the market for small quantities of permits is likely to be reasonably well-functioning; however, a major expansion or entry of an oil refinery, an offshore oil terminal, or an electric utility generation facility would be especially difficult to accommodate because so few sources have sufficient numbers of permits to be potentially significant sellers to the new source.

A second problem in anticipating the extent of a problem of market thinness is that there is likely to be a systematic tendency to underestimate the possibilities for transactions. A substantial source of demand and supply in the market for permits will be factors that are not measurable in advance. Examples are innovations in abatement technology, entry, exit, contraction and expansion of polluting entities, and opportunities for more efficient abatement methods that may be known to existing sources but that have not yet appeared in the public domain (for example, process changes).

In Los Angeles the problem is even more difficult because the local air pollution control authority has explicitly adopted the policy of attempting to write standards in inverse order of their costs per unit abatement. Thus, with few exceptions, the standards in place are the least expensive abatement methods available, and the pending standards are the least expensive remaining possibilities. Consequently, most of the demand for trades, and the gains from a permits market, are unlikely to be measured using existing cost information. Therefore the extent to which the thinness of the market is a potential problem is likely to be overstated. For example, given historical natural gas supplies and no abatement methods other than those whose costs are known publicly, the annual cost savings from a competitive reallocation of the emissions permits that are currently in place is estimated to save only about $20 million per year in abatement costs, which is about 7 per cent of the total.[19] This indicates a strong possibility of a thin market indeed; however it is sure to be an underestimate of the potential savings and hence the desire to trade.

Whether the market is thin, initially and in the future, again depends on the design of the system. A few examples illustrate this point. (1) If existing emissions (or some proportion of them) are simply made tradable, a thin market is a more likely prospect than if an auction process is used for the initial allocation. (2) Fine-tuned, multiple-market systems are more likely to face a problem of thinness than single markets defined over a broad geographic area. (3) If permits are perpetual with no periodic reallocation process, a decision to make a major purchase or sale would then require that the firm wishing to create a market undertake the time and expense of organizing and negotiating a trade. At the other extreme, if permits have a fixed life and are reallocated by auction, a convenient time and place is established for facilitating major re-distributions of permits should changes in underlying economic and technological conditions warrant it.

Selecting a Design: Conclusions

The preceding discussion should make clear that selecting a design for a system of marketable emissions permits is not a purely technical, scientific matter. Working out the details requires considerable judgment, including an assessment of which risks a political entity would prefer to run. The following observations present an analysis of two polar cases: a design for sulphur oxides emissions in Los Angeles, an area in which information is comparatively rich, and a design for the general problem of emissions in control in an information-poor environment.

In Los Angeles, market imperfections apparently are a far more important design issue than is the selection of appropriate definitions for the geographical extent of a permits market. Fine-tuning the system in terms of multiple markets for sulphur emissions promises little gains, yet there will be formidable problems of transactions costs and market structure. Consequently, a system in which permits are simply stated in terms of allowable quantities of sulphur dioxide equivalent emissions anywhere in the region appears to be the most desirable.

The Los Angeles air shed has a relatively large number of sources producing a small quantity of emissions, but only ten firms account for about 85 per cent of the total. Consequently, imperfectly competitive and thin markets are a potential problem for large transactions. The implication is that the method selected for initiating and maintaining the system should encourage an active, competitive market.

The most attractive method for the initial allocation is an auction mechanism. This provides a thick market (all permits are transacted in the initial distribution) and, because all polluters are placed on the same side of the market, it minimizes the likelihood of monopolistic imperfections. The mechanics of the proposed mechanism are as follows. Each source would be asked to write down the number of permits it would seek to purchase at each of several prices. The firm would be free to choose as many price gradations as it wanted. It could write down one price-quantity pair (for example, X tons per day at any price up to $\$ Y$ per ton). It could provide a step function of several jumps, such as X tons per day for prices between $\$ Y$ and $\$ Z$ ($\$ Y$ larger), and $X + W$ tons for prices below $\$ Z$. Or, it could bid a continuous demand function for permits. Permits would then be allocated to the highest bidders at the quantities requested, descending down the price bids until the permits were completely allocated. Among the bids not receiving any permit allocations, the one with the highest bid price determines the price of all permits (that is, the allocation mechanism is a second-price auction). This process is the most likely theoretically to produce a competitive allocation of the permits.

A separable equity issue accompanying the auction is the allocation of the net costs of the permits. Whereas the permit price determined above could actually be paid to the state, an alternative is to pay the revenues according to a previously arranged provisional permit allocation, as described above. As a political matter, the chances of implementing a tradable permits system are probably greater if the revenues do not accrue to the governmental treasury, and if the provisional allocation of the rights to receive the revenues from the permit auction does not reward firms who have been most resistant to current environmental regulations. For example, if ownership rights for purposes of allocating the auction revenues were based upon emissions under current standards, firms that had succeeded in fighting regulation or that had managed to induce regulators to impose relatively undemanding standards on them would receive relatively large quantities of rights in emissions in comparison with firms that had been more cooperative and engaged in more costly abatement techniques. From an equity standpoint, provisionally allocating the permits prior to the auction on the basis of either pre-control emissions or the expected competitive allocation are both superior. The latter approach – estimating the competitive allocation and granting ownership in permits on the basis of it – is more difficult, for it requires establishing in a formal regulatory process what the cost-minimizing allocation would be. This is comparable to setting source-specific emissions standards and could be upset by the procedural requirements of the regulatory process. If any single firm objected to the allocation, the entire system could be delayed by continuing litigation until its appeals were resolved.

The primary difficulty with a system based on pre-control emissions is that for one important source – oil refineries – the methods that they would adopt today with no regulation would produce far less emissions than the best methods of 1970. A method based on pre-control emissions would, in any event, end up giving most of the permits to oil companies, who would then probably sell them in large quantities and high profit to public and municipal utilities. This does not seem to be very acceptable politically.

Obviously, the equity aspects of initialization are thorny. Perhaps the best alternative is to base allocations on an amended list of existing emissions, with the few remaining uncontrolled sources being put through an emissions standard process before the initial allocation of tradable permits is made. Whatever the choice, the allocation would proceed as follows. The ratio of target emissions to the baseline emissions would be calculated. Each firm would then receive a provisional allocation of permits equal to this ratio times its baseline emissions. New or expanded sources would receive allocations based upon actual emissions when operations began.

After the provisional allocation is made, each firm would make bids on permits, and thereby receive a final allocation of emission permits according to its bids at the price of the highest excluded bid. The firm would pay for these permits at the established price, and receive revenues at the same price for the permits which it held provisionally. The net payment for a particular source would be the product of the auction price and the difference between its final allocation based upon the bidding procedure and its provisional allocation based upon pre-control emissions. For all firms taken together, the net payment would be zero.

To provide a continuing opportunity for entry and expansion, permits could be separated into vintages according to useful life. The permits would be declared the binding control on emissions beginning at a specified date after the auction – perhaps a year or two after it takes place to give sources ample time to engage in capital investments to accommodate their permit holdings. All permits could then be valid for another fixed period after the system is in place, such as for an additional year. Then, a pre-designated portion of the permits could expire each year – for example, 10 per cent. Prior to the expiration date, the regulators would determine how many permits would be issued to replace the expired ones, based upon considerations of cost and air quality. The new permits could be allocated by the same auction procedure as was used for the initial allocation. Provisional allocations for purposes of distributing auction revenues would be based upon holdings of the expiring permits, but the final allocation would be based upon a second-price auction.

Between the formal auctions, government regulators could maintain a public file of the current holdings of permits of various vintages, and could serve as a clearing house for information about firms that wish to buy or sell their holdings. More risk-averse firms (or firms wanting a long-term emissions commitment) could seek to sell permits with short remaining lives and buy permits with longer lives. Entry and expansion of polluting sources could still take place through the clearing house; however, the presence of an annual auction would probably end up being the primary mechanism for a new major source to acquire the necessary permits.

The preceding mechanism appears to cope best with the specific design problems for the case at hand. A key element of the Los Angeles problem, however, is the finding that the geographic allocation of emissions does not make much difference in terms of satisfying air quality objectives. In the absence of information about the relationship between emissions and air quality, or in a world in which localized effects are understood and known to be potentially important, how might the design of the system differ?

The mechanism described above has several features that are well-suited to the case of poor information. First, the periodic auction is the best way to protect against market imperfections owing to either market concentration or market thinness. Second, the concept of having some of the permits expire each year is especially appropriate when the relationship between emissions and air quality is poorly understood, because the process by which expiring permits are converted into new ones allows the regulator continually to adjust the number of permits (and hence air quality). Of course, the more uncertain are regulators about the emissions to air quality relationship, the greater is the degree of variability in the number of permits that they would desire. One method for achieving greater potential for variability is to have two types of permits: long-term (perhaps ten years, as above, or even perpetual) and short-term (as short as one year). Whereas under the system described above only 10 per cent of the permits expire each year, with a two-permit system a much higher proportion could be assigned to the short-term category and therefore varied in quantity from year to year. A second use of short-term permits would be to facilitate an economically efficient approach to achieving the ultimate air quality objective. Regulators could announce a strategy to reissue short term permits at some ratio of new to expiring permits that is less than one, thereby gradually winding down the total emissions in the area. The process could be based upon an emissions target that is established before the system begins to operate (assuming the relationship between emissions and air quality is known well enough to make this feasible), or the winding down process could be open-ended, with regulators announcing a fixed percentage reduction in short-term permits until ambient air quality standards are achieved (or changed).

The preceding arrangements still leave unsolved one potential failing of a market in permits: the possibility of localized effects from a single or a few sources that elect to buy a large number of permits rather than to abate. Because this result in the context of a permits market is a consequence of a cost-minimizing process of reducing emissions, the appropriate response to the problem may be to allow some degree of localized violations of air quality standards. Nevertheless, in the context of existing air pollution regulation, rather than regulation seeking to make some sort of optimal trade-off between benefits and costs, the ambient air quality standard is an inflexible policy objective.

If enough firms contribute to a localized effect, one possible solution is a system of multiple permits markets. This would require a formal regulatory determination of the coefficients relating emissions to air quality for the relevant sources and localized pollution hot spots. As long as the number of these localized problems is relatively small, allowing firms to participate in only a few markets, this approach may prove workable. But it would require a substantial evidentiary burden on the regulators in defining the permits, the markets and the mathematical relationship of sources to each. In the absence of good information about the relationship between emissions and air quality, regulators may not be able to sustain such findings legally, or may be able to do so only after a long legal battle.

A second, probably more fruitful approach is to set up a permits market, but to overlay minimum standards on the sources that are suspected of having important localized pollution effects. Only very large sources or sources emitting at or near ground level can be expected to cause a violation of ambient air quality standards all by themselves; hence regulators could deal on a case-by-case basis with these sources. The idea would be to let the permits market allocate emissions, but to set an upper bound on the number of permits that could be held by some specific sources or a lower bound on stack heights. These standards would be set according to the same procedural and evidentiary requirements that apply to the present source-specific regulatory standards; however, the process of implementing them would not need to delay the implementation of a general permits market. The long legal process to set an upper bound on a particular source could be underway while the market operated, and could be directed only at the major sources that in equilibrium were observed to hold a greater number of permits than the proposed upper bound.

Any of the preceding systems – numerous short-term permits, some standards overlaying the market for permits – creates uncertainty among emissions sources in picking an optimal abatement strategy, or indeed in being willing to experiment with a change in the regulatory system for controlling emissions. Uncertainty about the future state of regulatory stringency affects the selection of abatement methods by a regulated entity – both the total amount abated, and the choice among capital-intensive technologies versus changes in operating procedures. In general, uncertainty should make firms somewhat more reluctant to abate at all, and somewhat more likely to adopt more flexible abatement methods that allow relatively inexpensive adjustments in emissions as policy changes occur.

One good argument for a stable regulatory policy is to create a more certain decision-making environment for regulated firms. But if long-term goals cannot be very accurately stated, either because the benefits of improved air quality are uncertain or because the relationship between emissions and air quality is poorly understood, regulatory policy will produce a more efficient result if this uncertainty is transmitted to businesses by the regulatory system. A system that does not specify the long-run emissions goal, but that makes some measured change in emissions over time (and that is ambiguous about the ultimate stopping point), will be more efficient if it encourages more flexible abatement methods. Consequently, although the politics of the situation may prove intractable, a design criteria for situations in which the amount of emissions to be allowed in an area is unknown ought to be to construct a permits system that conveys this uncertainty to polluting entities.

DIRECTIONS OF CHANGE IN US POLICY

In the late 1970s, the Environmental Protection Agency began seriously to consider – and then to encourage – a policy of 'controlled trading methods' in air pollution regulation. The idea was to introduce some elements of a market – and its attendant flexibility – into the standards-setting mode of regulation. Three such methods have been developed and, to a limited extent, implemented: 'bubbles', 'offsets' and 'banks.'

As discussed above, current regulatory practice is to set a standard for each source, with a source defined as a point from which emissions are released. For large, complex manufacturing processes, such as oil refining or steel making, a single plant can have several separate sources. The bubble policy is an attempt to introduce some relaxation of the exclusive focus on specific sources. It enables a firm to reduce emissions below the standard from one source and increase emissions from another at the same location if the effect is a net improvement in environmental quality. The term 'bubble' was adopted to evoke the notion of placing a bubble around an entire plant and treating it as a single source rather than as a series of independent sources.

Bubbles are intended to deal with cost-minimizing reallocations of emissions among sources at the same facility. A similar concept for trade-offs between two facilities underpins the second policy, called offsets. An offset is a reduction in emissions below the standard in one facility that more than compensates for an increase in emissions at another in the same general area. An offset is more like a normal market relationship, for the mechanism by which one firm induces another to reduce its emissions is to pay compensation. Because the offset policy is oriented towards trade-offs between two firms, the details of the transaction are expected to be the result of bilateral negotiations, rather than a transaction in a continuously operating centralized market.

Still closer to a normal market is an emissions bank. The bank policy provides a mechanism whereby a source can receive credit for an excess reduction in emissions without actually finding someone to whom it can sell the emissions reduction. If a firm beats its emissions standards, it receives a credit in the emissions bank. Normally the amount of the credit is some fraction (near to but less than one) of the reduction in emissions below the standard, so that the process effectuates a net reduction in emissions. Other firms, seeking to receive emissions permits, can then purchase the banked credits by negotiating an agreement with one or more depositors.

All of these new policies are conceptually like tradable emissions permits in that they allow economic considerations to guide some reallocation of emissions permits. But all are part of the standard-setting process, rather than a substitute for it. Each trade must be approved by regulatory authorities in the normal permitting process. This normally requires information about the abatement technology to be used at both the point where emissions are reduced and at the source increasing emissions. Moreover, except for the bubble policy, these methods take existing emissions standards as a baseline: neither trading partner in an offset or bank exchange can end up emitting more than the existing source-specific emissions the standard allows. Offsets and banks are seen as means for allowing entry and expansion of pollution sources when the source would cause a reduction in air quality even if it was in compliance with source-specific standards. Thus, new or expanding sources can use offsets and banks to purchase emissions permits for the emissions they would release after having adopted the best abatement technology available to them. These policies do not relax uneconomic differences among old source categories, or between new and old sources, that are present in the existing system of source-specific standards.

Offsets and banks also suffer from the absence of a formal method of organizing the market. Each depends on bilateral negotiations, and each can expect infrequent transactions because only new or expanded major sources are candidates to engage in trades. Consequently, the transactions costs for trades can be expected to be high, and problems of market imperfection are likely to emerge.

Finally, the status of traded emissions permits is secondary to permits inherent in existing source-specific standards. The EPA guidelines for the controlled trading methods include provisions for situations in which ambient air quality standards are not satisfied after all sources are controlled. In general, if environmental quality objectives are not attained, all emissions permits are to be regarded as provisional and subject to change. But traded emissions permits are to be the first to be examined for re-definition. For example, the guidelines governing the emissions banks – the most market-like of the three options – state that local air pollution control agencies are to select among four alternatives if air quality objectives are not realized: (1) a moratorium on the use of permits obtained through the bank, (2) a revision on a source-by-source basis of the number of permits from the bank that are necessary to allow a given quantity of emissions (for example, a depreciation of the value of a permit), (3) an across-the-board depreciation of the value of all traded permits, or (4) a forfeiture of all traded permits.[20] Thus traded permits are required to bear the brunt of the uncertainties in environmental policy. Obviously, polluting entities can be expected to be reluctant to risk substantial capital investments on the validity of traded emissions permits.

The new trading methods offered by EPA should properly be regarded as a supplement to a continued primary reliance on source-specific standards. For the reasons given above, they are not appropriately characterized as a system of marketable emissions permits. Instead, they are a mechanism whereby sources can collaborate to obtain some changes in source-specific emissions standards from local regulators, subject to some important conditions about the kinds of changes that are feasible and the long-term status of the revised standards. They do not abandon the premise of the existing regulatory structure, which is that in order to control pollution one must directly control every polluter.

The argument for these changes in regulatory policy – assuming that the problems with the existing system are major – must be primarily political, based upon the idea that controlled trading options are a necessary step in the transition from the old system to a new, market-oriented one. In this light, the controlled trading options have one major advantage over the designs discussed in the previous section: not everyone has to participate in the system and face the uncertainties inherent in it. Local regulators can continue to set standards for every source, even when trades take place. A polluting entity can choose to satisfy its current source-specific standards, avoid subjecting itself to a market process, and presumably live happily ever after in a blissful but expensive world of relative regulatory certainty. Assuming that regulators can avoid a policy catastrophe, such as observing continued failure to satisfy ambient air quality standards and then voiding all traded permits, the presence of a functioning and profitable permits trading system can induce more firms to enter offset or bank arrangements. And, as experience is gained, environmentalists and local regulators can develop more faith in decentralized decision making and exercise less and less scrutiny over the details of each transaction. Moreover, areas that do relax the source-by-source review process and essentially permit any reasonable trade will gradually be rewarded by the flexibility the system allows for economic growth, perhaps forcing more reluctant regulatory authorities to go along.

The major problem with this line of reasoning is that the idea of marketable permits may sink because the new trading methods are so procedurally freighted, so limited in applicability and so burdened with uncertainties over the long-term value of the permits. Too timid a reform leads to few transactions and market imperfections that undermine the efficiency of the trades that take place. Even in the absence of a policy catastrophe, the system could prove so cumbersome that it is uninteresting to polluting entities and hence does not lead to the gradual transition to a true market system.

In any event, at some point it is likely to be desirable to make a major alteration in policy, regardless of which transition path to a market system is followed. That is the regularization of a market situation – such as an auction – that avoids source-by-source review and that facilitates trades by providing a thick market with low transactions costs. This is the key to substantially improving the efficiency of the environmental regulatory process in the USA. Moreover, the method for implementing this change is the principal design issue that has thus far been ignored by policymakers and that must be addressed if an economically rational regulatory method is to be put in place.

NOTES AND REFERENCES

1. The research reported in this chapter was supported by a grant from the California Air Resources Board. The author gratefully acknowledges the helpful comments and criticisms on an earlier draft by Glen R. Cass and Robert W. Hahn.
2. For some data on these points, see *Cost of Government Regulation Study for the Business Roundtable* (Arthur Anderson, Inc. (Chicago) and Business Roundtable (New York) 1979).
3. Annual reports of the US Governments Council on Environmental Quality show steady but slow decline in the concentration of most air and water pollutants.
4. For a detailed study of this issue, see Lester B. Lave and Eugene P. Seskin,

Air Pollution and Human Health (Baltimore: Johns Hopkins University Press for Resources for the Future, 1977).

5. For a more complete discussion of the nature of the regulatory process and how process affects policy, see Roger G. Noll, 'Breaking Out of the Regulatory Dilemma: Alternatives to the Sterile Choice', *Indiana Law Journal*, vol. 51, (1976) no. 3, pp. 686–99.

6. For a more complete discussion of the problems of the present regulatory system, see Allen V. Kneese and Charles L. Schultze, *Pollution, Prices and Public Policy* (Washington DC: The Brookings Institution, 1975).

7. See Bruce A. Ackerman and William T. Hassler, *Clean Coal/Dirty Air* (New Haven: Yale University Press, 1981).

8. For a well-documented sample, see Richard E. Ayers, 'Enforcement of Air Pollution Controls on Stationary Sources under the Clean Air Act Amendments of 1970', *Ecology Law Quarterly*, vol. 4 (1975), no. 3, pp. 441–78.

9. For descriptions of European regulatory systems with contrasts to the American process, see Blair T. Bower, 'Mixed Implementation Incentive Systems for Water Quality Management in France, the Ruhr and the United States,' Conference on International Comparisons of the Implementation Process in Environmental Regulation, March 1981; and Steven Kelman, *Regulating America, Regulating Sweden* (Cambridge, Mass: MIT Press, 1981).

10. See J. H. Dales, *Pollution, Property and Prices* (Toronto: University of Toronto Press, 1968); W. David Montgomery, 'Markets in Licenses and Efficient Pollution Control Programs', *Journal of Eeonomic Theory*, vol. 5 (1972), pp. 395–418; and Thomas H. Teitenberg, 'Transferable Discharge Permits and the Control of Stationary Source Air Pollution: A Survey and Synthesis', *Land Economics*, vol. 56 (1980), pp. 391–416.

11. For a more complete treatment of this subject, see A. Michael Spence and Martin L. Weitzman, 'Regulatory Strategies for Pollution Control', in Anne F. Friedlander (ed.), *Approaches to Controlling Air Pollution* (Cambridge, Mass: MIT Press, 1978); and Marc J. Roberts and A. Michael Spence, 'Effluent Charges and Licenses under Uncertainty', *Journal of Public Economics*, vol. 5 (1976), pp. 193–208.

12. For a comparison of the effects of taxes and bounties on entry, see R. Talbot Page, 'Failure of Bribes and Standards for Pollution Abatement', *Natural Resources Journal*, vol. 13 (1976), pp. 677–704.

13. For a complete analysis of this problem, see Robert W. Hahn, 'An Assessment of the Viability of Marketable Permits', Doctoral dissertation, California Institute of Technology, May 1981.

14. For a more complete discussion and description of the cost data, see Robert W. Hahn, 'Data Base and Programming Methodology for Marketable Permits Study', Open File Report 80–8, Environmental Quality Laboratory, California Institute of Technology, 1981.

15. For a detailed description of the model, see Glen R. Cass, 'Methods for Sulfate Air Quality Management with Applications to Los Angeles', Doctoral dissertation, California Institute of Technology, December 1977; and Glen R. Cass, 'Sulfate Air Quality Control Strategy Design', *Atmospheric Environment*, vol. 15, no. 7, p. 1227.

16. For more details about the choice of emissions limits and the various simulations, see Robert W. Hahn and Roger G. Noll, 'Designing a Market for Tradable Emissions Permits', in Wesley Mogat (ed.), *Reform of Environmental Regulation* (Cambridge, Mass.: Ballinger, 1982).

17. For a more complete analysis, see Hahn and Noll, 'Designing a Market for Tradable Emissions Permits'.

18. See Cass, 'Methods for Sulfate Air Quality Management with Applications to Los Angeles'.

19. Calculations in Hahn, 'An Assessment of the Viability of Marketable Permits'.

20. *Emission Reduction Banking Manual*, Emission Reduction Banking and Trading Publication BG200 (US Environmental Protection Agency, September 1980).

Index